Becoming a Dynamics 365 Finance and Supply Chain Solution Architect

Implement industry-grade finance and supply chain solutions for successful enterprise resource planning (ERP)

Brent Dawson

<packt>

BIRMINGHAM—MUMBAI

Becoming a Dynamics 365 Finance and Supply Chain Solution Architect

Copyright © 2023 Packt Publishing

All rights reserved. No part of this book may be reproduced, stored in a retrieval system, or transmitted in any form or by any means, without the prior written permission of the publisher, except in the case of brief quotations embedded in critical articles or reviews.

Every effort has been made in the preparation of this book to ensure the accuracy of the information presented. However, the information contained in this book is sold without warranty, either express or implied. Neither the author, nor Packt Publishing or its dealers and distributors, will be held liable for any damages caused or alleged to have been caused directly or indirectly by this book.

Packt Publishing has endeavored to provide trademark information about all of the companies and products mentioned in this book by the appropriate use of capitals. However, Packt Publishing cannot guarantee the accuracy of this information.

Group Product Manager: Alok Dhuri
Publishing Product Manager: Kushal Dave
Senior Editor: Ruvika Rao
Technical Editor: Jubit Pincy
Copy Editor: Safis Editing
Project Coordinator: Deeksha Thakkar
Proofreader: Safis Editing
Indexer: Pratik Shirodkar
Production Designer: Arunkumar Govinda Bhat
Marketing Coordinator: Deepak Kumar and Mayank Singh

First published: June 2023

Production reference:1160623

Published by Packt Publishing Ltd.
Livery Place
35 Livery Street
Birmingham
B3 2PB, UK.

ISBN 978-1-80461-149-4

www.packtpub.com

I've been wanting to write a book for a very long time but never really had the opportunity. I'd like to dedicate this book to my amazing fiancée, Violeta, for giving me the motivation and courage to go and try things I was always hesitant to try before. This is only the first of many new accomplishments to come. I am a better person because of you, and I feel more confident in myself. I'm proud of you and of myself because of all the successes we have had... all since I met you.

– Brent Dawson

Foreword

I have known Brent for over 3 years since we met in the Microsoft Business applications community via common interests.

Since then, we have interacted about Microsoft stack products at community events (user groups, conferences) and personally.

This book *Overcoming Challenges in D365 Finance and SCM Projects* tells you the most important things you need to know about running a D365 project, from identifying if you need the software, to the completion.

Technical information is expressed in a very understandable manner with architecture concepts, configurations and customizations with examples, security and integration considerations. However, this is not all that is covered in the book. Brent also describes how to make a project a success by describing how to manage the human element of the process, which often can be a downfall of a project despite technical brilliance.

Technical know-how and experience are evident in the book, but I knew that as I have consulted with Brent multiple times in the past.

If you are considering using D365 finance and SCM in your organization and you are a functional consultant or seasoned architect, then you will get to know what the bigger picture of the project looks like or at least most likely find something that has got a different angle to it.

Sincerely,

Laurynas Merkelis a.k.a. Larry

Low Code platform Architect

Contributors

About the author

Brent Dawson is the owner of and principal consultant at Digital Ducttape Ltd. He is certified in many different areas, including D365 F&SCM Solution Architect, TOGAF (enterprise architecture), **Microsoft Certified Trainer (MCT)**, and **Certified Information Systems Security Professional (CISSP)**. Brent has over 25+ years of teaching and classroom experience. His focus is mostly on Microsoft Dynamics 365 **Finance and Supply Chain Management (F&SCM)**, Power Platform, and ethics in IT. He has an impressive 30+ years' experience in the IT industry and has worked in many different facets of IT, including end user, system, and security architecture. Originally from Canada, he currently lives in London in the United Kingdom. He has completed and helped to create several certifications and accreditations in the IT industry, including authoring various exam questions and setting certification exams for Microsoft and ISC2. His extensive knowledge sets him apart in industries such as oil and gas, manufacturing, finance, transportation, and the public sector.

Brent is also a frequent speaker at Microsoft and community-based conferences. He has previously spoken at Microsoft Ignite, Scottish Summit, and South Coast Summit on Microsoft D365 F&SCM, and Syracuse and Northampton universities on IT ethics. He's always willing and available to speak at conferences.

> *I want to thank a few people. My family (Dad, Mom, Phil, and Janice) for convincing me to stay in computer science at university, Doug for making me believe that IT wasn't all about programming, and Leon for introducing me to the world of dynamics architecture. I also need to thank AJ, Chris, Alison, Jeff, Ewan, Kaila, Larry, Malin, and all the rest of the Bespoke Badgers. You are the most supportive and excellent group of people I've ever had the opportunity to know.*

About the reviewer

Rahul Mohta brings 20+ years of expertise in ERP consulting, implementation, and pre-sales, focusing on Microsoft Dynamics 365 F&SCM.

He has diverse and rich experience, working with customers and partners globally, enabling them to realize the full value of their future Dynamics platform.

Rahul strives to work as a solution leader and trusted advisor, playing diverse roles and working extensively in both the functional and technical domains.

Table of Contents

Preface — xiii

Part 1: Architectural Considerations and Best Practices for D365 Finance and SCM

1

Overcoming Challenges in D365 Finance and SCM Projects — 3

How do we get started?	3	What can we do to fix it?	15
Who wants this software?	4	How to be an SA	16
How to get started?	5	Conclusion	17

2

Understanding the Microsoft FastTrack© Process — 19

The Success by Design methodology	20	Who does what in the project?	28
Cloud-first	20	FastTrack engagement	29
Data-first	21	The role of the SA	30
Phased approach	21	A FastTrack engagement case study	30
What is Microsoft FastTrack for Dynamics 365?	24	The initiate phase	31
Customer requirements	24	Conclusion	35
Partner requirements	25		
Engagement	25		
Implementation guides	26		

3

Dealing with Integrations   37

What are integrations?   38
What components make up an integration?   38
Data integration patterns   39
Custom services   40
Batch APIs   40
OData   40
Dataverse   41
Virtual entities   43

Why do integrations fail?   44
Working in silos   44
Data dependency   44
Not understanding interface complexity   45
Understanding integrations   45
Resistance to change   45
We always blame the software   46

Case study   46
Integrating two ERP systems   46
DW for a racing team   47
Solidworks to D365   47
Power Automate   48

Ways to fix integration issues   48
Change-tracking   48
Budget properly   48
Tool selection   49
Planning your strategy   49
Creating the team   50
Standardization   50
Testing, testing, and testing   50

Conclusion   50

4

Efficient Security Design   51

Why is the cloud different?   52
What does security look like in D365 F&SCM?   53
D365 security architecture   53
Extended data security   54
Security reports   54
Segregation of duties   59

External reports   60
How to best set up security   60
Architecture   61

Conclusion   75

5

Planning for Successful Data Migration   77

What is data migration?	77
Types of data	78
Data locations	78
Data migration methodologies	79
Data management	80
Data management framework	81
Data entities	82
Data mapping	83
Data tools	84
Creating a migration strategy	84
Prepare for data migration	85
Data import and export strategy	86
Validating data output	86
Cutover plans	87
Data migration best practices	88
Case studies	90
So, what are the reports?	91
Conclusion	93

6

Licensing Challenges   95

Understanding the Microsoft licensing model	95
Where can I get the licenses from?	96
Dynamics license types	97
Base versus attached licenses	97
Other licenses	98
But I'm an administrator?	99
How do we know what license to get?	99
Plan out subscription requirements	100
Dynamics 365 Licensing Guide	100
The Users page in System Administration	101
Custom security	102
Subscription estimator	102
ISV, External, and other license types	104
Multiplexing	105
Assigning licenses	106
License reporting	107
Security configuration diagnostics	109
Real-world example	109
Conclusion	110

Part 2: From Solution Design to Deployment – Practical Advice

7

How to Plan a D365 F&SCM Project — 113

Project management	113	**Project structure**	122
The project layout	115	Steering the project	122
Project management tools	116	Project reports	123
Prepare to start	116	Risks	124
Project team	116	Stage gates	124
Governance	118	Change boards	124
Framework	120	Responsible, accountable, consulted, and informed	124
Risks	120	Business processes	125
		Project checklists	126
		Conclusion	127

8

Learning the Client's Business — 129

Success by Design	129	**LCS tools**	141
Where to start?	130	Business process modeler (BPM)	142
Let's speak the same language	131	**Implementation of requirements**	143
LCS BOM	132	**Case study**	144
Identifying the business processes	132	**Conclusion**	145
Dynamics 365 F&SCM TOM	134		
Why understand the TOM?	135		
Business process optimization	136		
Solution modeling	139		
Fit-gap analysis	139		

9

Collecting Project Requirements — 147

Where do we start?	**148**	Active listening	154
Why out of the box?	148	Using diagrams	156
Let's talk a bit about development	149	Where are we?	156
Understanding the differences	**150**	**Create the solution blueprint**	**158**
What tools are available?	150	**Conclusion**	**163**
Okay, so what's next?	**154**		
Let's listen to the client	154		

10

ALM Tools and Applications — 165

Azure DevOps	**165**	**Task Recorder**	**173**
Version control	167	Task Recorder for security configuration	174
Release pipelines	168	RSAT	176
Project management	169	Visual Studio	178
Testing	170	**DevOps examples**	**180**
Dynamics LCS	**172**	Creating a project	180
Environments	173	Best practices	185
		Conclusion	**186**

11

Human Change Management — 187

What is human change management?	**187**	**Why do employees need to know what's coming?**	**191**
Identifying stakeholders and their needs	188	The Change Curve	193
Developing a change management strategy	189	**Human change methodologies**	**194**
Communicating the change	190	Prosci ADKAR Model	195
Training and development	190		
Reinforcement and sustainability	191		

Who is best to lead change?	197	Case study 2 – the good project	200
Change tools	198	**Conclusion**	**201**
Case studies	**199**		
Case study 1 – the bad project	199		

12

Building a Blueprint Solution — 203

Knowing what goes into a solution blueprint	**203**	Plan for long-term support and maintenance	207
		Review and iterate	207
Understanding the blueprint	204	Project roles	208
Assess the suitability of the blueprint	204	**Expressing user requirements**	**209**
Customize the blueprint	205	**What to include in the blueprint**	**211**
Establish a strong governance structure	206	Responsible, accountable, consulted, and informed	213
Develop a detailed implementation plan	206	Project budget document	214
Ensure adequate training and skill development	207	**Living documents**	**215**
Implement monitoring and evaluation mechanisms	207	**Best practices**	**216**
Foster collaboration and knowledge sharing	207	**Conclusion**	**217**

13

Deploying the Project Solution — 219

Building the blueprint solution	**219**	Case study	234
Design pillars of solution architecture	220	**How should it look?**	**235**
Strategies	221	**Conclusion**	**237**
Go-live preparation	**234**		

Index — 239

Other Books You May Enjoy — 250

Preface

Many ERP projects are doomed to failure, whether it's due to bad planning, incorrect resource scoping, or just a lack of knowledge of what a system can do. Organizations that implement large ERP projects will always look for ways to deploy a system that is free from bugs and geared toward making their organization more efficient and profitable.

Focusing on Microsoft Dynamics 365 Finance and Supply Chain Management solutions architects, this book will present some of the more challenging areas that lead to project failure or cost/time overruns. It will present a discussion of the major causes that can cause a project failure, and it will offer some observations from the field that can be a guide to help maneuver past any issues toward a successful outcome.

Who this book is for

This book is for aspiring Microsoft D365 finance and supply chain solutions architects looking to take up the challenges of integrating different systems, configuring security models, complex data migrations, licensing, and overall system design based on client requirements. Furthermore, this book serves as a valuable guide for experienced solution architects seeking to expand their skill set and enhance their expertise in tackling complex challenges within the field.
What this book covers

Chapter 1, Overcoming Challenges in D365 Finance and SCM Projects, starts the book with a high-level discussion about the most common roadblocks that can happen during an ERP project.

Chapter 2, Understanding the Microsoft FastTrack Process, introduces the Microsoft FastTrack process for Dynamics projects. We will look at the structure used to complete a project based on Microsoft's best practices.

Chapter 3, Dealing with Integrations, examines the potential issues that can arise when working with integrations between Dynamics 365 F&SCM and other software applications.

Chapter 4, Efficient Security Design, discusses how to set up security configurations in an organization.

Chapter 5, Planning for Successful Data Migration, explores the major impacts and pitfalls related to data migrations and data translations when moving to D365.

Chapter 6, Licensing Challenges, delves into the types of licenses used in D365 and how to assign them based on job type, as well as security roles.

Chapter 7, How to Plan a D365 F&SCM Project, examines how to prepare for successful project deployment.

Chapter 8, Learning the Client's Business, discusses how to best capture a client's requirements, as a successful project is always about knowing what the client needs.

Chapter 9, *Collecting Project Requirements*, explores how to get a client to work with an architect to kick-start a project, including how personnel will be assigned to work on the project.

Chapter 10, *ALM Tools and Applications*, delves into the Microsoft recommended tools that should be used during the execution of a project.

Chapter 11, *Human Change Management*, discusses many issues that can happen when proper corporate change management is excluded from a project.

Chapter 12, *Building a Blueprint Solution*, examines what needs to be entered into the solution blueprint.

Chapter 13, *Deploying the Project Solution*, gathers together everything we discussed into a logical cheat sheet that you can use to get your project off on the right foot. We'll look at the timelines you should follow so that the project starts successfully and stays on track until the final go-live.

Download the color images

We also provide a PDF file that has color images of the screenshots and diagrams used in this book. You can download it here: `https://packt.link/omA3u`.

Conventions used

The following text conventions used throughout this book.

Bold: Indicates a new term, an important word, or words that you see on screen. For instance, words in menus or dialog boxes appear in **bold**. Here is an example: "The **Security duty assignments** report gives a view of all the duties that are part of a role."

> **Tips or important notes**
> Appear like this.

Get in touch

Feedback from our readers is always welcome.

General feedback: If you have questions about any aspect of this book, email us at `customercare@packtpub.com` and mention the book title in the subject of your message.

Errata: Although we have taken every care to ensure the accuracy of our content, mistakes do happen. If you have found a mistake in this book, we would be grateful if you would report this to us. Please visit `www.packtpub.com/support/errata` and fill in the form.

Piracy: If you come across any illegal copies of our works in any form on the internet, we would be grateful if you would provide us with the location address or website name. Please contact us at `copyright@packt.com` with a link to the material.

If you are interested in becoming an author: If there is a topic that you have expertise in and you are interested in either writing or contributing to a book, please visit `authors.packtpub.com`.

Share Your Thoughts

Once you've read *Becoming a Dynamics 365 Finance and Supply Chain Solution Architect*, we'd love to hear your thoughts! Scan the QR code below to go straight to the Amazon review page for this book and share your feedback.

https://packt.link/r/1804611492

Your review is important to us and the tech community and will help us make sure we're delivering excellent quality content.

Download a free PDF copy of this book

Thanks for purchasing this book!

Do you like to read on the go but are unable to carry your print books everywhere? Is your eBook purchase not compatible with the device of your choice?

Don't worry, now with every Packt book you get a DRM-free PDF version of that book at no cost.

Read anywhere, any place, on any device. Search, copy, and paste code from your favorite technical books directly into your application.

The perks don't stop there, you can get exclusive access to discounts, newsletters, and great free content in your inbox daily

Follow these simple steps to get the benefits:

1. Scan the QR code or visit the link below

`https://packt.link/free-ebook/9781804611494`

2. Submit your proof of purchase
3. That's it! We'll send your free PDF and other benefits to your email directly

Part 1: Architectural Considerations and Best Practices for D365 Finance and SCM

In this part, you will get a view of the areas that most often cause the greatest number of issues during the execution of a D365 F&SCM ERP project. In addition, you will also learn the best practices and suggestions to resolve these issues, based on the experiences of myself and other solution architects that I have worked with over the years.

This part has the following chapters:

- *Chapter 1, Overcoming Challenges in D365 Finance and SCM Projects*
- *Chapter 2, Understanding the Microsoft FastTrack Process*
- *Chapter 3, Dealing with Integrations*
- *Chapter 4, Efficient Security Design*
- *Chapter 5, Planning for Successful Data Migration*
- *Chapter 6, Licensing Challenges*

1
Overcoming Challenges in D365 Finance and SCM Projects

Every book needs to start somewhere. As I was sitting and planning out what to put into this book, I was trying to figure out what causes me the most lack of sleep in a project – meaning, what issues come up during a project deployment that cause the most issues and the most grief between consultants and clients?

I have been involved in Microsoft Dynamics projects for over 10 years now. Every project, no matter how hard you try to plan to avoid issues and problems, ends up with at least one major issue. Many, if not most, ERP projects are doomed to failure.

Whether it's due to bad planning, incorrect resource staffing, or just a lack of knowledge of what a system can do or what a client wants, organizations will eventually run into something that causes a project to go completely off the rails. This, of course, will have not only a negative impact on timelines and budgets but also on the project team's morale.

If we're going to be successful, then we need to understand what we can do to help avoid issues and make our work as good as can be.

How do we get started?

That's an interesting question, isn't it? How do we get started? Well, basically, someone must decide, "We need to become more modern in our organization; otherwise, we'll be left behind." The point and goal of an organization is to deliver a product or service to a customer and, ultimately, make money.

It's totally possible to make money using old-fashioned systems – account books for accounting, order books to manage orders for customers, and printed flyers for customers, but it's not really all that efficient. How much time does an employee spend handwriting out these types of documents, and how much space is then required to store those documents? If an organization is to keep, let's say, seven years' worth of financial data for tax purposes, how many filing cabinets, or file storage boxes in a warehouse, do we need to keep all that information? And then what happens if you need to find one document from a box that contains data from six years ago?

Alternatively, maybe an organization has several different systems they work with but don't have the ability to share data. This can cause a number of issues, including duplication of work, extra spending on supplies and maintenance, and potentially missing payments from customers and to vendors.

At some point, someone (usually in the finance department) will visit IT and suggest that they look at a way to improve how the organization operates. Depending on the size of the organization, a committee will be created that will come up with a way to improve operations.

From there, a technology roadmap will be created, and ultimately, a budget will be allocated so that a new digital transformation can occur. But what if you have no idea how or what needs to happen to get to a desired destination?

With so many different types of software available on the market, most organizations can't make an educated decision without assistance from someone (usually a company that specializes in ERP deployments) who has many years of experience working with technology. So, you find a few people who have experience in leading organizations with their technology roadmaps, interview them, and finally, hire someone to help guide you on the journey.

Now that you have a leader in place (with the guidance of a consulting company), and a good idea of how you want to proceed, you start to look at different software tools, technologies, and partners to help you deploy a solution. You made an important decision in this process – for instance, you really like Microsoft products and would prefer to stick with those technologies, including tools such as Azure and Power Platform, because you trust the company and believe that their technologies will be well supported far into the future.

You can now announce to the company that it is going to migrate its current systems to Microsoft Dynamics 365.

Who wants this software?

Microsoft Dynamics 365 is a cloud-based software platform that allows an organization to integrate its processes into a single, integrated platform. Microsoft **Dynamics 365 (D365)** provides applications to help manage customer relationships, including D365 Sales (used to manage the sales cycle), D365 Marketing (used to manage marketing campaigns), D365 Customer Service (used to manage customer information and services), and D365 Field Services (used to manage and assist technicians' schedules and appointments).

There are also two **Enterprise Resource Planning (ERP)** systems. One of these applications is called **Business Central (BC)**. This is a small- and medium-business version of an ERP system that is suited for a company with around 100 to 250 users. The application consists of three modules:

- A Finance and Operations module based on a previous application called **Microsoft Dynamics NAV**
- A sales module
- A marketing module

The enterprise edition of their ERP application is called **D365 Finance and Supply Chain Management**. This application is made up of several modules, including Accounts Payable, Accounts Receivable, inventory management, and asset management. Other enterprise applications include Project Ops for project operations and financial management, Human Resources to manage all users from a human resources perspective, and Commerce, which is used to manage both brick and mortar and online retail stores. Microsoft is also in the process of preparing other tools that will be released in the near future to cover areas such as intelligent order management, Microsoft Supply Chair Center.

Now that an organization has selected D365 Finance and Supply Chain Management, its next step is to find an implementation partner. Microsoft has many different partners who can do the deployment, but you want to find one that will not only do the work for a customer but also become a partner in the deployment of their system. By becoming a partner, the consultants have a vested interest in deploying the best system possible.

As a part of the selection criteria when picking a partner, you need to check out their work and references. One of the things that the customer needs to find out is whether the partner is eligible for Microsoft's architectural support process called **FastTrack for Dynamics 365**: `https://learn.microsoft.com/en-us/dynamics365/fasttrack/`

Success by Design is a methodology that prioritizes communication between Microsoft and the partner to provide a successful project. There are specific requirements that both the customer and partner must meet to be eligible to take advantage of FastTrack. We will take a detailed look at FastTrack in *Chapter 2*.

How to get started?

Once the customer has decided on the partner and the deployment methodology, they have been through the FastTrack design process, and has a blueprint, it's time to get to work. But where do we start?

I believe the first thing that needs to happen is to start showing people in the organization how the system works – not from the point of view of the solution that has been agreed upon but just the system's look and feel, and how some of the processes work by default. When you create the first dev/test environment, you have the option of installing the demo data for the Contoso Corporation. With this system, you can show the organization what the system will do.

As an example, let's say that one of the processes that has been identified needs to be improved is the expense management process. Currently, in your organization, you do everything on paper. A user would go away somewhere that they can do the expense and couldn't do a claim until they came back to their office.

Let's say you need to go and attend a conference. You have your travel (flights/trains/mileage), hotel, and meals for the days you're away. You might also have other items expensed, such as stationery and photocopying.

When you get back to the office, you first make photocopies of all the receipts from your trip, then fill out a spreadsheet that lays out all the expenses in date order, and print and sign the spreadsheet. Once that's done, you need to put it on your manager's desk with the receipts and wait for them to review and sign the expense report.

Now, a few different scenarios could happen:

- The manager reviews the expense report right away and everything is correct, and he forwards it off to the finance or HR department for reimbursement, and you get the money back on your next payday.
- The manager reviews the expense report and realizes you forgot to add two receipts that are needed before the expenses can be approved. Therefore, he takes the report back to you, you fix it, and then you resubmit it.
- The manager is away on holiday for two weeks, so you submit the expense report, but you're now going to have to wait an extra two weeks to have the expenses reviewed and submitted for payment.
- The amount of the expenses is higher than the level that your manager can approve, so they need to submit the expenses to their manager for approval. In addition, all the preceding scenarios above could still apply.

There are lots of different ways that this process can fail because of its manual nature. And this is just the submission process. We have even looked at the finance side – knowing which budgets the expenses come from, the expense policies that need to be applied, and so on.

Now that we've identified the business process that needs to be executed, how do we take that manual process and input it into D365 Finance?

In D365 Finance, there is a specific module for expense management. In this module, we will set up many features including the following:

- Expense policies
- Budget allocations
- Expense processing
- Expense reporting

For a user, there are many different expense types that they can choose from, including a standard expense report, cash advances, and travel requisitions.

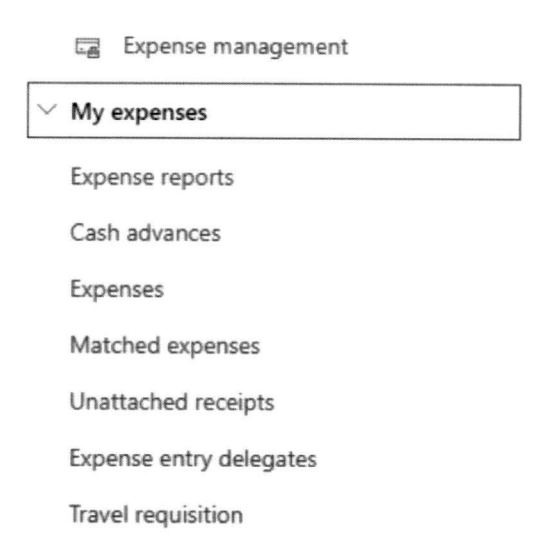

- Expense management
- My expenses
  - Expense reports
  - Cash advances
  - Expenses
  - Matched expenses
  - Unattached receipts
  - Expense entry delegates
  - Travel requisition

Figure 1.1 – The D365 Expense module

Once in the expense module, we need to select and create a new expense report.

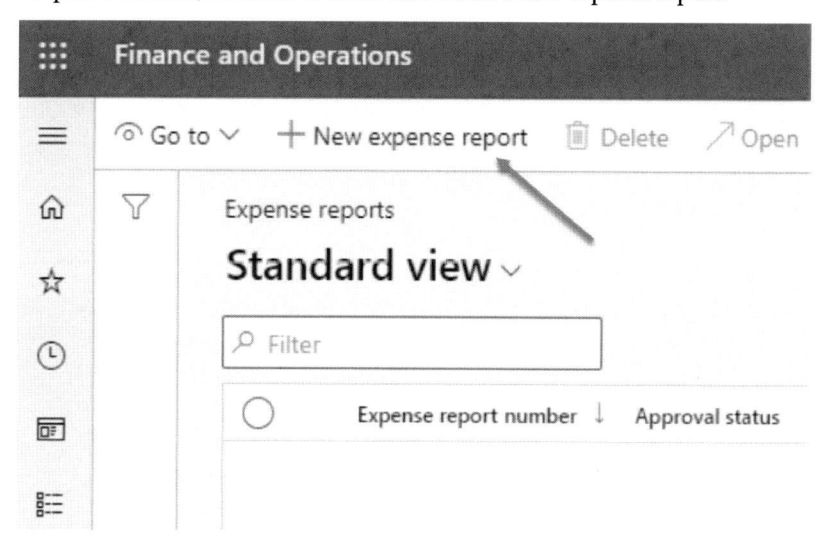

Figure 1.2 – The New expense report button

To submit the expense report to the system, you will fill out a form that lets you select the expense category and the amount, separate taxes (if required), and attach scanned copies of receipts.

New expense report

My view ⌄

Purpose	Location
Conference	MainOffice

Map to travel requisition	Travel requisition amount

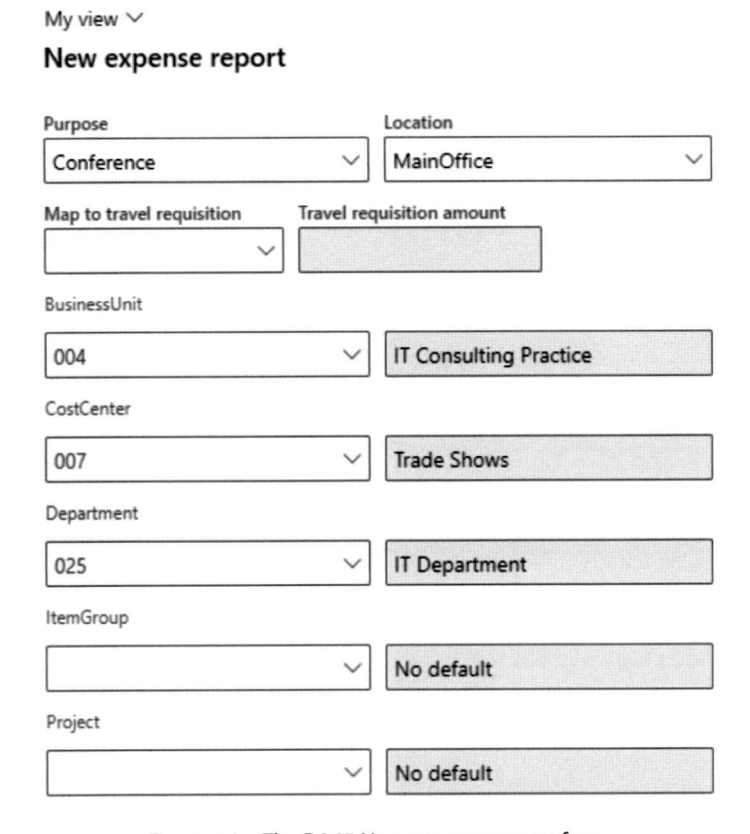

BusinessUnit

004	IT Consulting Practice

CostCenter

007	Trade Shows

Department

025	IT Department

ItemGroup

	No default

Project

	No default

Figure 1.3 – The D365 New expense report form

Finance and Operations

Save | Go to ⌄ | Add unattached expenses | Distribute amounts | Header receipts | Print ⌄ | Email report

BRENT DAWSON : 000056 | Standard view ⌄

Expense report for Brent Dawson - 000056, Conference

Expense report header

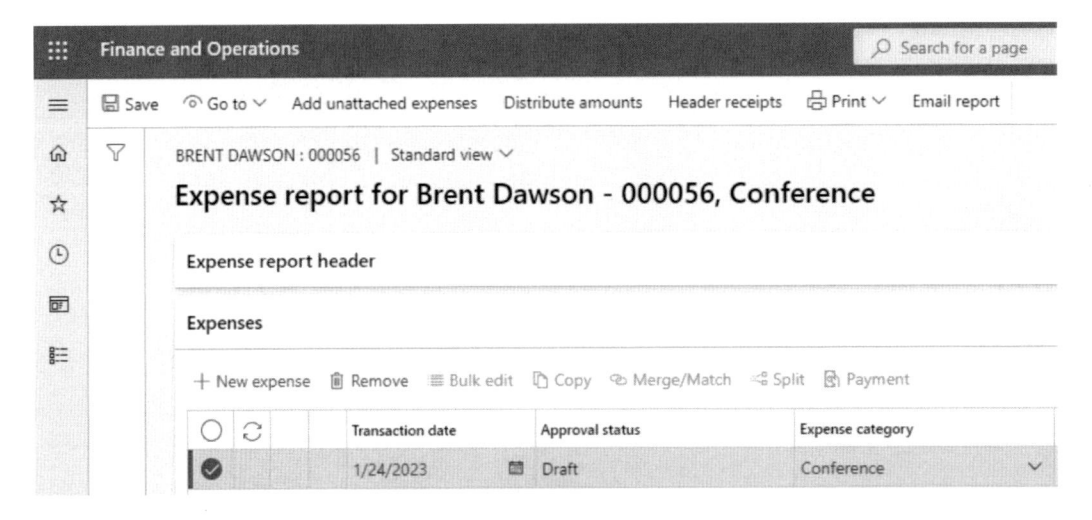

Expenses

+ New expense 🗑 Remove ≡ Bulk edit 📋 Copy ⊗ Merge/Match ⊰ Split 💲 Payment

Transaction date	Approval status	Expense category
1/24/2023	Draft	Conference

Figure 1.4 – Expense line items

Once you have entered all the values for the expense report, you can refresh the screen to update each of the expense lines. After you refresh the screen, you will see the **Submit** button appear in the top menu.

Figure 1.5 – Submission of an expense report

You are able to add some notes to the expense report for the reviewer.

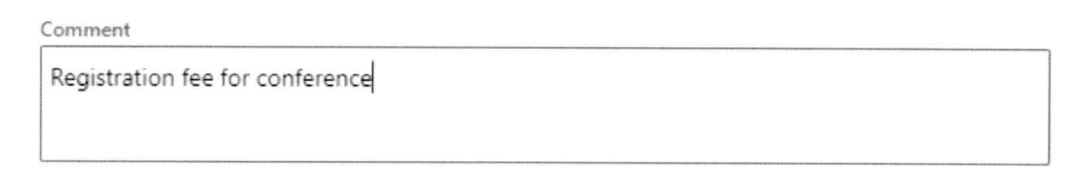

Figure 1.6 – The Expense report submit comment field

To help with the process of approving the expense report, we will implement an expense management workflow. The workflow involves manually passing the expense report around for approvals, signatures, and payment. An example of a workflow is here:

Expense flow

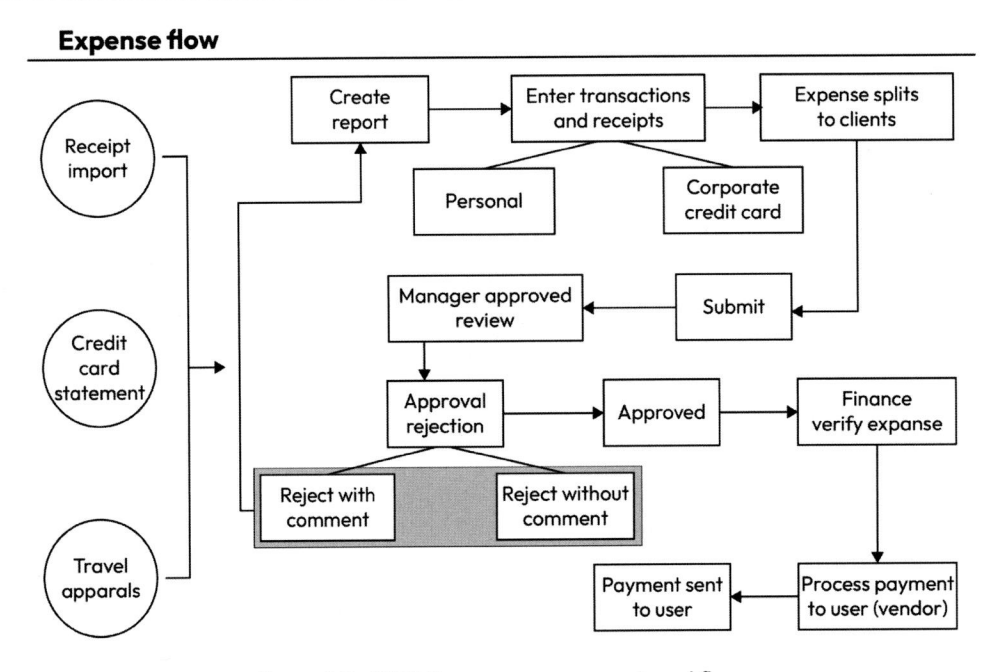

Figure 1.7 – D365 Expense management workflows

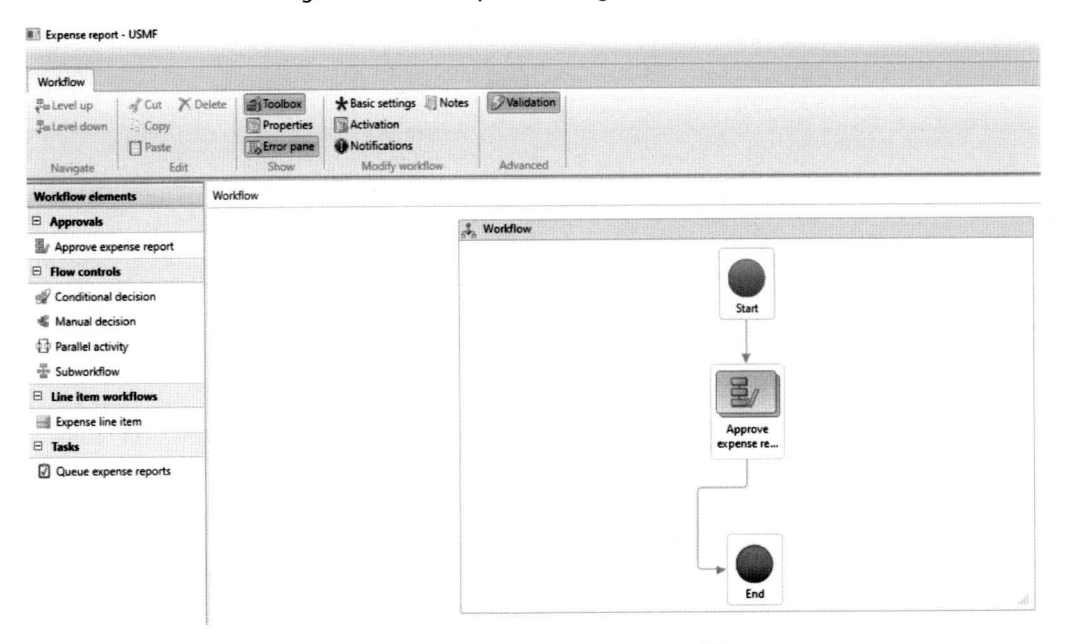

Figure 1.8 – A D365 Expense report workflow

We've now made the process of submitting expenses less work for the submitter, the approver, and the payor.

How to get started? 11

Once the expense has been submitted, we can go and look at the history of the workflow to see where it is at any given time. In this case, we will click the **View history** button, and can see the status of the workflow.

> **Note**
> It's also possible to add a business event to the system that can call an external Power Automate flow, allowing for an expense approval without having to log in to F&SCM.

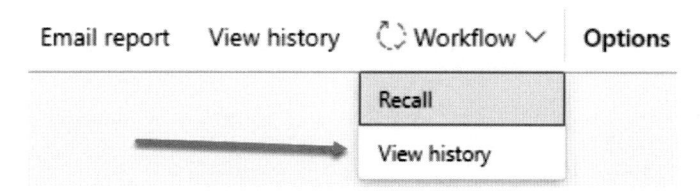

Figure 1.9 – The View history button

The following screen shows the status of the workflow. In this particular case, the expense report still sits in pending status.

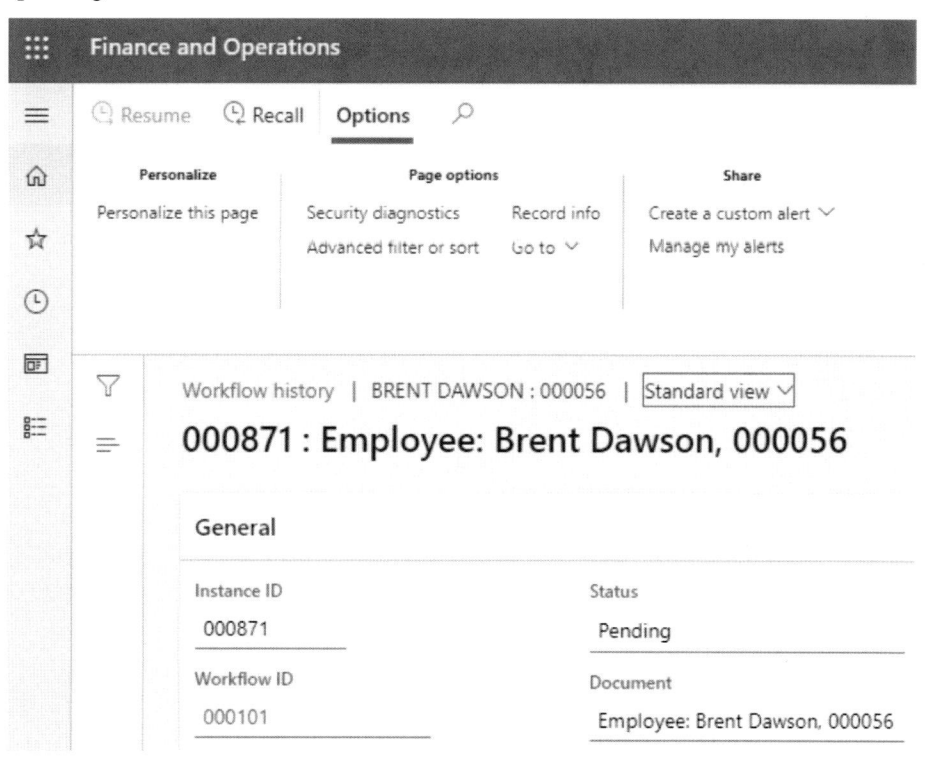

Figure 1.10 – The expense workflow history

If we want to see who the report is currently with, we can scroll down the page and see who the work item is currently assigned to. In this case, it's assigned to **Julia Funderburk**. If we have the correct permissions, such as System Administrator, we can reassign the work items to a different user.

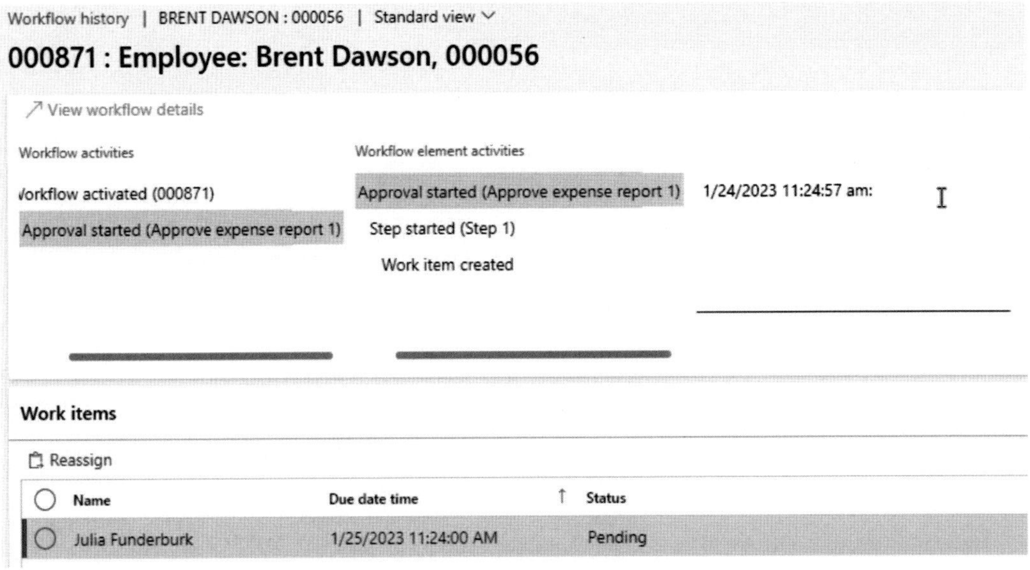

Figure 1.11 – The workflow work item assignment

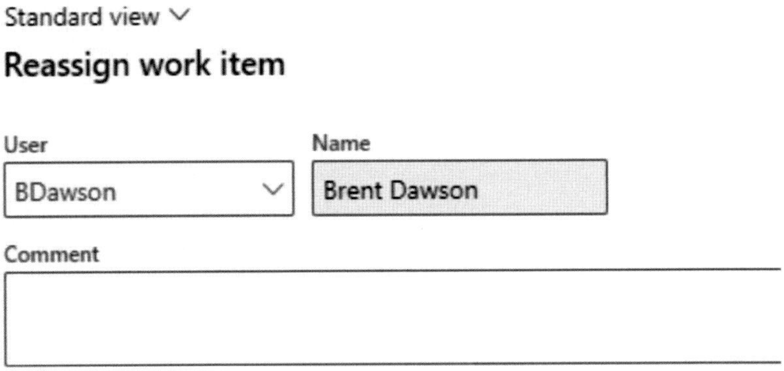

Figure 1.12 – The workflow reassignment dialog

Now that I've reassigned the approval to myself, we can go back to the home page of D365 and see it listed under the **Work items assigned to me** list.

How to get started? 13

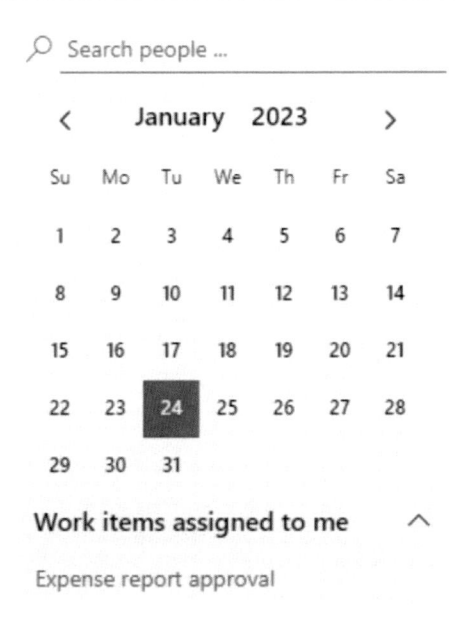

Figure 1.13 – The Work items assigned to me list

When we open the task that needs to be completed – in this case, the expense approval – we will be taken directly to the expense report approval screen. We will click on the **Workflow** dropdown and select one of the options. For this example, we'll select **Approve**.

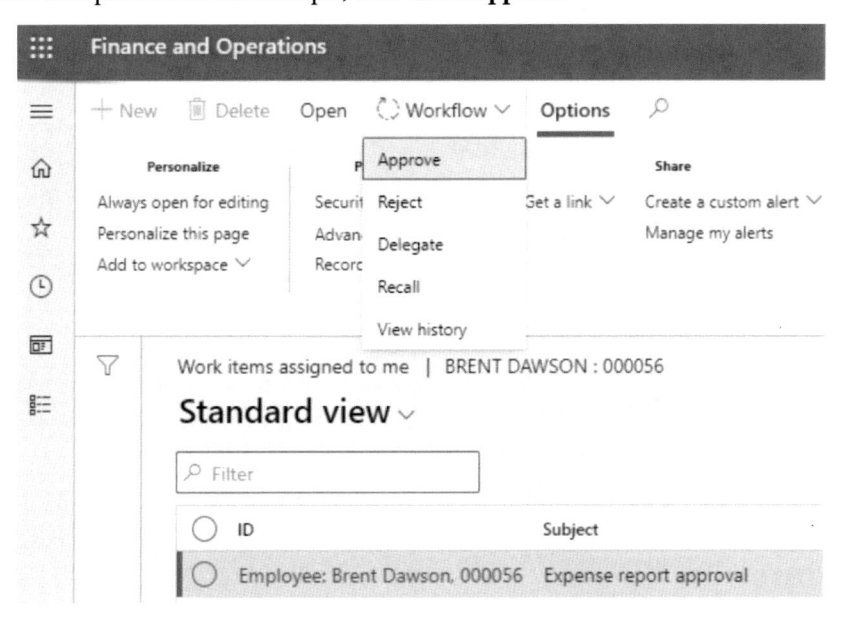

Figure 1.14 – The workflow approval screen

Standard view ∨

Expense report - USMF - Approve

Comment

Figure 1.15 – The expense approval comment screen

Finally, we can look at the **Expense reports** page, and we can now see that the status of the workflow is set to **Approved**.

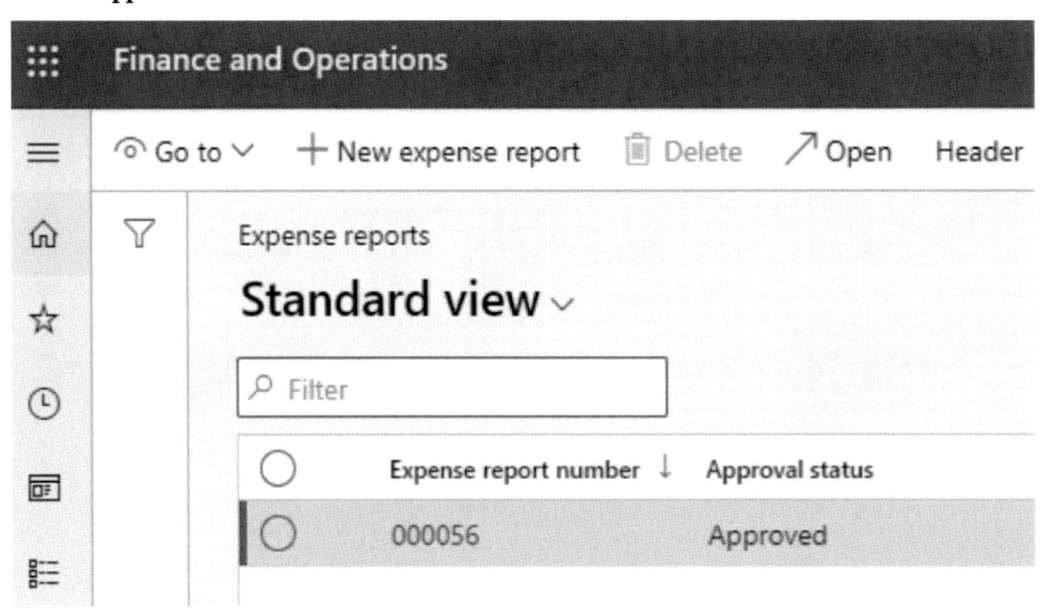

Figure 1.16 – The approved expense report

The previous example is just one of many business processes can that be implemented and automated in D365. This was a simple example, but as we go through the book, we'll look at more complicated examples that can see many more issues pop up.

Let's say that, as we start to implement the preceding solution, the customer comes to us and says, "You know how we decided that we were going to use the expense module to track our expenses? We decided that we want people who work for one of our legal entities to submit their expenses in a different legal entity when they do work." That brings in several complications.

First and foremost, how do we track any financial information for a worker who does work for a customer in our system? If they must submit their expenses to the company that they are doing work for, but their timesheets to the company that is their actual employer, how do we know that the expenses are not being submitted twice? And which company pays the expense? And who do they pay them to? And in what format?

These types of situations can occur regularly. Even though you've been through the process of discovery, situations such as these will show up completely out of the blue. The next and most important question is, how do we fix this issue?

What can we do to fix it?

When I was planning out the chapters of the book, I was looking at it from the point of view of how I fix things if they go sideways or, better yet, how to prevent those things from happening in the first place. I was trying to figure out the areas where most of the problems occur and things that we can do to help prevent or fix the most common issues.

There are many ways that a project can get out of control, for lack of a better term. Generally, when an organization and a partner put together what a project will consist of, there is a pretty good idea of what the project is supposed to accomplish. Generally speaking, the point of the project is to introduce the system into the business to improve its efficiency, save money, and help the company to improve its financial status.

The sales team of the partner and the customer agree on what the solution will look like in general terms, including which of the D365 F&SCM module will be deployed, some basic configurations of those modules, data management and migrations, reporting, and potentially, the inclusion of ISV modules or application integrations between F&SCM and some other application(s). Note that these applications may be legacy applications, running on hardware in the company's data center, or newer cloud-based SaaS solutions. We will have a long discussion about integrations in a later chapter.

As most salespeople aren't technically qualified to create the **Statement of Work** (**SOW**) on their own, they will get the help of a **solutions architect** (**SA**) to help with scoping out the solution and a project manager to assist in costing the project. Once this is completed, the solution and plan are handed over to the delivery team. As the project plan at this stage is a very high-level plan, the project manager will, with the assistance of the SA, fill in who will do what specific tasks at what point in the project.

However, one of the things we tend to find out after the SOW between the two sides has been worked out and signed is that people have their own agendas, and they want their issues dealt with in a specific way. If we go back to the previous example of the expense report, we need to come up with a solution that will fix the business process.

At this point, those on the project might start pointing fingers at each other and attribute "blame" for the incorrect solution. At this point, as the SA, it is your job to calm everyone down and come up with a way to implement the customer's requirement, but you should also be able to explain and negotiate a potential change to the way they perform that specific business practice.

In this case, if you can show the customer how the method they wish to use causes issues in areas such as expense payments, reporting, tax collection, and several other areas, you may just be able to convince them that maybe there is a better way to execute this process. The SA needs to be politically savvy enough to be able to negotiate with the customer to do things more conventionally.

How to be an SA

As you go through the different chapters of the book, you'll notice that we focus on the role of the SA. But what is an SA, and how do you become one? It's not that hard a role, but it should be given to someone with many years of experience and deployment projects under their belts.

The SA is one of the leaders of the project.

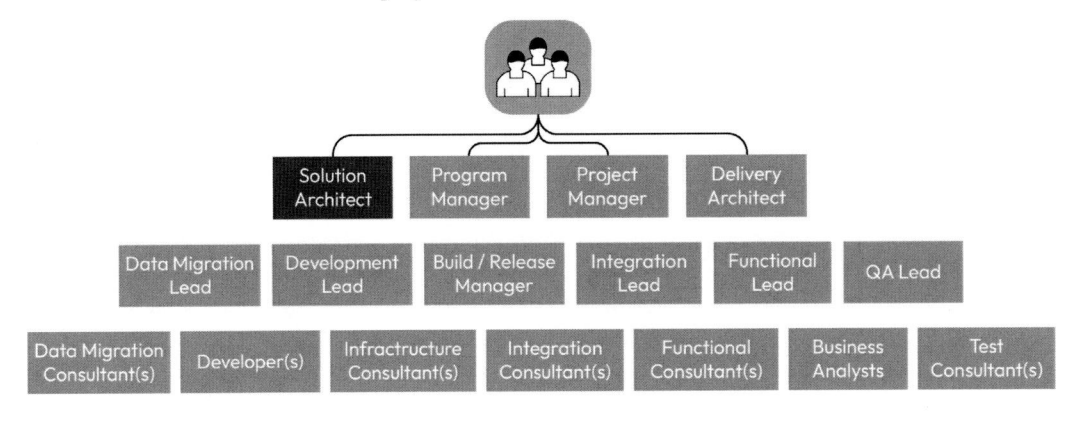

Figure 1.17 – An example of a project team

They need to have a deep technical and functional knowledge of the D365 Finance and Supply Chain Management application. They also should have extensive knowledge of technologies and applications that could potentially integrate with D365. As the team leader, the SA is the point person who project members will contact for any issues that may arise during the project timeline. They also need to have a level of soft skills to be able to work and communicate with people about the project solution, as well as the tasks that need to be completed during the project.

As an SA, you are also the point person when it comes to issues that happen during the project. As we mentioned previously, as the solution blueprint is a living document, you will have the opportunity to modify it during the deployment. When changes need to be made, usually a change request is created and signed by the customer, so you have in writing that the customer agrees to the change and, depending on how the project is funded, will pay for it.

In the end, the SA is the person who is the most technically knowledgeable and is able to make design decisions across all areas of the project, including development, configuration, security, licensing, storage, data migration, and go-live tasks. It's also helpful if the SA understands the customer's business (if not in detail, from at least an industry level). Above all else, a really good SA is a master of collaboration within their team and across the organization.

A SA will also need to be an excellent problem solver. No one knows all the answers to every question, so they need to be comfortable with doing research or asking colleagues for assistance with any challenges they come across. They also need to be able to distinguish the difference between a problem, a design issue, and a bug.

And lastly, an excellent SA will always be an eternal optimist and level-headed. They can't let anything get to them. They are the team leader, and if it looks like they are doing something wrong, that will filter down to the rest of the project team and have a negative impact on the team and the delivery of the application. You need to be able to have that human touch that will let you successfully interact with your team members. You must always be positive and happy, even when disaster is staring you in the face.

Conclusion

Now that you've read this first chapter, you're probably thinking to yourself, "Do I really want to do this? Do I really want to read the rest of this book? Do I really want to be an SA???" I promise you, if you do continue reading, you'll hear lots of examples of when things go right and when they go disastrously sideways. Most of these examples are from projects that I've been involved in, but many come from people in the community who have shared their experiences with me at conferences, in presentations, or in one-to-one conversations. By the end of the book, you'll hopefully know how to avoid situations where a project can fail.

Hopefully, at this point, you'll see how the role of an SA is important in making a project a success. In the next chapter, we're going to look at the Microsoft FastTrack for Dynamics 365 project methodology. The goal we will attempt to achieve is to see how you can work within the methodology to successfully implement your D365 F&SCM projects.

2
Understanding the Microsoft FastTrack© Process

In the past, doing a Microsoft Dynamics implementation was based on a process called **Sure Step**. Sure Step was a methodology created by Microsoft for use when working with Dynamics AX 2012. This methodology sets out what processes need to be completed and followed, and in what order, to complete a successful deployment. There are several workflows, project templates, maps (used to create processes), and implementation tools included in the tool.

The methodology flow looks something like this:

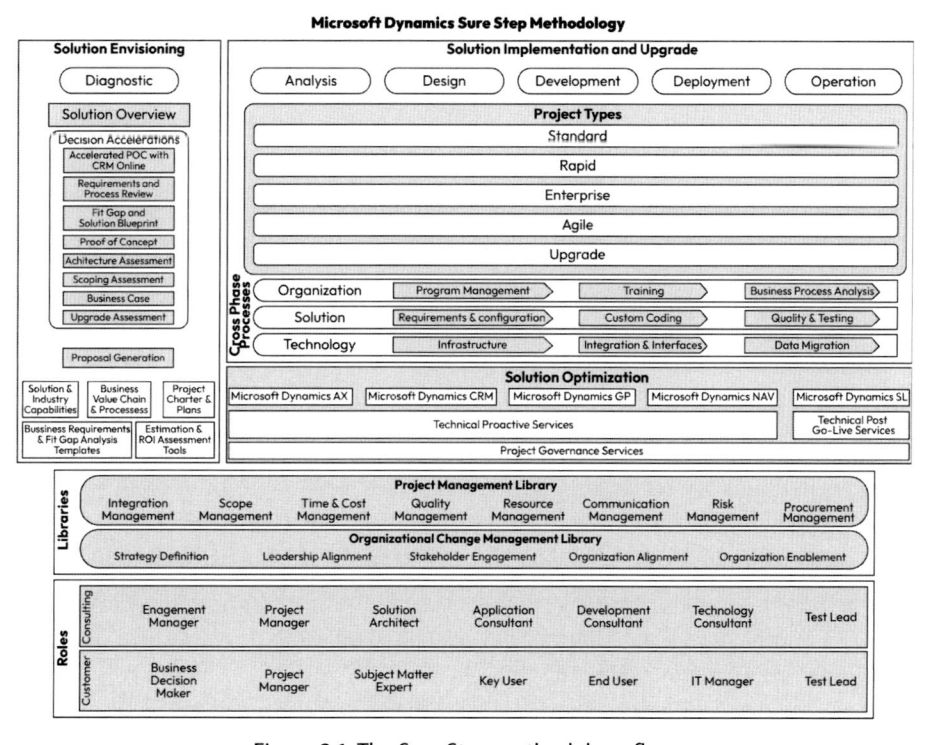

Figure 2.1: The Sure Step methodology flow

The Success by Design methodology

Before we can dig into what FastTrack is, we need to have a good understanding of what the *Success by Design methodology* is. Success by Design lays out the methods and processes that should be followed, including the best practices identified by Microsoft, to have a successful deployment of a solution. The key is that it is not a project management methodology like Microsoft's previous version, called Sure Step. Also, it doesn't necessarily follow a specific project management methodology. It will work just as well with agile as it does with waterfall.

Let's break out the processes involved and get a good understanding of how Success by Design works in practice.

Cloud-first

Today, everywhere that you read about technology, you will see that everything is related to the "cloud." This is known as the "cloud-first" strategy. This strategy is based upon the concept of putting all of your systems, computers, servers, and applications into a hosted environment, where the provider manages all of the infrastructures and the customer is responsible for managing their data and access to it. That might be a very simplistic way of looking at it, but at a high level, that's really all it is.

Organizations will start to buy space in cloud systems and move their applications to those spaces. No longer will they have to spend money internally on data centers, software licenses, power, cooling, and storage. They will now start to use that same money to pay for space and applications in the cloud.

One of the platforms provided by Microsoft is Dynamics 365. This platform provides two basic functions:

- First off, it provides ERP functionality with the finance, supply chain, human resources, and commerce tools needed for an organization to function
- The second set of functions includes more of the customer engagement functions, such as sales, marketing, and field services

The first observation you can make about the "cloud-first" philosophy is how an organization spends its money. Previously, a company would have a large capital expense budget that was used to purchase servers, software licenses, and desktop computers. Once these items were paid for, they were listed as a fixed asset to the organization, which means that they could depreciate the value of those purchases over a number of years, allowing them to reduce the tax requirements that they had to pay to their local governments.

Cloud deployments now mean that we no longer have these capital purchases but, instead, take all of those funds out of the CAPEX side of the business and move them to the OPEX side of the business. We now pay for services based on consumption of those resources, rather than paying for them upfront, all at once.

Now, in reality, what I just said isn't exactly 100% correct. In theory, that's how it works, but in reality, there are different ways to work out how the whole licensing of resources works. In a later chapter of the book, we'll delve into a deep discussion about licensing.

Data-first

Another philosophy that has become popular is the idea of data-first. This philosophy is based on the idea that an organization should focus on the processes and technology around the data that is created and consumed. Dynamics 365 has a data-first strategy where you merge frontend and backend business functions together, such as an e-commerce website and a supply chain system that fulfills the orders that customers make.

The advantage of these types of systems is that they are configurable, allowing customers to be able to get the most out of their investments. Also, this idea lets companies make these changes without having to use the old method of pulling out a complete system and replacing the whole thing with something new. Furthermore, it allows for an organization to keep existing systems in place and then integrate that data with newer, more advanced cloud-based applications.

One concept that follows the data-first philosophy is the ability of an organization to view its data and use it, without having to worry about the technology that's used to access it. They understand that the data itself is more important than the tools used to work with it. This is the type of organization that is the most mature in its organizational structure. Going forward, it will find it very easy to implement new and advanced technologies.

Phased approach

The Success by Design methodology is a phased approach. The phases are used to break a project into smaller projects that let you succeed in smaller increments, allowing the whole project to be successful.

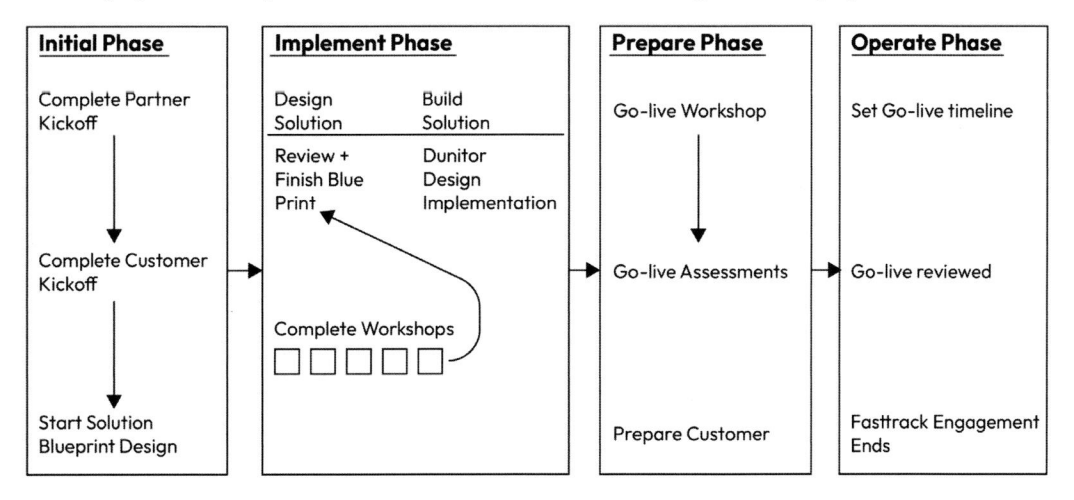

Figure 2.2: The Success by Design phases

The four phases of the process are as follows:

1. **Initiate**: This phase gets the ball rolling for a project
2. **Implement**: The project team starts to implement a solution
3. **Prepare**: This phase has a completed solution that needs to be deployed to user access
4. **Operate**: This is post-deployment and involves offering support for a production environment

Initiate

The point of the initiate phase is to get the people together who will work on a project. This will be both experts from the partner and **Subject Matter Experts** (**SMEs**) of the customer. Both the project manager and solutions architect will guide and lead the process of identifying the requirements for the solution. One of the project processes that will be discussed and agreed upon during this phase, if it hasn't been agreed to in the **Statement of Work** (**SOW**), is which project methodology will be used. There are a number of different project management types that can be used. In previous projects, many companies used a waterfall methodology.

The waterfall methodology is a very linear process. In this methodology, you spend the beginning of the project collecting the requirements. Once all of those requirements are collected and the solution is created, you go back to the project plan and update the work breakout structure, assigning the tasks needed based on the requirements. So, as long as there are no changes to the solution, this point should be the last time you make major changes to the project plan.

The more common project methodology that is followed currently is the **agile** method. Agile is a methodology where you break a project down into small chunks, and the overall project is completed in several stages or iterations. Each of the iterations is intended to finish a specific part of the project and then move on from there. Also, agile is intended for the project team to learn what they did well in the previous iterations and bring those forward to later ones.

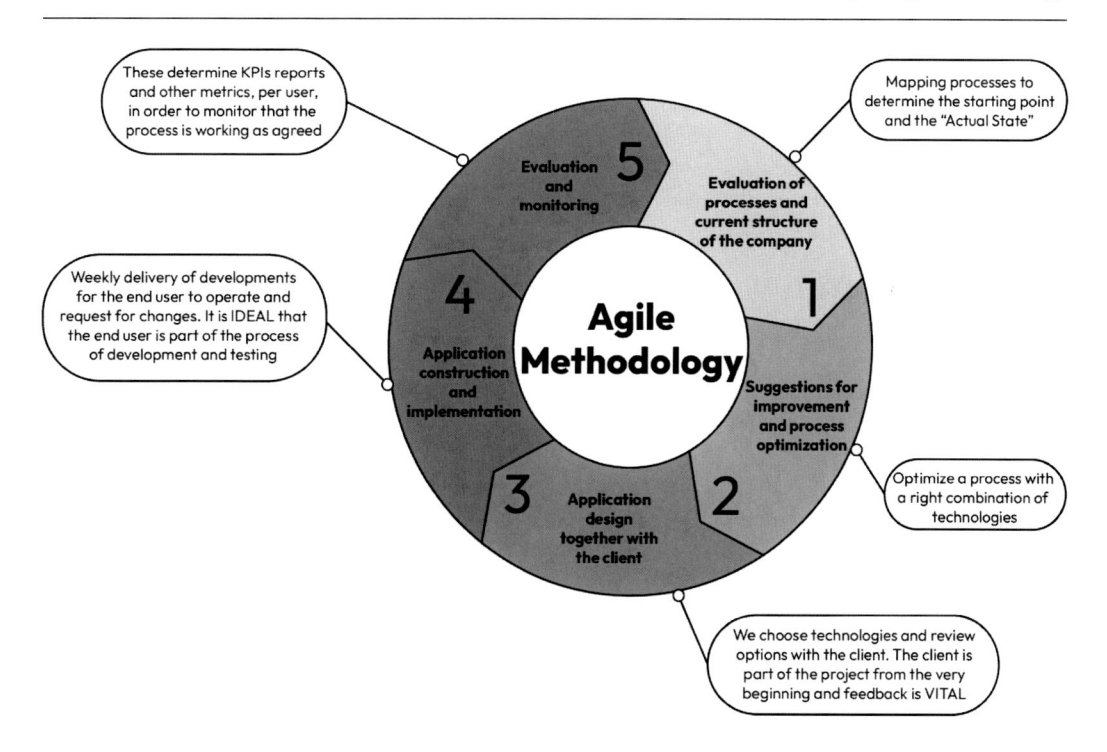

Figure 2.3: An agile project management methodology

However, in reality, Dynamics 365 projects don't really work well with either of those methodologies in their pure form. In most cases, you will have a hybrid approach that will contain some waterfall methodology – that is, the creation of the solution and gathering all of the requirements at the beginning – and agile iterations, where you break the deployment into smaller parts and complete each one before moving on to the next iteration.

Implement

The implementation phase of a project involves completing the tasks needed to build the solution that was agreed on earlier in the project. During this phase, there will be constant reviews of the work that has been completed to make sure that it falls within the scope of the solution. If you're using the agile approach, at the start of each iteration, a review of tasks for the next iteration will be agreed upon, the project plan will be updated, and task assignments will be created.

At the end of the iteration, you'll look at what you've completed, which has been tested and merged into the solution code management tool.

Prepare

In the prepare phase, the solution has been built. At this point, the customer's SMEs will start to test the solution. The scripts that will be used to test the solution are created near the beginning of the project, when the requirement-gathering sessions were completed. The testing scripts can be run either as a manual or automated process.

It's usually a good idea to run through all the scripts at least once manually. Once you have gone through all the scripts, you can then configure them to run automatically so that when future updates are added to the system, you won't have to take the SMEs away from their daily jobs to test the updates. This, of course, will happen monthly when you deploy the updates.

Operate

In this phase, the solution has been tested and signed off by the customer. It's in production, and the users are working in the system. At this point, the project team is disbanded, and support is handed over to the operations teams. This phase doesn't end until all the deployment is rolled out, especially during a multi go-live project. You can still hand off the deployments that have gone live, but this phase continues until all deployments are completed.

What is Microsoft FastTrack for Dynamics 365?

As mentioned previously, Microsoft has created a project program called FastTrack for Dynamics 365. The point of this program is to integrate architectural expertise from Microsoft into an organizational project. The support happens all through the length of the project – from requirement gathering to go-live support.

The purpose of the program is to make sure that the solution that is created for the customer fits within what Microsoft deems to be best practice. However, you can't just start using FastTrack unless you are accepted (let's look at what that means next).

Customer requirements

There are very specific requirements that customers need to meet to be eligible for the FastTrack program. The requirements are as follows:

- The deployment partner they select is qualified in FastTrack
- They must be nominated by their implementation partner to Microsoft for approval
- The minimum annual spend on Dynamics licenses needs to be more than $100,000 USD

Besides the requirements listed here, the customer must also be purchasing products from the Dynamics flatforms in either Customer Engagement or Finance and Supply Chain Management.

Partner requirements

- They must select an implementation partner who is certified in FastTrack
- A gold or silver partner status must be maintained by the partner in the Cloud Business Applications competency
- The FastTrack Success by Design training must be completed successfully by all the project team members, including the solutions architect, project manager, and all functional consultants

If all the requirements are met, a dedicated Microsoft Solutions Architect is assigned to the project and works with the project delivery team throughout the scope of the project to make sure it goes smoothly, following Microsoft's best practices.

If a customer doesn't meet the minimum requirements needed for Microsoft support through FastTrack, they are still able to use the self-service resources. These resources include forms, PowerPoint presentation templates, data templates, and assessments.

Engagement

Prior to 2001, Microsoft solution partners had to have revenue from licenses between $100,000 and $300,000, which then gave them access to the FastTrack implementation portal. This portal can be used to track the success of projects and get access to the FastTrack team at Microsoft. It also allows you to manage the project statuses, timelines, go-live tasks, and access to support staff for any issues or risks that could impact the project.

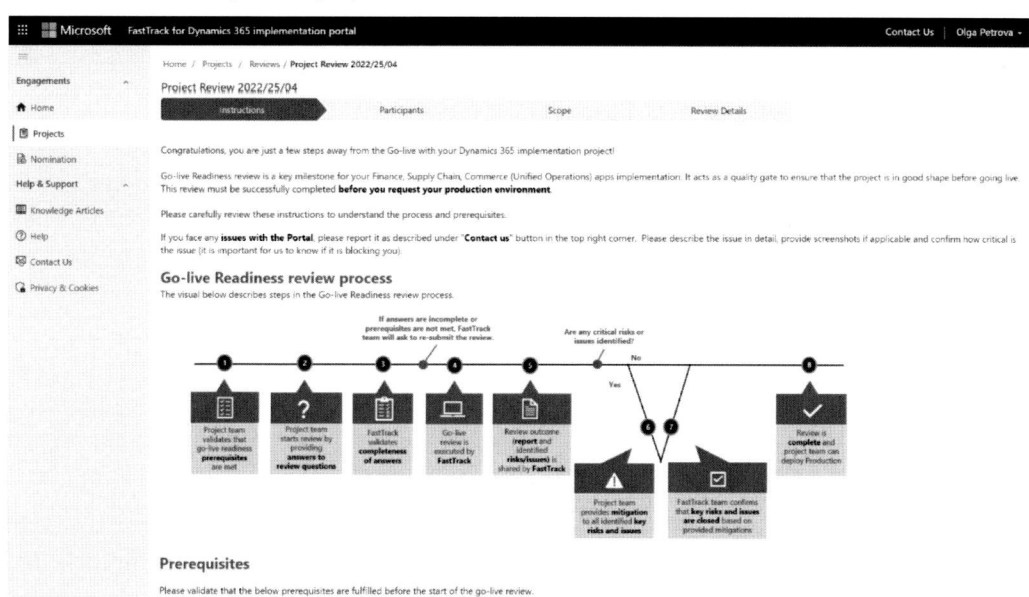

Figure 2.4: The FastTrack for Dynamics 365 implementation portal

As of January 1, 2021, to be considered eligible for FastTrack, your project will need to be nominated by a partner. It will be reviewed by the regional FastTrack lead, and they will determine whether the project will get full FastTrack support from Microsoft. If they accept it, then you will get access to the portal and all functional support that goes with it. If your project is not selected, as listed previously, you can still take advantage of the publicly available resources for FastTrack. It's also possible to have an exception created for your project by the regional lead.

One of the biggest advantages is the ability to directly access senior technical resources, primarily for technical support. Also, if you fall within the specified threshold, you get a dedicated Microsoft Solutions Architect to work with you throughout the length of the project. This is incredibly helpful, especially during the blueprinting and go-live preparation phases of the project.

As mentioned previously, Dynamics 365 FastTrack can be accessed in different ways. The three types of access include the following:

- **FastTrack workshops**: These workshops are scheduled to help when the project is at its most critical, such as at the beginning when requirements are being captured, and at the end when you are preparing to go live.
- **Techtalks**: Techtalks are a set of videos that do a deep dive into the contents of the software, how to configure specific components, and the methods that project managers and solution architects should follow to deliver a project successfully. In some ways, that is what this book is doing as well – presenting areas that are troublesome and finding ways to fix those issues.
- **Success by Design**: Success by Design is the methodology that is used to complete Microsoft Dynamics 365 deployments. It is based on several thousand successful deployments and uses those deployments as learnings for your project.

Implementation guides

A feature of FastTrack that is useful for everyone, regardless of Microsoft's assistance or not, is the Implementation Guide. This guide has been compiled by a number of Microsoft Solutions Architects and provides examples and best practices to configure D365 F&SCM, to properly determine requirements for the solution blueprint, and to assist project team members, including the solutions architect, project manager, program managers, and anyone else who is involved with the project.

The two main parts of the guide cover organizational change management and the foundations of solution design.

Organizational change management

In a later chapter of this book, we'll do a deep discussion about the concept of human change management. However, one of the most important ideas on which extensive work is required is the idea of organizational change management. A technology project isn't always just about technology. This is especially the case when an organization brings in a completely new system or technology.

If an organization brings in an ERP system for the first time, it is essential that the staff is properly prepared for the new system. But sending out an email to the staff saying, "*Hey, on Feb 2, we're going to be starting to use our brand-new, incredible ERP system. Hope you're excited about the new changes*" is not a very good way to inform the staff about what they are about to experience.

Organizational change management's goal is to properly prepare staff for changes. This will include such processes as surveys, demo presentations, update emails, and pre-deployment training. You want to involve the staff and frontline workers in the project as much as possible. Question and answer sessions are also an important way for the project team to properly understand how the staff might use the new applications.

The preferred methodology for organizational change management is by PROSCI. It defines change management as "*the application of a structured process and set of tools for leading the people side of change to achieve a desired outcome.*" The idea of how a change will impact users is something like the following chart.

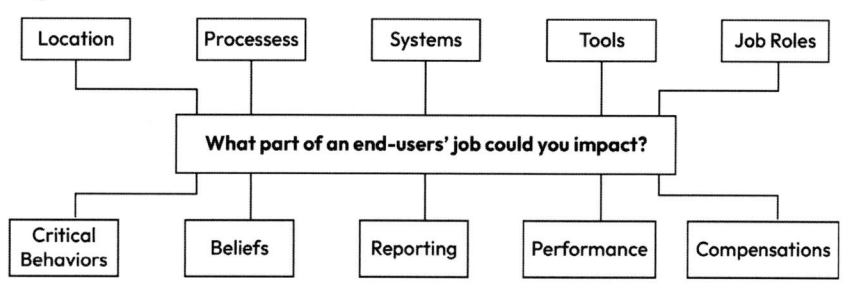

Figure 2.5: How a change affects a person's job

Solution design

You can never be successful in a project unless you know where you're going. Much like when you're going to drive to a place you've never been before, you need to have a map of how to get there. If you're of a certain age like I am, you used to go down to your local map store or travel association and pick up maps of where you were going to go.

Traveling on the main highways and motorways was pretty straightforward because you could look at the map and say, "*I'm taking this major highway to get to the city I want to go to.*" But when you got there, it was a bit trickier, because you couldn't be looking at the map while you were driving to find the destination. Having someone traveling with you who was able to read the map and give directions saved you from potentially having an accident.

When GPS came along, not only did the new device remove the requirement for someone else to be with you in the car, but it also showed you the map and also verbally told you where you should turn and how far ahead that turn was. It also happily announced when you had made it to your destination.

The same goes for when an organization implements new technologies and applications. There needs to be a vision of how it will get to that end goal. The implementation of a new ERP needs to fit into that vision. This can be assisted by an organization having a technology roadmap. This roadmap gives the project team guidance in terms of how the technology should be implemented, and it also makes sure that future technology implementations work with the ERP system.

All of the architectural decisions that are made must complement the technology roadmap. These are all gathered and created during the requirement-gathering phase of the project.

Who does what in the project?

We've looked at the high levels of the FastTrack program. We next need to look specifically at what the different types of engagement are for the program. Not every company will have the same processes or access to the FastTrack program, so we need to understand who does what.

When looking at a project, it's not just the implementation partner that needs to have specific tasks assigned to them. There are three different groups of people that will need to have tasks assigned during the project. These groups are the implementation partner, the customer, and Microsoft. Let's look at the specific tasks assigned to each group.

Partner tasks

The implementation partner will be the primary contact with Microsoft. They are also responsible for all the tasks related to implementation, including the following:

- Requirement-gathering
- Solution blueprint design
- Business process gap management
- Custom code development
- Data migration tasks
- Security configuration
- Initial customer training
- Documentation
- Go-live deployment

All these tasks are executed in combination with the tasks that are the primary responsibilities of the customer and Microsoft.

Customer tasks

The customer also has several tasks that are assigned to them. Having a dedicated group of individuals from the customer side can help to make a project more efficient. In a future chapter, we'll discuss the consequences of not having dedicated project team members for the customer business units.

The customer's tasks include the following:

- Project management and program management
- Blueprint and gap review and approval
- End user training, notification, and utilization after going live

Microsoft tasks

As FastTrack is a program that involves technical and functional resources from Microsoft, there are also tasks that are associated with them. These tasks include the following:

- Guidance on both the solution blueprint and the technical design of the system
- Managing a go-live workshop
- Making recommendations and modifications to a solution to match D365 best practices
- Creating an access gateway to all technical resources internally at Microsoft

The key to Microsoft's role is supporting the implementation partner's solutions architect. They will be there for advice and should not do, or be expected to do, the solution blueprint design. They will have input based on document reviews, but they should not be expected to do the work for the project.

FastTrack engagement

As we mentioned previously, there are different types of engagement. If you fulfill the correct amounts of licenses and the implementation partner has the minimum income, then you'll have access to the FastTrack methodology.

Because no two projects are the same, the amount of involvement of the Microsoft solutions architect will vary. If the solution architect from the implementation partner is a FastTrack Recognized Solution Architect, then they will need less communication and involvement with Microsoft's solution architect. If the implementation partner SA is not **FastTrack Recognized Solution Architects** (**FTRSA**)-certified, then the Microsoft SA will be more involved. This involvement can be completed virtually or, if required, in person.

If you don't qualify, Microsoft still recommends that you follow the methodology; it will just be done either on their own or with people from your implementation partner. Microsoft has made the Success by Design guide publicly accessible.

The role of the SA

It's important to understand that it's not just the SAs provided by Microsoft that are available to a project under FastTrack. Microsoft can provide support from many of the Microsoft departments. Based on the type of request that is made, you can communicate with one of the following:

- **Customer service and support**: This is where you submit support tickets for any bugs in the system that you are not able to get solved yourselves.
- **Customer success managers**: This group of people assists a customer to validate that an implementation matches the requirements that the customer has. This group will also work with the customer to validate that a system works as expected post-deployment.
- **Customer engineers**: This group helps to validate that a solution works the way it was designed by completing performance testing, solution blueprint review, and code reviews and testing.

Also, any of these groups can bring in further support within Microsoft to help support the project. They can get help for things such as ISV integrations, updates to product roadmaps, and testing strategies to further test deployments.

A FastTrack engagement case study

Now that we have an understanding of what FastTrack is and how it can be used, let's show some examples of what we can expect. In this case study, we'll walk through how that methodology can be used for a short project and what types of output we can expect.

Background

You are the owner of a company that manufactures barbeques. You've been in business for about 25 years and have a wide range of products that sell all over the world. You currently have an ERP product that you have had for about 10 years. The software is outdated and has been heavily customized to allow you to run your business. The software is only used to run your finances and purchasing for the company. You have a separate application that you use for inventory and warehouse management.

The company leadership has decided that they will implement a new system based on Microsoft D365 F&SCM. They will move away from the current two applications and put all business operations into D365. Your CIO has been in contact with Microsoft, who has looked at your high-level project plan and has decided that you would be eligible for FastTrack, depending on which implementation partner you choose. They have provided you with a list of four partners that would be able to take advantage of FastTrack. You have been allocated a budget of $5,000,000 to complete the work.

After interviewing the partners, you decide to work with ABC Solutions. This company seems to have the best resources for your project and also qualifies for the FastTrack program. ABC created a SOW, and you both agree to everything and sign the contract.

Let's speed forward slightly, and imagine that your project has been approved and added to the FastTrack program. After a short time, Microsoft assigns a dedicated SA to your project, and you're ready to get started. A project kickoff is scheduled, and all the leading people of the project are to attend. From the customer side, this would include the CIO, the program manager for your company, the assigned project manager, and the senior business leaders. These include the finance director, procurement manager, head of engineering, warehouse director, IT director, manufacturing director, and maintenance director. We have a dedicated project admin, who will work with the project manager and be responsible for tasks such as scheduling meetings and organizing documentation. Generally, the CIO or whoever the project's executive sponsor is will attend the first meeting to give a bit of a pep talk, or set out what they see as the successful outcomes of the project.

From the ABC Solutions company, it will be the salesperson who worked on the SOW, the partner project manager, the SA assigned to the project, and all of the members of the project team. From Microsoft, we will have the assigned SA.

At our production facility, we've dedicated a large area to the project room. There are a few small offices for the senior members of the project team and a large room with computers for use by the members of the project.

At this meeting, we lay out the structure of the project, the roles that each of the individuals will play, and our expected timeline. After this meeting, we have the first set of requirements meetings scheduled.

Now, let's take a look at what we can expect during each of the phases of the project. This will be based on Success by Design.

The initiate phase

We've started this phase by having the project kickoff meeting. Now, we will have a number of meetings to gather all of the requirements for the project.

> **Best practice**
>
> It's best if you break meetings down into smaller parts and focus on specific areas that need to be recorded. I recommend you break them down by module, then by department, and maybe further by function.
>
> As an example, have one meeting for two to three hours dedicated specifically to the accounts payable module and all the processes in that area. Then, do the same for accounts receivable. You can have a single meeting that comes with functions, such as budgeting, reporting, cash and bank management, and any other functions that they may have. Each of those meetings may be longer than two or three hours, but I wouldn't recommend having a single meeting longer than three hours, with at least two breaks during that time. The longer people have to sit and focus on something, the harder it gets to keep their attention. More but shorter meetings are preferable. Also, bring snacks and coffee – trust me, it helps.

Now, we need to figure out how many workshops we need and who should be there. By this time, you will have identified who will be your SMEs in each of the departments and assigned those individuals to the project. These are people who matter most during the workshops, as they will be able to inform the SA what, outside of regular business processes, must be included in the solution.

> **This really happened…**
>
> I was once on a project where the company's entire sales staff was six people, so they were all invited to the sales workshop. Also, the director of sales and the finance manager were in attendance. As we worked through the business processes, one of the salespeople brought up a situation where a customer may make a big purchase, in which they would give them an extra discount and make some guarantee on product availability.
>
> The funny part about this requirement was that neither the director of sales nor the finance manager had any idea that this was happening. At that point, the salespeople were told that this shouldn't be happening anymore and that it was no longer a requirement. The point of this is to make sure you have all the people that you think will have an impact on the requirements.

Workshops

The next step is to determine the number of workshops. Because we will be implementing just about every module in F&SCM, we will need to have a large number of workshops. Here is a list of workshops that will be needed:

- An ALM strategy
- BI and analytics
- A cutover strategy
- A data migration strategy
- Gap analysis
- Integration designs and requirements
- Reporting requirements
- Security requirements
- A testing strategy (including the creation of testing scripts)
- A solution blueprint review

> **Note**
>
> This is the minimum number of workshops by a function that a project requires; there may be others. If, for example, you decided to implement dual-write, you should have a separate workshop related to that topic. There should also be a separate workshop related to any customizations you will need to develop.

We've now come to the end of the initiate phase of the project. Now, we will move on to the implementation phase.

Implementation

In this phase of the project, we will accomplish three tasks:

- First, we will finish the solution blueprint design and get an agreement with everyone that it's what will solve the problem. This is where the Microsoft SA comes in. They will do a final review of the solution and comment, if required, on areas that either don't follow best practices or should be reconsidered. This is also an opportunity for the business to reconsider its business process and potentially change it to map to the functionality of the application better.
- Second, by the midpoint of this phase, we'll have the finalized design in place, including any development that may be needed based on the business processes in the blueprint. There will also be several implementation workshops held during this phase. The point of those workshops is to try and get rid of as many risks as possible before the building of the solution starts. Again, this is an opportunity for the business to reconsider its business processes and make changes as required.

    As an output of this phase, we should have process diagrams created for all of the business processes. The following is an example of the type of flowchart that will be created.

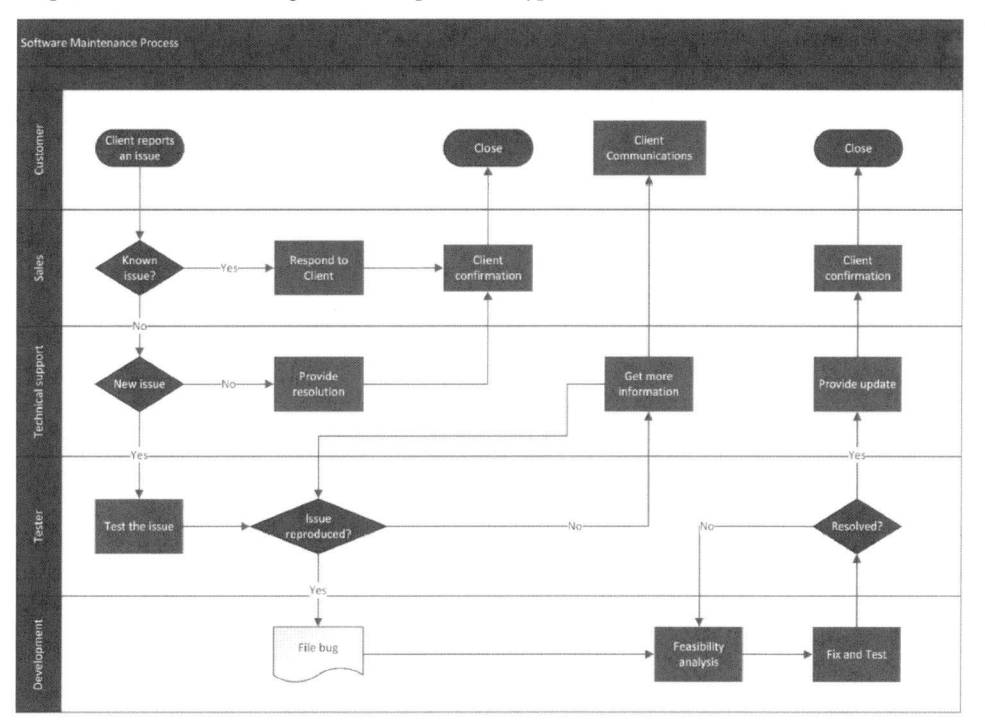

Figure 2.6: A cross-functional flowchart

- The third accomplishment is the final build of the solution. Also, in this phase, comes testing, testing, testing, and more testing. We'll discuss testing strategies later in a later chapter, but I believe there should be the following types of tests:

  - **Unit testing**: This testing is done because the units are implemented by the functional consultant and also tested by the SME
  - **Code testing**: This testing is done by the developer for the custom code they create, and it is then tested in the unit
  - **Testing phase one**: This is UAT testing, completed by the SMEs without any data or integrations enabled
  - **Testing phase two**: This is the second round of UAT testing that is completed with demo data and security roles in place
  - **Testing phase three**: This is the third round of testing that includes all of the preceding, plus any integrations that have been put into place
  - **Testing phase four**: This is an optional phase, but it can be used to do a final end-to-end test of the system if any potential bugs were discovered in the previous testing phases

At the end of this phase, we've completed testing the solution and are all in agreement that it works as needed, based on the requirements. Next, it's time to get this into production.

Preparation

It's at this point that everyone becomes a bit nervous. Did I test it well enough? Did we include all of the business processes we have in the company? Is it really going to work?

Hopefully, at this point in time, we've answered all those questions and can now prepare to go live. In this phase, we will hold more workshops, but these will be specifically for how to get the system up and running and ready to use on go-live day. This is where the Microsoft SA becomes very useful.

The SA will go through in detail what is needed for the system to be ready to go live. They will also assist in getting your production environment set up and a copy of your complete solution moved to the production systems. Once production has been completed, we want to do a simple smoke test of the environment to make sure nothing has changed, but by this point, the system should be hands-off. The following diagram shows a typical go-live timeline.

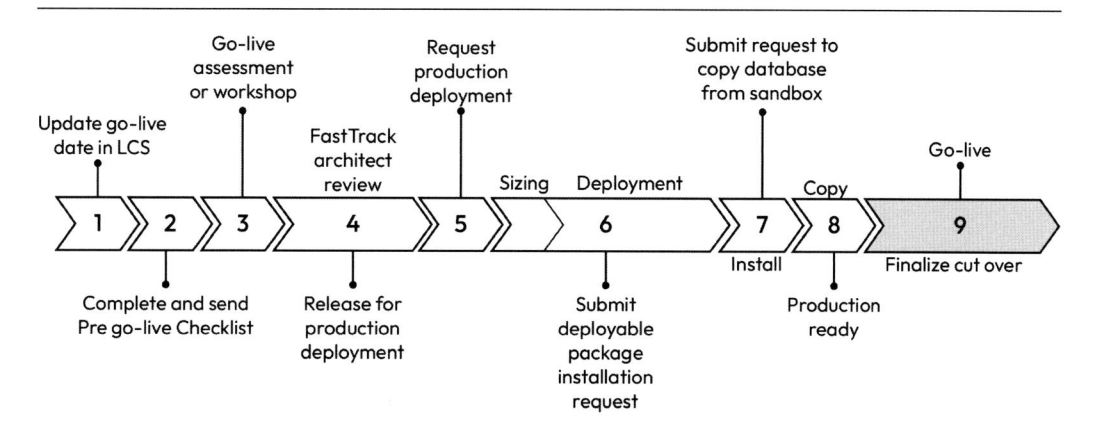

Figure 2.7: The go-live timeline

If we go back to the barbeque company, it would be at this point that an outage is declared on the existing system. Nothing new can be placed into the old system. That doesn't mean the business stops functioning, but any new sales should be recorded in Excel and then manually entered into D365 once the system is declared live. This way, you don't have to worry about any extra data migrations from the old to the new system.

We're now live, and believe it or not, IT WORKS!!! Congratulations to everyone who was involved directly with the project. Everyone did an excellent job. Now, we move on to the post-go-live phase.

Operate

Now that we're up and running, we need to maintain the system. There is an old age that goes, *"All's well that ends well"*. At this point, our FastTrack experience is over. The Microsoft SA leaves the project once go-live has been completed. All other project resources are also released at this point. All that remains is for the senior project staff to have a post-go-live review of the project. This is a learning experience for both the customer and the partner.

Conclusion

The purpose of this chapter was to explain and demonstrate the processes of the Dynamics 365 FastTrack program. Here, we looked at the Success by Design methodology, discussed who should be on a project team, what the roles are of the customer, implementation partner, and Microsoft in a FastTrack project, and how each of the phases in the project should be executed.

In the next chapter, we'll start to look at some of the areas where I saw and experienced solution and deployment issues. We'll start by looking at integrations, which, based on my experiences, seem to be the area that always causes the most problems and biggest delays during a D365 implementation project.

3
Dealing with Integrations

No matter how much we would like companies to use a single platform to do all their work, we know that is unreasonable. Companies have many different applications and platforms that will need to be supported post-Dynamics deployment. As an example, a company might have an existing Unix-based system that they have poured lots of money and effort into keeping available and running. They may look at this system and say "I've spent so much money on this; I'm not ready to retire it". In that case, you'll have the project requirement to share data that exists in that legacy system.

Of the four areas in a project, integration tends to cause SAs the greatest number of headaches.

D365 Integrations

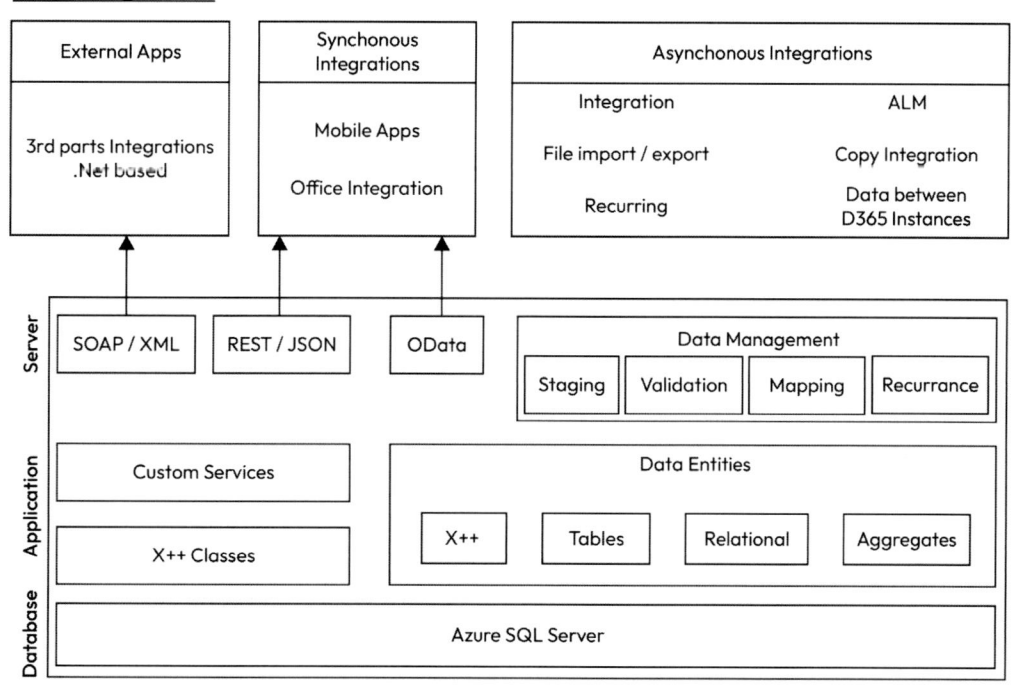

Figure 3.1: Integration platforms

What are integrations?

When completing the project requirements phase of the project, it's very important that you identify what integrations you'll need. Knowing what the applications are and where they are located will help you make a determination as to the type of integration required, but we need to understand what integrations are.

Integration is best described as a method that allows for the transmission of data between different applications. These applications can be on different platforms, such as on-prem or cloud, can be on different operating systems such as Windows or Unix, and can be managed by different companies. Integrations are a very powerful way to allow for data sharing throughout a company.

The problem is that integrations can be very challenging. If you don't look at the reasons why you would need an integration, you may end up getting yourself into a situation where you didn't plan on needing one, only to discover at a later point that you now need to get data from a different system. Of course, this does two things to the project:

- First, it adds extra tasks to your existing project plan
- Second, it can mess up go-live dates

The solution architect is the person on the project who is responsible for identifying, documenting, and organizing the integrations needed for a project. They need to understand which systems need connections and then what type of connection will be required.

What components make up an integration?

Early in the process of determining the requirements, one of the most (if not the most) important ones is knowing which systems will be retired and which will be continued. If we go back to our discussion in a previous chapter on the company's technology roadmap, we need to use that to guide us when gathering the requirements. If we decide that there are some systems that we just can't remove, then there is our way of knowing whether we need integration.

Now, just because we have many different systems doesn't mean that we will be replacing all of them, or having to share data between them. It's quite possible that we will have a system that is there for a specific task that doesn't need any data to be added to F&SCM or doesn't record information past instant reporting. As an example, airports have temperature detection systems that record the temperature at the runway level and two depths below the runway. This is used to determine when chemicals need to be spread across the surface of the runway to prevent planes from sliding when landing. (I don't know about you, but I really don't want the plane sliding off the runway when I land… I want my flights to be uneventful.)

This type of system doesn't record historical data, it's only an in-the-moment tool. So why would we want to record any of that information in the ERP system? Some may argue, "*Well, if we know this information, we can integrate it with the asset management module and have it notify us when we should put down antifreeze.*" Well, yes, in theory, that could be something you might consider, but there is already an existing system that does that for us… called the *weather service*.

As the solution architect, you need to take these systems and understand which pieces of data you need. Once you've determined a system that does require an integration, first, you need to identify the requirements of the systems, which components are needed, and how they need to be configured.

Integration Components

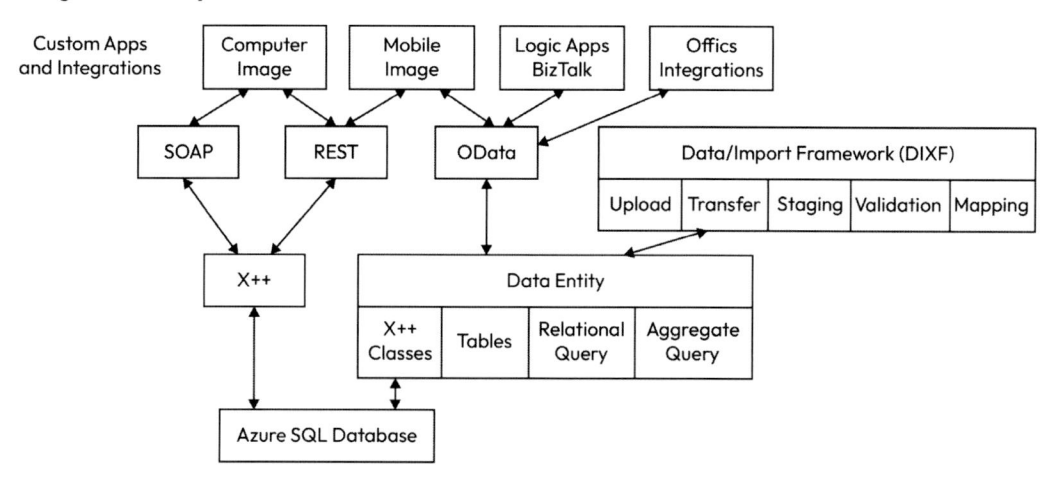

Figure 3.2: Integration components

The preceding diagram shows all of the components needed to successfully set up and configure an integration with F&SCM. When planning the integration, you need to understand how the data will be transferred, what the data looks like on both sides of the integration, and how it will be consumed in F&SCM.

Data integration patterns

There are two different types of integrations that can be used. One-off patterns are generally configured as data packages in F&SCM. We'll discuss those in greater detail in *Chapter 5*.

The second type of integration is recurring. These integrations are configured as APIs using a number of different communications methodologies. They are also file-based so that the data is transmitted as a file between systems. These APIs include the following:

- Custom services
- External web services

- Office integrations
- Data management packages
- **Open Data Protocol (OData)**
- **Dual-write (DW)** Dataverse integrations
- Batch APIs

Let's take a look at a couple of these types of integrations and why we need them.

Custom services

To allow data to be sent out of F&SCM, you can set up custom services. These services will always be created in either SOAP as a SOAP endpoint or in JSON as a JSON endpoint. Custom services take advantage of being highly customizable and transferring large amounts of data between systems. Also, custom services are used when you want to implement synchronous communications. As a reminder, synchronous communications allow for data to be sent in real time or on a scheduled basis. Examples include video or phone conversations.

Custom services are best recommended when you need to create a synchronous integration that needs to be highly customized. Equally, these are best used when you're working with low to medium levels of data transmission, require near real-time updates, and are being used specifically for system-to-system integration. As an example, you would use a custom service when connecting a system that uses a JSON or SOAP endpoint to allow data to flow in and out of an application. Using an in-house web app written in ASP.NET would facilitate this type of connection.

Batch APIs

Batch APIs are primarily used with large data transmissions. This is run as a batch job, importing or exporting hundreds of rows of records into and out of F&SCM. This is specifically when you need to schedule the data transfers at a time when the system is not heavily used. It also uses asynchronous communications to quickly transfer the data from one system to another. An example of an application that would use a batch API would be when moving a large amount of data to a database from a legacy system that needs to be imported as part of a data migration to F&SCM.

OData

OData is a protocol used to transfer data between systems. It is based on **Representational State Transfer (REST)** to create, delete, update, and read data in various systems. As an example, OData is the primary protocol used when communicating between Excel and F&SCM. Both JSON and HTTP communications take advantage of OData's data transfer capabilities.

OData works well when transmitting low to medium data volumes and near real-time data transfers are needed.

Dataverse

Because we can communicate with different systems via several different methods, mostly based on OData, batch APIs, or custom integrations, we also need a way to share information within the Dynamics 365 platform. Let's first understand why we would need an integration platform for Dynamics 365 apps.

Dynamics 365 F&SCM is based on a data structure that has been around for several years. When Microsoft purchased the software from its creator, Axapta, it kept the data structure of the system. I mean, why change it if it's not broken, right? The CE family of applications, including Sales, Field Services, and Marketing, is based on Dataverse.

Dataverse and F&SCM are incompatible with others unless a data translation is undertaken. The biggest advantage of the Dataverse is that it has many features, including the ability to create Power Apps. A virtual data source in Dataverse is how F&SCM is represented, and using the virtual data source, allows users to edit, delete, update, and read data in Dataverse from F&SCM. There are two ways you can share data between F&SCM and Dataverse, which we will examine next.

Data integrators

Data integrators use point-to-point connections to integrate between F&SCM and Dataverse and specifically for F&SCM and D365 Sales. This tool has several limitations, including the fact it's a one-directional integration, which means that you can only transfer data from F&SCM to Dataverse.

The advantage of using the data integrator is that it does allow you to have integrations from multiple sources into Dataverse, making it highly customizable, and allowing for data conversions as a part of the integration. Its best feature is its ability to transmit high volumes of data, but not in real time. Because this is a scheduled or manually executed integration, there will be a difference in the data of the connected systems.

Via the AppSource website, there are three pre-defined templates that can be installed:

- A project service automation template
- One for field services updates
- One for a sales-to-cash sales process

Each of these templates can be further customized by the company deploying them.

DW

A second way to integrate with Dataverse is by using DW. DW is a tool that provides out-of-the-box integrations to provide near real-time data transfers between D365 F&SCM and D365 Customer engagement applications, such as Sales and Field Services.

Dual write

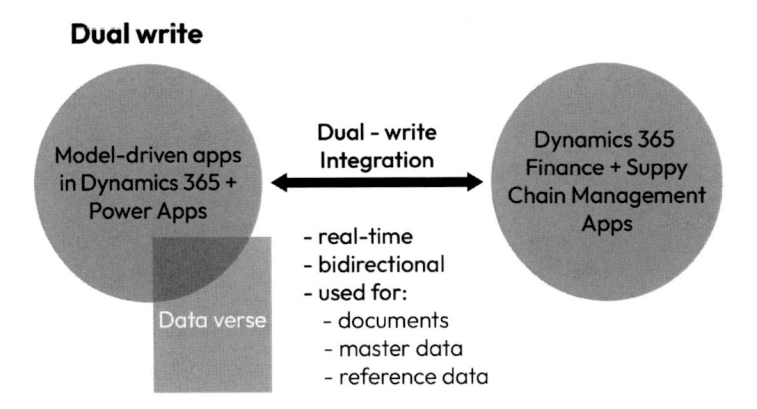

Figure 3.3: DW platform integration

DW has several features that make it the ideal integration choice when transferring data between the two Dynamics platforms. Because DW is native to the systems, it doesn't require any middleware to communicate between the systems, unlike data integrators, which do require a middle-layer tool. Some other advantages include the following:

- It offers you the ability to sync initial data between apps (if you have one app running and deploy the other one from scratch)
- You can start, pause, and catch up the sync at any time as required for offline/online modes
- It covers both standard and custom entities
- Notes and activities are expanded to support both customers and internal system users
- It follows the Microsoft policy of low-code/no code for Power Platform
- It allows users to extend data entities to Power Platform apps
- There is a bi-directional data flow between Finance and Operations and Customer Engagement Apps

Even though there are lots of advantages to using DW, there are some things that an SA needs to keep in mind when implementing the tools. First off, even though you can install both DW and data integrators in the system deployment, you can't mix the use of DW and the data integrator template for prospect-to-cash. Also, you are not able to transfer data between different legal entities in the system. So, if you have Company A and Company B, you can only transfer data within Company A and within Company B, not from A to B, and vice versa.

An example of why you would use this form of integration would be that you had a sales team that used D365 Sales to complete all telephone sales. The salespeople need to be able to see the inventory so they know whether there is stock of the items they are trying to sell.

The integration sends data from F&SCM to update items such as the inventory, price lists, and released products. It is used to send data from Sales to F&SCM so that items are sold and deducted from the inventory and released to the warehouse for picking and packing. DW is the easiest of the integrations to implement. It is an out-of-the-box tool that provides near real-time, bidirectional integrations. Because of the way it's designed, it will handle the differences in security, licensing, and topology between F&SCM and Dataverse.

When the integration between the D365 apps is in place, there are some major modifications made to Dataverse's database. These include the following:

- Date effectivity is added for defining record validity between a specific set of dates.
- The currency field is expanded to allow for up to ten decimal places for numeric values.
- A number of unit conversions are added for financial documents, including invoices, customer statements, purchase orders, and quotations.
- The ability to create notes and activities recorded in the database is increased to support external customers and internal system users, mostly employees.
- Dataverse is modified to allow for features in F&SCM to appear the same in Dataverse. These entities include contact information, parties, and contacts.

Virtual entities

Another method of working with data in external systems is by using virtual entities. These virtual entities make all users to work with data in other systems, without the requirement of replicating the data between the systems. This also allows the integration to function without the requirement of custom code to manage data transfer and communication.

With virtual entities, users can complete all standard data manipulation functions, including creating, deleting, and updating data. The advantage of using virtual entities comes when working with Power Platform apps for externally facing websites. This allows collaboration for several different types of business processes within the F&SCM platform. An example of this is the vendor portal. It allows users to manage vendor items, invoices, and communications without being a member of the tenant in which F&SCM is hosted.

A couple of other types of integrations we can use include the Azure integration services, based on Azure Service Bus. This allows companies to connect on-premises and cloud-based apps. This sets up secure message flow workflows to process and transmit data in real time. The connectors for this type of integration use triggers to generate the action to move data between applications.

Another integration type is based on Microsoft 365 tools, including Outlook, Word, Excel, SharePoint Online, and Teams. The integrations for these tools give you the ability to use the productivity capabilities that the Microsoft 365 tools provide.

The last type of integration is Business events. This type of integration is used to provide messaging features to external systems. The types of endpoints that are supported include HTTPS, Microsoft Power Automate, Azure Service Bus, and Azure Events.

Why do integrations fail?

As mentioned previously, integrations are one of the areas that can cause an SA grief during a project. There are several different issues that may cause the failure of a D365 integration. Listed here are the top 5 issues.

Working in silos

Unfortunately, many companies fall into this situation. They have separated out the way their company works so that it's easier to manage internally. This prevents the business units and IT from working together to take full advantage of how the integration will work. This happens mostly because neither side fully understands what the other side does and how they interact with the different systems that will utilize integration.

Data dependency

The single biggest reason to use integration is so we can transmit data between systems. When we're creating sales orders for customers, we need to have the following in the system:

- Information on products
- The total amount of product inventory
- The price of each item
- Which warehouse everything is located in

Where the information in your systems lives will determine what dependencies you have on the data. As an example, let's say that you migrate all of the warehouse management functionality to D365 SCM. The business has decided that it will keep its existing **transportation management system** (**TMS**), which it uses to calculate shipping rates and schedule pickups.

To be able to properly track the costs for shipments and have them correctly appear in the **general ledger** (**GL**) account for transportation, you'll need to be able to access the data from the TMS and have that data extracted and imported into D365 Finance. If you don't understand what the data in the TMS looks like, which fields contain the specific data, and how you're going to be able to access that data from that application, your integration will fail to provide the information and feature the business requires.

Not understanding interface complexity

Have you ever looked at a problem and thought "How hard can it be?!" I've done that lots, thinking that I've done something before and it can't be that difficult. Usually, when I have that attitude, about 5 minutes into the development of the integration, the developer will call me and ask me whether I actually know what I'm doing. Creating and architecting integration is a complex process. Understanding that complexity is very important for two reasons:

- First, and most importantly, you can give the developer a design document that makes sense and is easy for them to interpret and create
- Second, understanding the complexity means that you understand what the data is, how it's to be used, the best way to work with that data, and how to test to make sure the integration is working properly and efficiently

Both the project team and the business need to understand how the data model works. Quite often, the partner will have no idea what the data model looks like and will have to investigate the structure. Either IT or the business unit will have to assist the SA to understand the structure and how best to work with it. This design should not only be a written document but also a diagram showing the data structure, workflows, and data interfaces.

Understanding integrations

It's important for the client and the project team to understand that the integration is not just a standalone tool. Integration is a component that needs to be created as part of the overall system.

Resistance to change

I find it rather funny the number of organizations that want to bring in a new ERP system but really don't want to change. I once worked on a manufacturing project where they had a very old ERP system and were upgrading to D365 F&SCM. Quite often during the discussions about configuration and requirements, they would say, "It has to work the same as it does right now… our users aren't supportive of change." When someone tells me that, it makes me wonder why we are even doing this project to begin with. D365 F&SCM has many new and advanced features that older ERP systems don't, and if you're not will take advantage of them, then why bother? Another comment I hear is that the new system must work exactly the same for things such as customers, sales, discounts, and so on.

If an organization is not willing to adapt to change, that makes it very difficult to create a new system for it. This also happens with integrations. A company may have technology in place that it's used for a long time and invested heavily into. Let's say that system is Microsoft Biztalk. Biztalk is a great tool for doing EDI transmissions between different systems, but it's not really good at transmitting large datasets from one system to another. If a company is set that this will be the integration middle-layer tool, it automatically restricts its ability to bring in modern technology.

The technologies that are being used need to work between systems and the middle-layer tools need to be adaptive and scale to what the new technologies require. Business decisions about what technology to use, as a part of a resistance to change, can have a major negative impact on the project.

We always blame the software

No matter how wonderful the software is, we can't always blame it for failure. In most cases, the reason the integrations fail is due to a lack of data governance on how the data is to be used, the personal political ambitions of staff members, and a lack of clear understanding of current business processes and documentation on how those processes work. If you want to avoid any type of deployment issue, you need to clearly understand what your data is, how it needs to be processed, and what it's supposed to look like once it's been processed. It might sound a bit silly to say, but my hero Albert Einstein's quote fits perfectly here: *"If you can't explain it simply, you don't understand it well enough."*

Case study

Of course, the point of this book is to help you get out of situations in which you might have issues. So, let's look at a couple of real-life examples of how and why integrations failed and how they were fixed.

Integrating two ERP systems

As we mentioned earlier in this chapter, one of the major issues with integrations is knowing your data. You need to know what data is stored in the application you're wishing to integrate with, how it's used, and who is using it. I worked on a project for a client who decided they wanted to implement a new property management system in their company. Originally, they had an ISV offering loaded into the D365 system. However, the property management department didn't have a say in the selection of the ISV, and to be honest, they never really liked it to begin with. When it was purchased, the ISV had to make several modifications to its software to work the way the property people wanted.

After a couple of years of using this tool, they finally decided that they wanted something that would work the way they did. After some research, they found a new standalone, SaaS-based application. The tool worked well for what it was intended to be used for. There was one problem, however. The software was basically a separate ERP system that had its own AP and AR functions.

The reason this was complicated was that the finance department, which made all the decisions about money and needed all the property rents to be recorded in the GL, needed the D365 system to be the system of truth. So, allowing for this, we needed to set up an integration between the property management system and D365, which would let the numbers in the AP and AR modules be replicated between the two applications. Now, that being the solution, there were several issues with this solution.

First, the data format in D365 is very different from what it was in the property management software. For us to move the data, we would have had to majorly transform that data for it to be accepted in D365. To do those transformations, there was a custom API created in the property management application that would expose data. To move and transform the data, a tool called **Dell Boomi**© was purchased. This tool sat there as middleware to do the conversions and transfer the data between applications.

After a long time, it was decided that the original plan of replicating the data between the two systems would have to be dropped and we could only transfer the AR data from the property management application to D365 because the property management software wouldn't accept any data transfers into the software via the integration. It took about 5 months into the project before we made that decision.

The lesson learned from this project was that trying to link together different ERP systems is not a wise idea. With all the differences in data types, data formats, and application configurations, trying to convert the data to fit into each application is way more complex than may be expected. I would recommend in that situation to replicate the data into a data warehouse in a data lake and then replicate that data to either D365 or the property management application.

DW for a racing team

I was asked by a co-worker to assist them in creating a connection between a D365 Sales and D365 SCM for when a race team uses specific parts during a race. These items would include things such as tires, filters, bolts, and so on. The goal of the integration was to set up special fields in Sales so that they could use sales orders to purchase items from inventory, which would be paid for by the race team after the race ended.

After reviewing this request, I suggested not doing this, as it would mean that they would have to create several new entities in the DW integration and it would be difficult and too much effort for DW to handle. For something like this, I suggested that they look at using a Power App, as there is a pre-configured connector for Power Apps and D365. In this sort of situation, use the type of application that best suits what you're trying to accomplish.

Solidworks to D365

Another project that I was involved in needed to add an integration that connected the CAD application Solidworks to D365. Solidworks was used by engineers to design new products that would be sold by a manufacturing company. In the CAD tool, they would do the design for parts and then they would create a **Bill of Materials** (**BOM**) list that would have all the parts. This was then used by the fabrication group to fabricate some of the parts, by the buyers to order the parts they couldn't fabricate, and finally by the production team to build the item.

The contents of the BOM needed to be transferred into the Product Information Management module in D365. This would add all of the items to the Released products menu so the buyers could buy the correct parts and the warehouse team could pick those parts for manufacture.

For this integration, we created a direct connection between D365 and Solidworks, as there was a pre-configured integration that would allow for this to happen. So, in this case, even though it was complicated, because there was a pre-defined integration, it made the data movement much easier.

When doing your work to plan out integrations, also keep in mind that sometimes the vendor will have a pre-created integration for you.

Power Automate

Since Microsoft has upgraded the Power Automate tools available in the Power Platform, being able to transfer messages outside of D365 has become much easier. However, many organizations have started to use it as a method of moving data between applications much like an integration. Power Automate was not designed for this purpose, and even though it can do the task, it's not the best option when working with many different applications.

Based on Microsoft's recommendations, Power Automate should never be used as an integration platform. If you are in a situation where it's suggested that Power Automate can be used, strongly advise against it. This will make your and the customer's life much easier in the future.

Ways to fix integration issues

Everyone you talk to on a project thinks they have the solution to solving integration issues. As we saw earlier in this chapter, one of several things can cause things to go a bit sideways. That doesn't mean it will be difficult to bring the project back on track. If you plan things properly, you can help to keep yourself out of situations where errors show up. As you'll see shortly, planning is the most important part of a project when it comes to implementing integrations.

Change-tracking

One thing that I've seen happen repeatedly is a misunderstanding of integrations in the sales cycle. If you do an incomplete job of scoping out the number and complexity of integrations, then the project will have issues trying to create and implement. One of the ways to help prevent issues during the creation of integrations is to create a change-tracking log. This can be done in either an Excel spreadsheet or in DevOps as a tracking log. It doesn't prevent pre-sales from mis-scoping this integration, but by using the log, you can track requirements for the integration during the design phase.

Budget properly

ERP projects are not cheap. If a company is planning on implementing integrations as a part of its ERP project, you'll need to allocate the correct amount of time and money to these tasks. From a resource point of view, you'll need to have the SA, who is the overall lead, a technical architect to manage the technical aspects of the solution, and a developer on the team to do the coding required to get the integration to work correctly.

For some of the integrations, such as when using DW or an Office integration, you can replace the developer with a functional consultant to complete the work. From the customer side, you'll need to have, at a minimum, someone from IT who can give you access to the needed systems and will also be responsible for managing the connection points, security, and access for the integration; a subject-matter expert from the business, to assist with what data is required and how it will be consumed; and an operational person from the IT department, who will ultimately be responsible for the management of the integration upon go-live.

Because there are several individuals in place working on these integrations, it's important that there be sufficient time put into the schedule for these tasks to be completed successfully. Obviously, a sufficient budget will also need to be in place for this work to be successful. At the time of the scoping of the project by the partner, the pre-sales consultants should have a deep understanding, based on previous experience, of how many hours it takes to implement different types of integrations.

Now, that's not to say that they will know that it will take exactly 3 hours to build a budget upload spreadsheet for Microsoft Excel, but they will have a good idea of how to estimate the time needed to complete each of the integrations for the project. Once that amount of time needed has been identified as well as which resources will be required, the cost for each of the integrations can be calculated and added to the project costs. It is always better to overestimate the time required than to fall short, especially if you have multiple integrations. If you underestimate each integration, the project can be put into a red state, based on time and cost.

Tool selection

The type of integration you need to develop will determine which tools are required. If you're creating a custom integration, you'll need a tool such as Visual Studio. You'll need to create the code and hook it into F&SCM. If you're creating an Office integration, you'll need to have access to the correct Office tool, the F&SCM module you're connecting to, and sufficient permissions needed to create the integration.

If a company has a requirement that its D365 implementation needs to have an Excel-like interface with custom fields specific to how their business functions, this will require a great deal of configuration and development. The integration will specifically need to have data mappings allowing the data to be loaded into D365 properly. This is a small example, but in many cases, these will be the types of integrations that need to be created and developed.

Planning your strategy

When completing the blueprinting for the project, one section that must be included is around integrations. In some cases, these integration tasks can be their own sub-project within the overall project scope. As part of this strategy, we need to look at how we will identify the integrations required and what each of those integrations needs to function correctly. A part of that integration requirement will be which platforms the integration will need to communicate with.

During the requirements phase of the project, the SA needs to work with the customer to understand how much data each integration will process, what would be the peak data amount to be processed, whether or not the data needs to be transferred in real time or whether there can be a delay in the transfer, and the type of integration that would best suit the type of data being used.

Also, as part of the solution blueprint, the SA will need to determine whether there are any licensing issues that will impact how the integration is developed. And finally, there must be clear and detailed explanations given to the customer so that they fully understand what the integration technology chosen will do, how it will connect, and what security and licensing issues they will encounter.

Creating the team

The integrations for a project are not only the responsibility of the IT department. Yes, they will be primarily responsible for the integration from the point of view of knowing how it functions, how it will process information, and how to connect systems, but we also need to ascertain how it will transfer data between the systems. The ideal team that will be needed for the creation and scoping of integration will be a combination of technical specialists and users from the business who will actually consume the information that the integration processes.

Standardization

As a consultant, you may have come across some of the other applications customers may want to integrate with in the past. Hopefully, you'll be able to reach back and use the knowledge that you've learned previously to help in the future, specifically when dealing with Office integrations. The more you can standardize these integrations, the more successful the project will proceed.

Testing, testing, and testing

There is nothing more important during a project than to test. I'm of the opinion that you can never test enough. Testing is not just a task that should be completed a couple of times near the end of the project but something that must always be done constantly. The testing needs to be completed when the integrations are created but must also be tested several times during the **User Acceptance Testing** (**UAT**). There should be at least three rounds of testing completed by the SMEs from the business. One last test should be done once the system is placed into production to make sure the connection points are still working.

Conclusion

In this chapter, I've aimed to point out the different types of integrations that we may have to work with during a project. And I hope I've pointed out some potential issues that could pop up during a project and how to fix them or prevent them from even happening. If you get this part of the project right, you'll look like a hero later on when users don't ever notice that they aren't working with data all in one single system.

In the next chapter, we will take a look at designing and setting up a security configuration. We will look at out-of-the-box versus custom security roles, table-level security, separation of duties, and how to properly set up access for external users. We will also look at examples of how to correctly set up security.

4
Efficient Security Design

I know in previous chapters, I've said *"This is the most important part…"*. Well, I'm going to do the same thing in this chapter. And I'll make a confession… security (and workflows) is my favorite topic to talk about. Now, you're probably saying to yourself *"There is something wrong with this guy!"*, and you wouldn't be wrong. When I started working in Dynamics, I started as an infrastructure administrator.

Back when I began, the administrator was responsible for setting up the infrastructure that Dynamics ran on, managing backups and environment replications, creating workflows, and setting up and managing security settings. Now that D365 has moved to the cloud, the job of the administrator has had a major change in responsibilities. Now, the administrator is more of a testing coordinator than someone who needs to actually manage the platform. But they will still be responsible for setting up and configuring (with the assistance of the business) security roles, duties, and privileges in the system.

In this chapter, we're going to discuss the following:

- How do we set up security in the cloud?
- What does security look like in D365 F&SCM?
- How do we manage the segregation of duties?

We'll also look at how to create a security configuration and what to do when an out-of-the-box security configuration doesn't fit a requirement. As a note, I'm not going to touch on licensing in this chapter. We'll be looking at that topic in detail in a future chapter.

Why is the cloud different?

If you've ever had to work in an environment that was in a local data center, you know that you are responsible for multiple layers of security, from the physical security of the data center to securing the application. When working in the cloud, this management of security must be done in cooperation with the cloud hosting provider. When working with D365, we must follow **Microsoft Trusted Cloud Principles (MTCP)**. The MTCP are made up of the following – security, compliance, privacy, and transparency. Microsoft is responsible for securing the environments, the infrastructure, and the virtual servers that D365 is run on. As an end user, you are responsible for who has access to the system and how the users access what areas.

The basis of access is around the idea of authentication and authorization. **Authorization** is how it is determined whether a person or service has the right to access a specific application. This is where a person's identity is validated. For D365, **authentication** is based on OAuth 2.0. OAuth is a JSON-based custom service that passes tokens that identify a user. When a person wants to connect to D365, they first get a connection to Azure Active Directory for that tenant. Once they are validated as a user in that tenant, they are then passed an authorization token that they can use to access resources.

When they connect to the D365 environment, this token is passed to show their authorization, and then from there, the application will assign the person access within D365. The following diagram shows the process of getting connected.

Client Computer

1. User wants to connect to a resource or application
2. Computer connects to AAD
3. AAD answers
4. Computer answers with IP address of application
5. AAD answers with IP address
6. Computer asks application for access
7. Application response with access

Azure AD

D365 Finance + Supply Chain Management

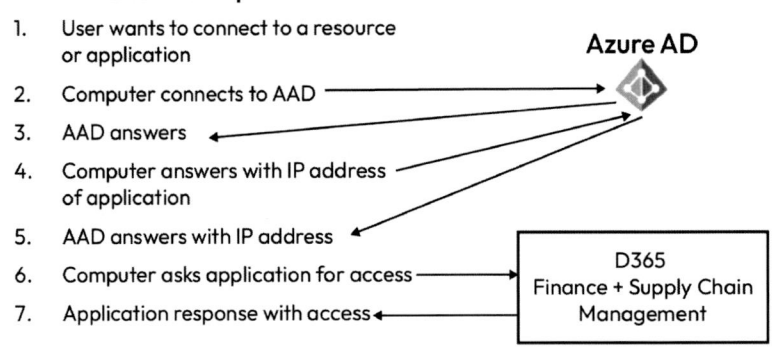

Figure 4.1: Authorization flow

The main concept that security follows is the concept of **Zero Trust**. Zero Trust is a security framework that makes a requirement that all users of the organization need to be authenticated, authorized, and validated on a continual basis for security access to be granted to access the application. Without this continual process being executed, a user could be hacked in such a way that once they are in the system, they could get access to the system, and cause problems. These could include deleting data, changing configurations, and removing user access (if they got Sys Admin access).

An additional method that can be used to enhance security when connecting to D365 is **Multi-Factor Authentication** (**MFA**). MFA is based on the idea of needing a second method of validating a user's identity. It could be based on something you know, such as a password, something you have, such as a device (i.e. a cell phone app or a one-time code generator), or something you are, such as your fingerprint. Usually, MFA is only used when a user is outside of their corporate domain. If they are logging in from home, or somewhere outside of the office, they will be prompted for secondary information. If they are connecting from their office network, the system can be configured to bypass the MFA requirement.

Once those configurations are set up, you can be assured that the security to get to D365 will be as secure as can be. Next, we'll look at how security works in D365.

What does security look like in D365 F&SCM?

Security in D365 F&SCM is one of the most important, but also complicated, jobs that an administrator must manage daily. No matter how much a business identifies and configures security during the project, there will always be some reason for it to change. Mostly, it's due to a lack of ability of out-of-the-box roles to fulfil a requirement. The security architecture is based on roles, duties, privileges, and permissions.

D365 security architecture

The security model is based on a hierarchy. The different levels represent differing degrees of detail. The following figure shows how the hierarchy is laid out:

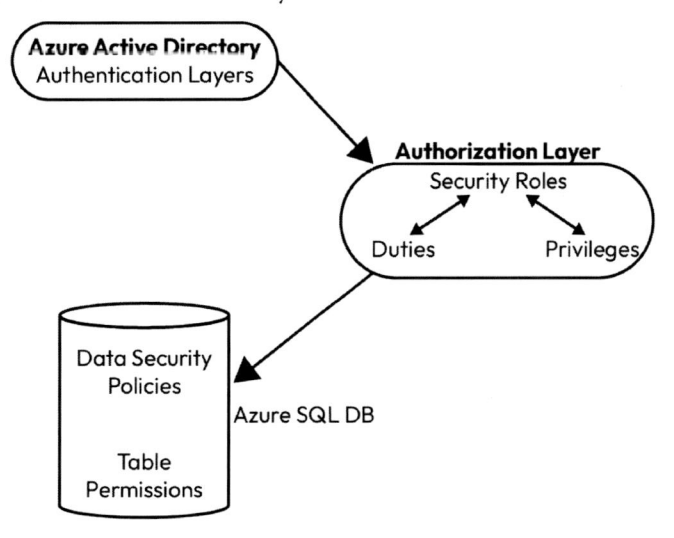

Figure 4.2: Security model in D365 F&SCM

The security model is designed in such a way that each level is responsible for a different piece of the system. The following make up the hierarchy:

- **Azure Active Directory**: This is the primary part that validates the user is authentic and authorized to access the application.
- **Roles**: The level grants access to Finance and Supply Chain Management.
- **Duties**: This level is made up of privileges that represent business processes. An example would be the processing of an invoice.
- **Privileges**: A privilege is made up of permissions and allows access to individual tasks such as deleting a sales order line.
- **Permissions**: These are securable objects in the system such as menu items and tables.

Extended data security

For most companies, the security architecture, as mentioned previously, is sufficient to secure their data. However, some companies might want to use an extra layer of data security. The extended data security model allows a company to add additional security at the data/table level of the database. This is accomplished by a developer restricting access to records based on a security policy that contains a custom security role.

Security reports

Once the security of the system is implemented, there are reports available to the administrator to see who is assigned to each of the security roles. These reports allow for the auditing of the roles, users, and overall security of the system. These reports can be viewed onscreen or exported in several different formats, including Excel, CSV, Word, XML, MHTML, and TIFF.

User role assignments

One of the reports is called **User role assignments**. This report generates a list of which users are assigned to which security role. The report can be filtered to show specific users to roles. The following is an example of a report.

User role assignments
Contoso Entertainment System USA

JULIA
365admin@ebecs.com   https://sts.windows.net/

System administrator   -SYSADMIN-
Maintains the Finance and Operations system, has access to all artifacts in the system, and cannot be modified

Organization type	Operating unit types	Organization name	Organization ID	Grant with children
Legal entity	None	ALL	ALL	No

ALICIA
ALICIA@contosoax7.onmicrosoft.com   https://sts.windows.net/

Budget clerk   BUDGETBUDGETCLERK
Documents budget events and responds to budget inquiries

Organization type	Operating unit types	Organization name	Organization ID	Grant with children
Legal entity	None	ALL	ALL	No

Buying agent   TRADEBUYINGAGENT
Documents purchase events and responds to purchase inquiries

Organization type	Operating unit types	Organization name	Organization ID	Grant with children
Legal entity	None	ALL	ALL	No

Employee   HCMEMPLOYEE
Worker in employment relationship with legal entities

Organization type	Operating unit types	Organization name	Organization ID	Grant with children
Legal entity	None	ALL	ALL	No

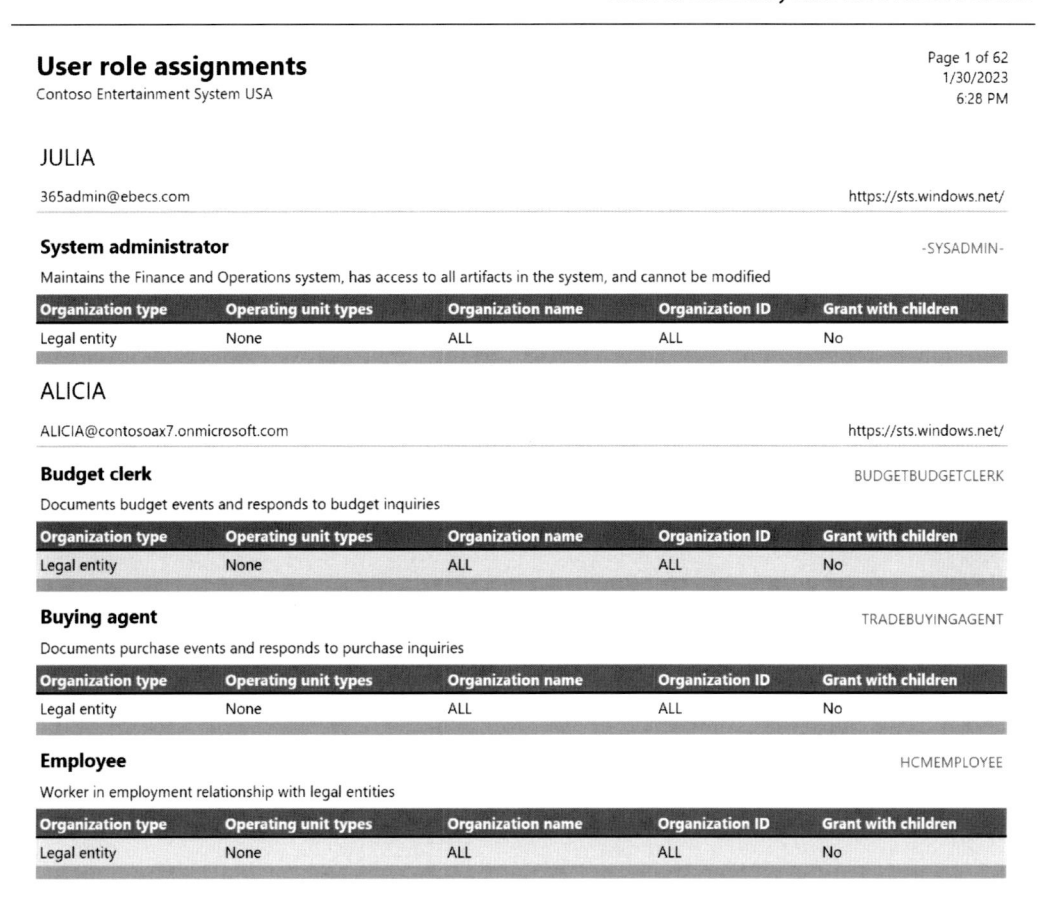

Figure 4.3: User role assignments report

If we want to view it based on a filtered user or list of users, we select the filter option:

Figure 4.4: User role assignments report filter

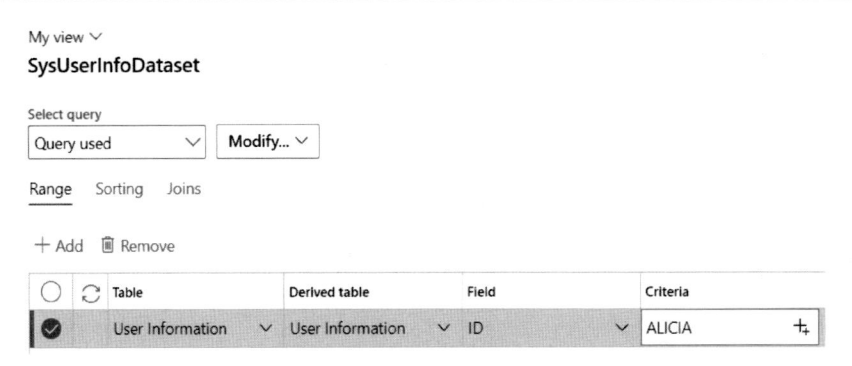

Figure 4.5: Filter settings

Security role access

The **Security role access** report shows a list of the permissions associated with a user for each specific security role. It shows all the combined permissions to give effective user permission.

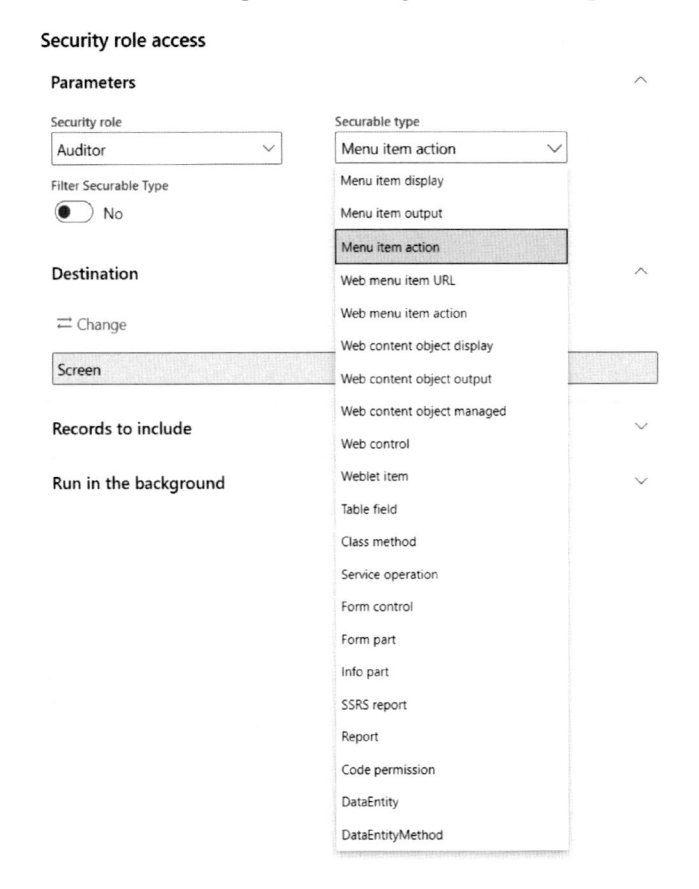

Figure 4.6: Security role access report parameters

And the report looks like this:

Security role effective access
Contoso Entertainment System USA

Page 3 of 8956
1/30/2023
7:18 PM

Auditor   Operations
  AUDITPOLICYMANAGER
  Menu item display

OBJECT	ACCESS	CHILDREN
ASSETCONSUMPTIONFACTOR	View	
ASSETCONSUMPTIONUNIT	View	
ASSETDEPRATE_JP	View	
ASSETDEPRECIATIONGROUP_W	View	
ASSETDEPRECIATIONPART	View	
ASSETDEPRECIATIONPROFILE	View	
ASSETDISCOUNTRATESCHEDULE_JP	View	
ASSETGROUP	View	

Figure 4.7: Security role access report

This report is useful to determine the level of access for each role, but it also shows you what license type would be required for this security role.

Role to user assignment

This report shows a collection of role assignments. This report shows which users are assigned to each role.

Role to user assignment

Contoso Entertainment System USA

Accountant

Documents accounting events and responds to accounting inquiries

CASSIE

Organization name	Organization type	Operating unit types	Organization ID	Grant with children
ALL	Legal entity	None	ALL	No

Louisa Allison

Organization name	Organization type	Operating unit types	Organization ID	Grant with children
ALL	Legal entity	None	ALL	No

OSCAR

Organization name	Organization type	Operating unit types	Organization ID	Grant with children
ALL	Legal entity	None	ALL	No

RetailServiceAccount

Organization name	Organization type	Operating unit types	Organization ID	Grant with children
ALL	Legal entity	None	ALL	No

STAN

Organization name	Organization type	Operating unit types	Organization ID	Grant with children
ALL	Legal entity	None	ALL	No

Figure 4.8: Role to user assignment report

Security duty assignments

The **Security duty assignments** report gives a view of all the duties that are part of a role. The following example shows some of the duties of the **Accountant** role:

Security duty assignments

Contoso Entertainment System USA

Page 1 of 397
1/30/2023
6:37 PM

Microsoft Dynamics 365 includes several features to help manage access to modules, forms, data, and reports. These features include user permissions, user group permissions, company accounts and virtual company accounts, domains, table and field access, and record level security.

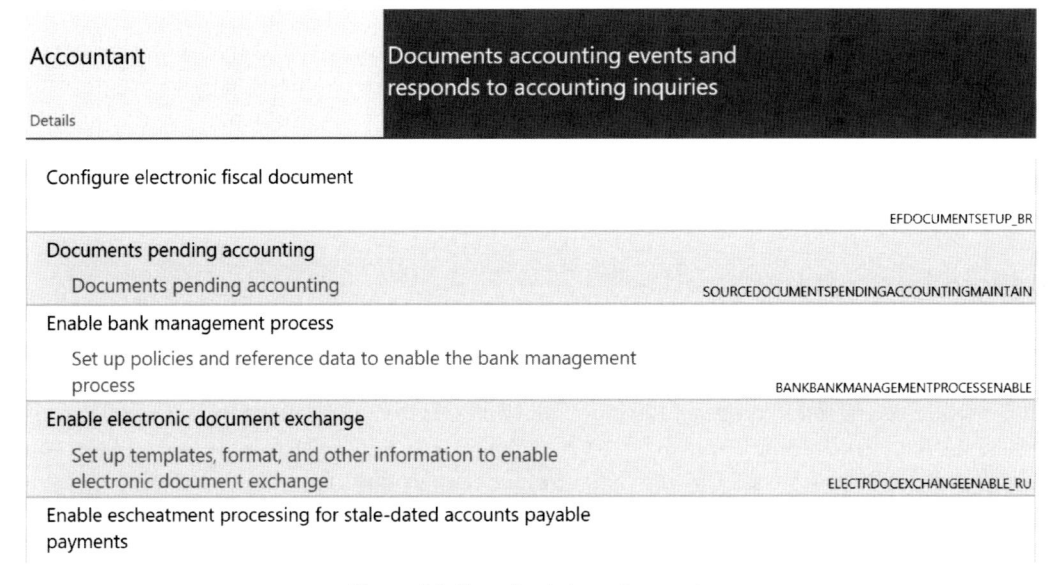

Accountant	Documents accounting events and responds to accounting inquiries	
Details		
Configure electronic fiscal document		EFDOCUMENTSETUP_BR
Documents pending accounting		
Documents pending accounting		SOURCEDOCUMENTSPENDINGACCOUNTINGMAINTAIN
Enable bank management process		
Set up policies and reference data to enable the bank management process		BANKBANKMANAGEMENTPROCESSENABLE
Enable electronic document exchange		
Set up templates, format, and other information to enable electronic document exchange		ELECTRDOCEXCHANGEENABLE_RU
Enable escheatment processing for stale-dated accounts payable payments		

Figure 4.9: Security duty assignments

Those reports will give you plenty of information related to the users and their security assignments.

Segregation of duties

One feature that will help to keep a company compliant with its auditors is the segregation of duties reports. The point of segregation of duties is having a method that will identify users and roles that have conflicting permissions. As an example, let's say that you have a person who was an AP clerk in the finance department, but is now an AR clerk.

Generally, this would be a conflict because they could complete tasks in both areas. So, if a user was an AR and AP clerk, they could create themselves as a numbered company, register it as a vendor, send an invoice for something that the company bought, create the invoice, approve it, and make a payment for the invoice. This would be a major problem as no one should be able to do both tasks in a system. Until an audit was completed, no one would know that type of activity was happening.

The system allows you to create rules for the system to follow to identify conflicts in the segregation of duties. You can also run reports that show current conflicts and any unresolved conflicts in the system.

External reports

There are two other locations where administrators can obtain security information:

- **LCS**: From here, you'll be able to view logs that contain information on user logins, distinct user sessions, all events for a user, and all events for browser sessions.
- **Databases**: Also, there are reports available at the database level that report on changes in the database, including update, insert, and delete. These reports show what has changed with specific data, such as a vendor's bank account, but also system performance.

Now that we've looked at what makes up system security, let's look at how to best implement it so that companies have efficient user access and proper system licensing.

How to best set up security

Microsoft has tried its best to set security roles so that a company doesn't have to modify them for their deployments. The problem is not every company has an accounting department, as an example. This would mean people executing individual roles and therefore, there will always be issues with segregation of duties. There will need to be some custom security roles created. So, before we show you how to create a new custom security role, let's give an example of why you would want to create one.

Let's say that you have a situation where, for some reason, salespeople have decided that they should delete an item from a sales order after it's been confirmed. Besides being a bad idea to begin with, here are some of the issues that can be created when that happens. First off, once a sales order has been confirmed, it reserves inventory in the warehouse. After that, a pick list is generated for the warehouse, and the warehouse workers will pick those items. If a salesperson has modified the sales line, either by changing the value or deleting the line altogether, the number of items shipped to the customer will be incorrect, and you may have to incur costs to get extra items returned or the cost of shipping missing items to the customer.

So, there are two ways to solve this problem:

- The first is, and it's not the best idea, to set up auditing so that you can see who is deleting items from the sales orders. Well, that's great as a training solution, but it doesn't fix the actual issue. You're still going to have missing or altered items on the sales orders, and it doesn't prevent any of the issues mentioned previously.
- The other option is creating a custom security role. Now, this part is tricky. We need to understand how a security role is created before we can make any modifications.

Architecture

As we saw earlier in the chapter, D365 F&SCM security is hierarchical. It layers permissions on top of each other until you get the configuration that the user needs. If we look at it from the point of view of the system, roles are assigned to users, duties are assigned to roles, privileges are assigned to duties, and permissions are granted to privileges.

Here is an example. In the **Accountant** role, we have the **Maintain fixed assets duties**, with one of the privileges being **Maintain fixed asset discount rates**. From there, we can see several permissions for everything from accessing menu items to accessing specific tables.

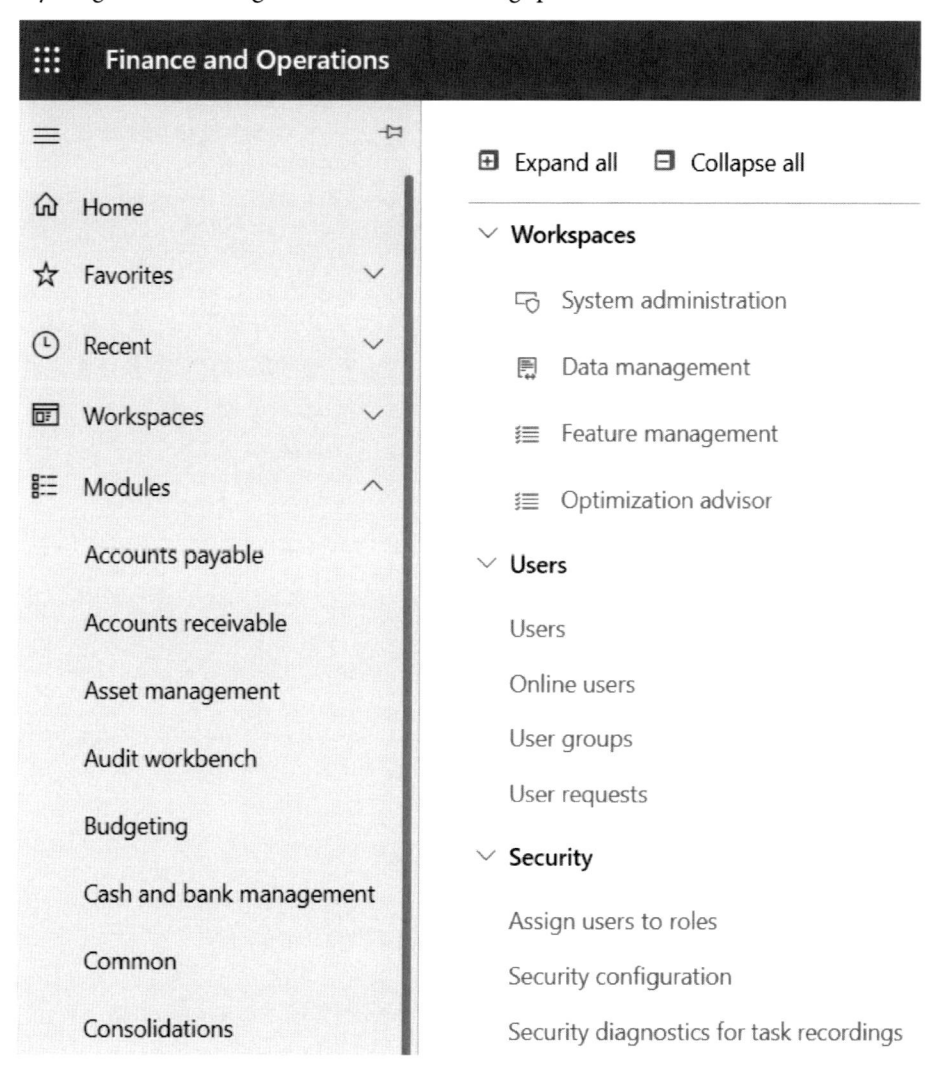

Figure 4.10: System administration main menu

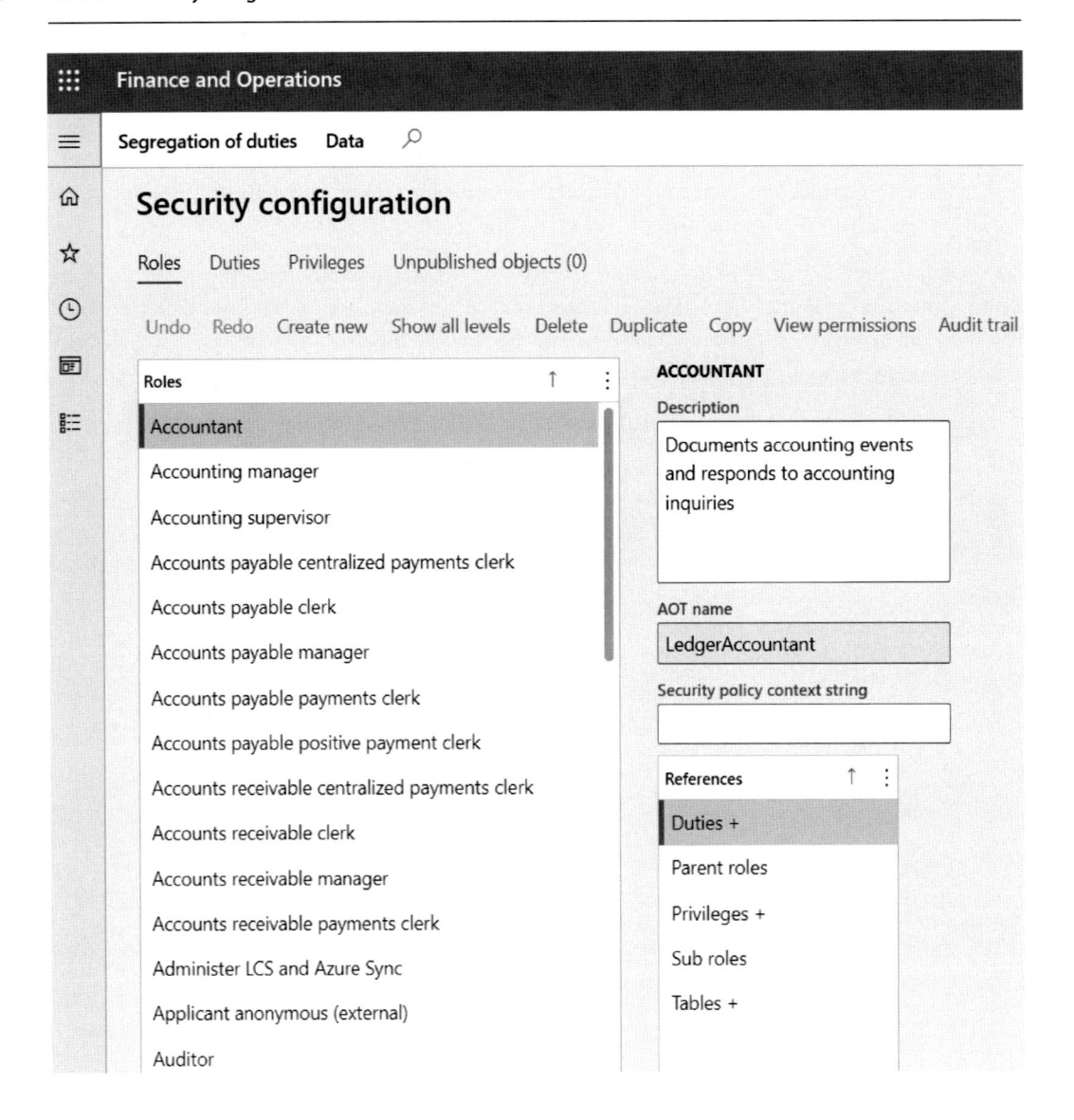

Figure 4.11: Security configuration – roles

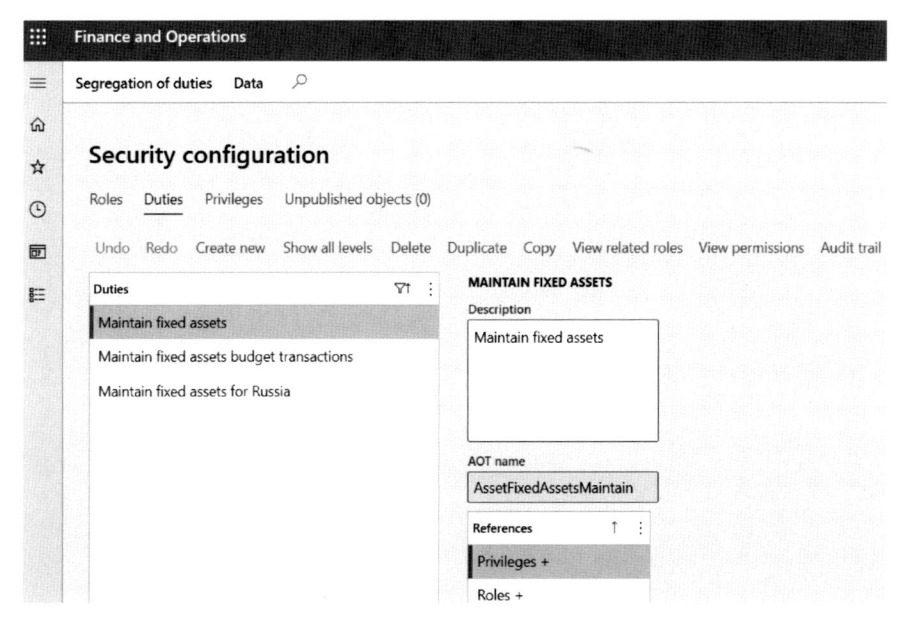

Figure 4.12: Security configuration – duties

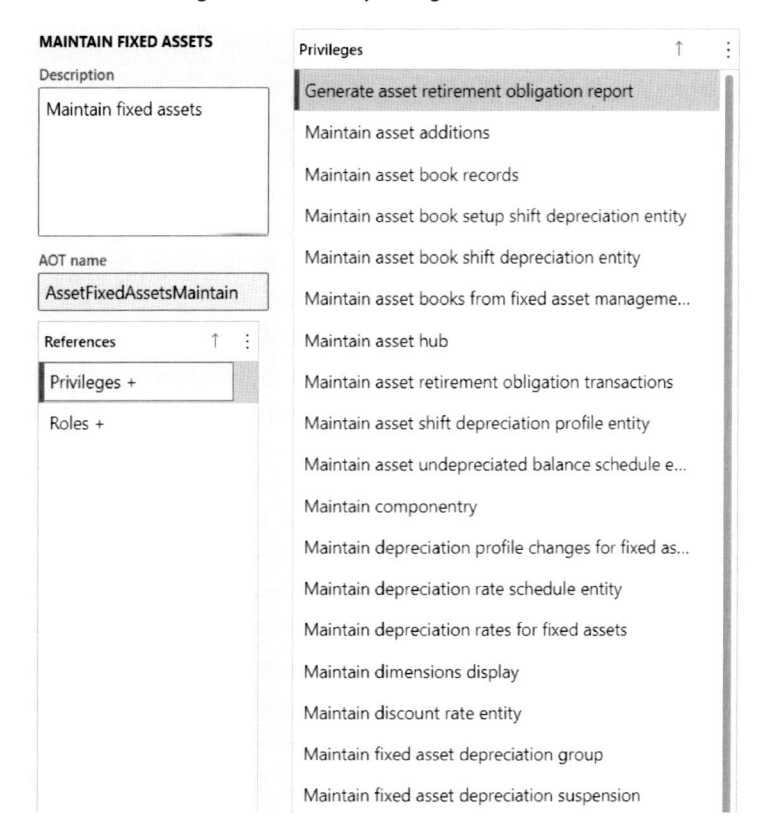

Figure 4.13: Security configuration – privileges

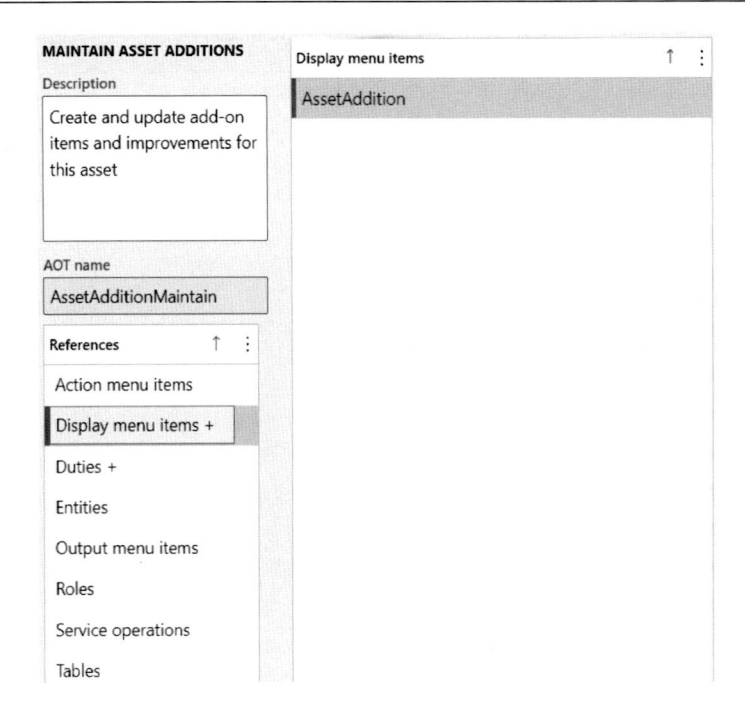

Figure 4.14: Security configuration – Display menu items

So now we're going to create our custom security role. But first… we need to figure out what it is we're going to modify. We don't want certain users to be able to delete items from a sales order. So, the best way to do that is probably by hiding the delete button. That makes sense because if you can't see it, you can't do it. But how do we know which button we need to hide? Well, that is the tricky part.

In my case, I have many years of experience working in the system and have gotten to know, more or less, where things are located. But what if you haven't got my level of experience? Is it going to be complicated or virtually impossible? Reassuringly, no – not really. What?

When I say not really, it's because you can do this in two ways:

- You can manually go through all the different options to figure out which privilege you need to edit to hide the button. That's not so bad, except there are at least four different duties that specifically have privileges related to the delete button. So that's not very helpful.

- But Microsoft has given you a tool to help with figuring out which items you need to modify. The tool is **Task Recorder**. Once you have created a recording, you can load it into the security diagnostics for task recordings. When you do this, it walks you through all the tasks and generates a list of the security settings that are produced when you click on the button, as an example.

So, now we can go and create a custom privilege, duty, and role for this. Use the following steps as an example for customizing your security roles.

Creating a security role

Security roles are a collection of duties and privileges. We can create a new test role such as **CreateCustomer**. The following steps can be used to create any new custom role:

1. Go to **System administration | Security | Security configuration**.

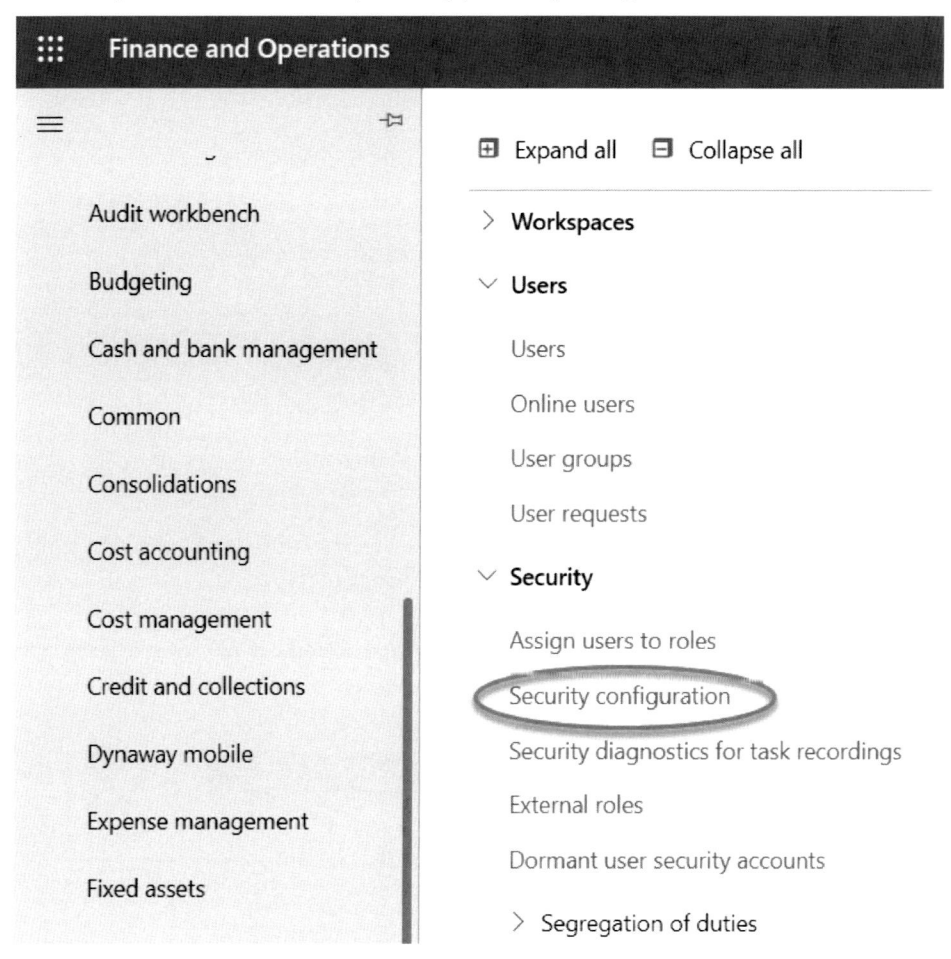

Figure 4.15: Security configuration tool

2. From the **Segregation of duties** page, click on **Create new**. In the pop-up box, enter the new role name, such as `CreateCustomer`, and then click **Ok**.

Efficient Security Design

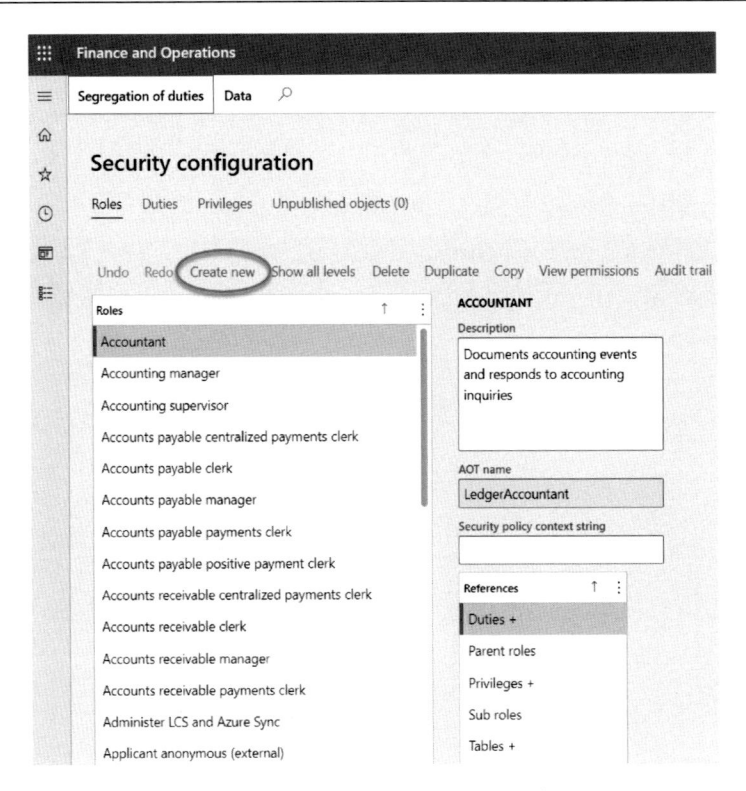

Figure 4.16: Create a new security role

3. Before you continue to the next phase, you'll need to publish the changes we've just made. On the menu, click **Unpublished objects**, then click **Publish all**. This will publish the new role and prepare it for further configuration.

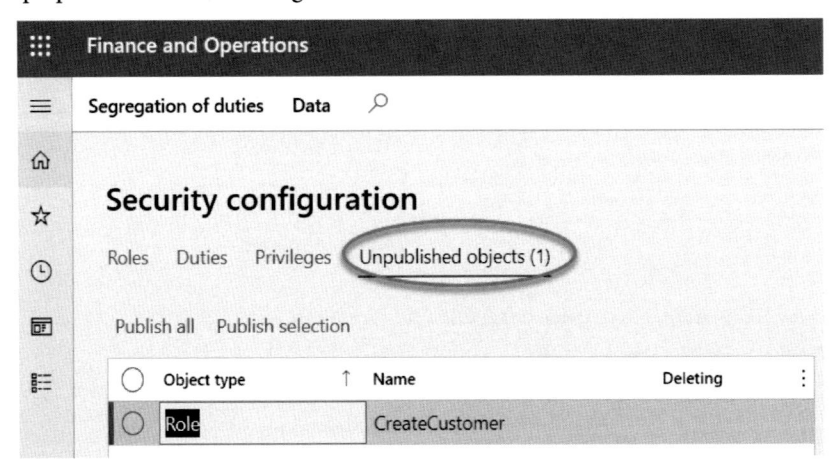

Figure 4.17: Publish new security configuration

> **Note**
> You cannot assign this role to a user until it has been published.

Creating a new privilege

A security privilege is a collection of entry points for menu items such as output menu item, action item, service operations, and so on:

1. In the previous screenshots, we've selected to create a new privilege called **CreateCustomerpriv**.

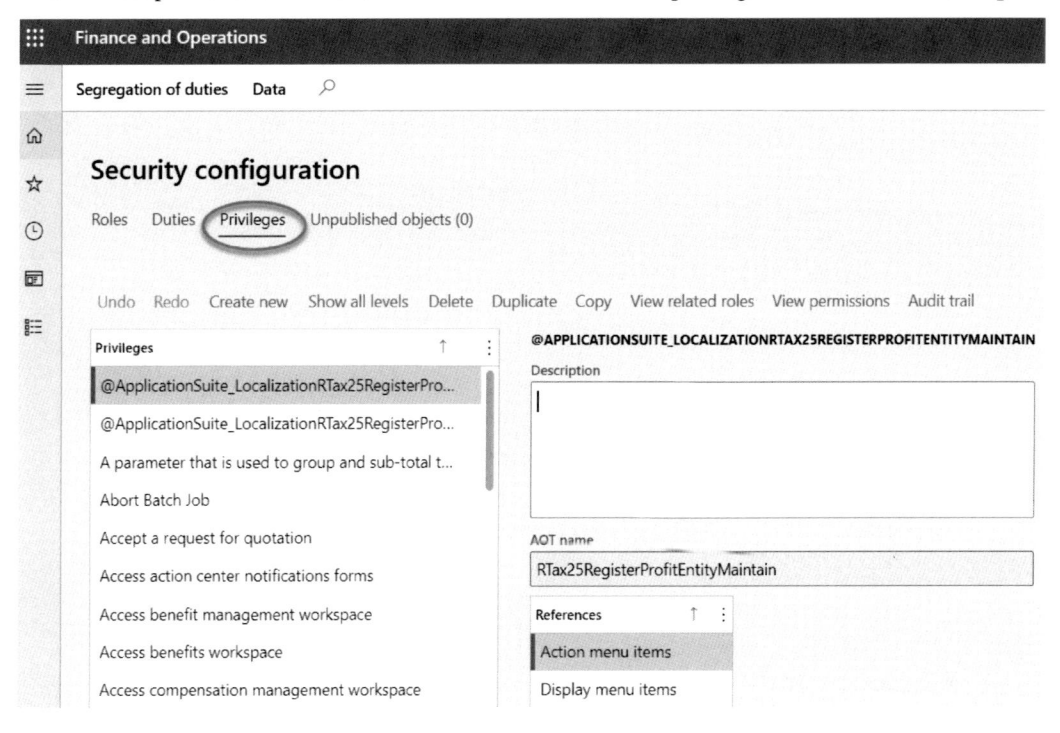

Figure 4.18: Create a new privilege

2. Next, we need to determine how we are going to configure the new privilege. In this particular case, we're going to modify **Display menu items**.

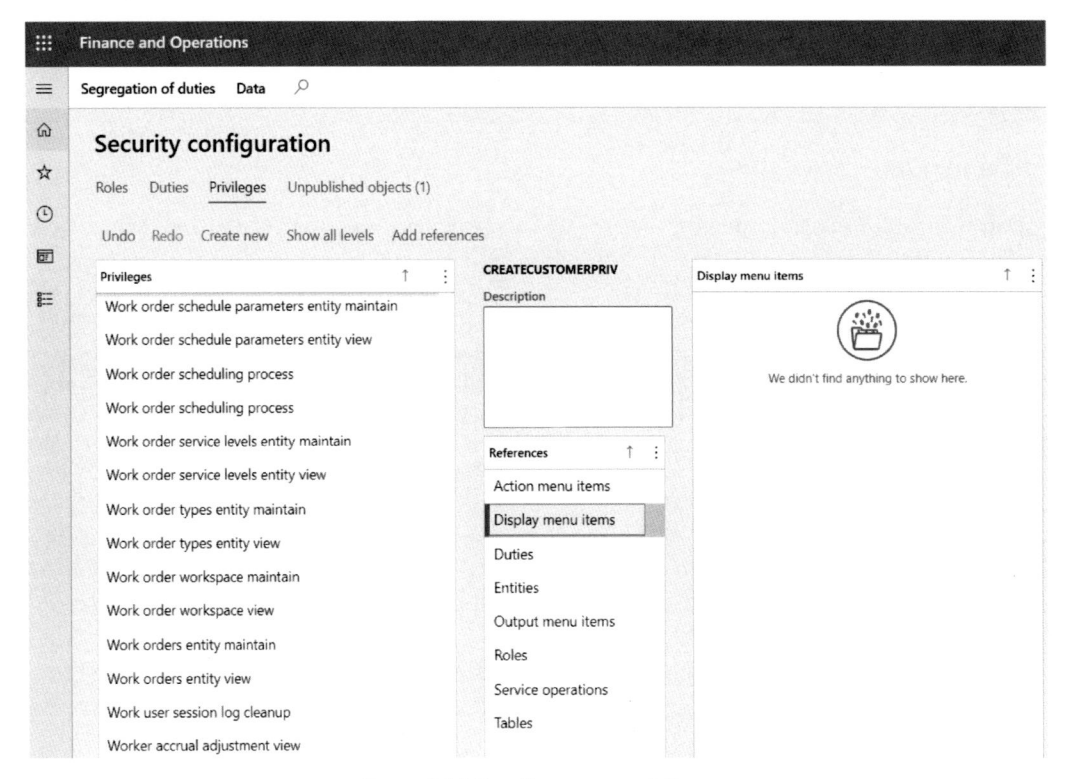

Figure 4.19: Creating a new privilege

3. For this example, we're selecting to modify the properties for the following menu items:

    - **CustTable**
    - **CustTableAddress**
    - **CustTableDetails**
    - **CustTableDocuments**
    - **CustTableEdit**

Figure 4.20: Select display menu items

4. Next, we are selecting **Grant** as the property. This will give the user permission to use these menu items.

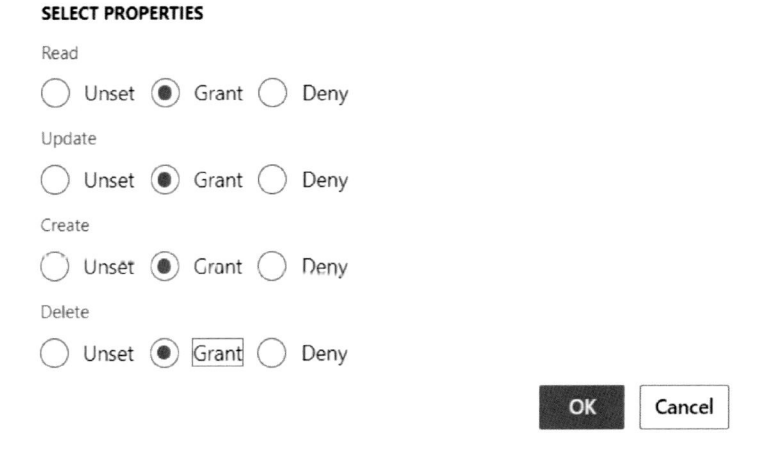

Figure 4.21: Select grant permissions for each of the display menu items

As we saw in the previous figures, there are four different menu-related options we can choose from. These include the following:

- **Action menu items for classes**, which allows a user to view the menu items
- **Display menu items for forms**, which allows a user to view menu items on a form
- **Output menu items for reports**, which allows a user to use menu items on output forms

70   Efficient Security Design

5. After we make all the changes, we need to make sure to publish all the objects.

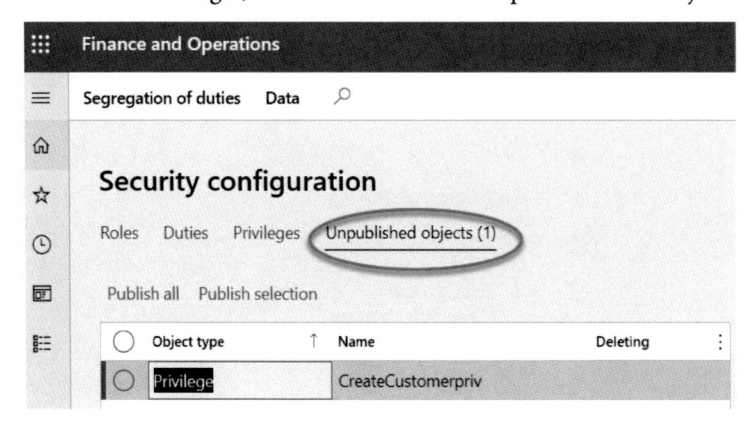

Figure 4.22: Publish security configuration

6. We are going to complete the same steps to create a new duty that we used to create a new privilege. In this example, we're going to create a new duty called **CreateCustomerDuty**.

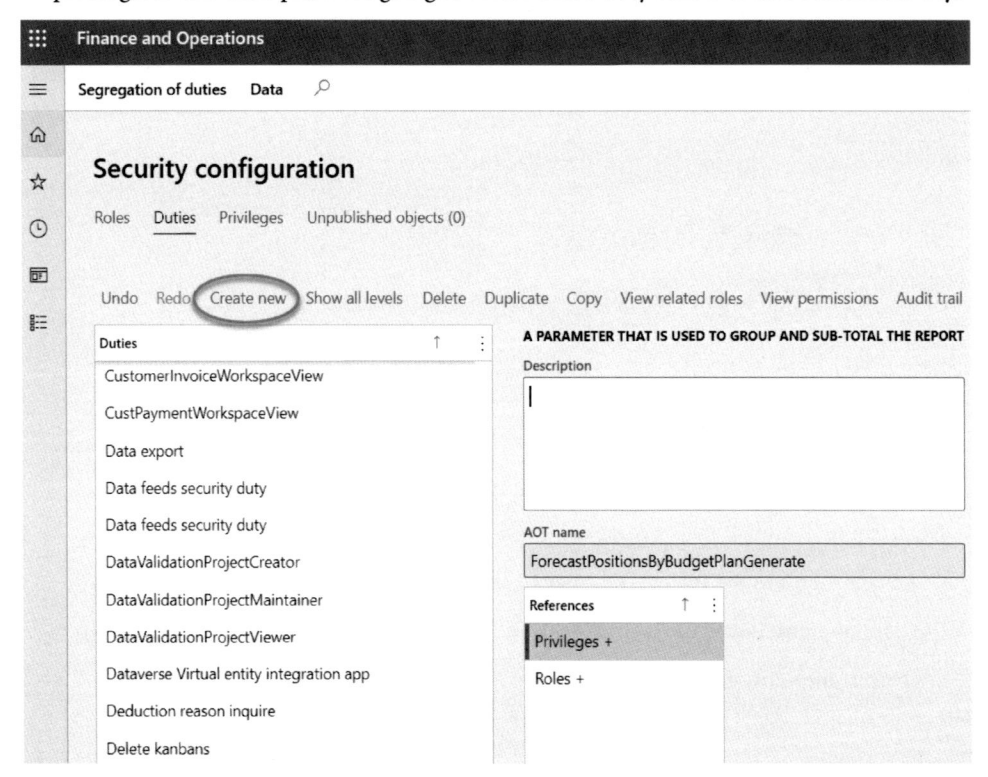

Figure 4.23: Create a new duty

What does security look like in D365 F&SCM?   71

7. After we've created the new duty, we need to select the previous custom privilege we created. To do that, click on the **Add reference** button, and select the privilege name. In this case, we're going to select the **CreateCustomerpriv** privilege. After we click **OK**, we will go back to the main menu, and we'll then add the new duty to the custom role we created earlier.

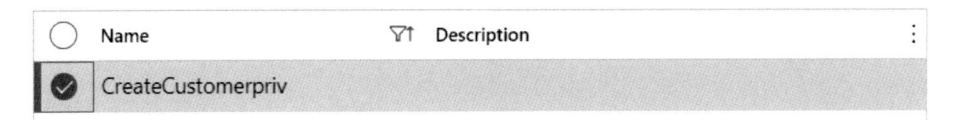

Figure 4.24: Select privileges

8. To continue the process, we're now going to add the new custom duty called **CreateCustomerDuty** to the new custom role, **CreateCustomer**. This will be completed by adding a new reference to the duty.

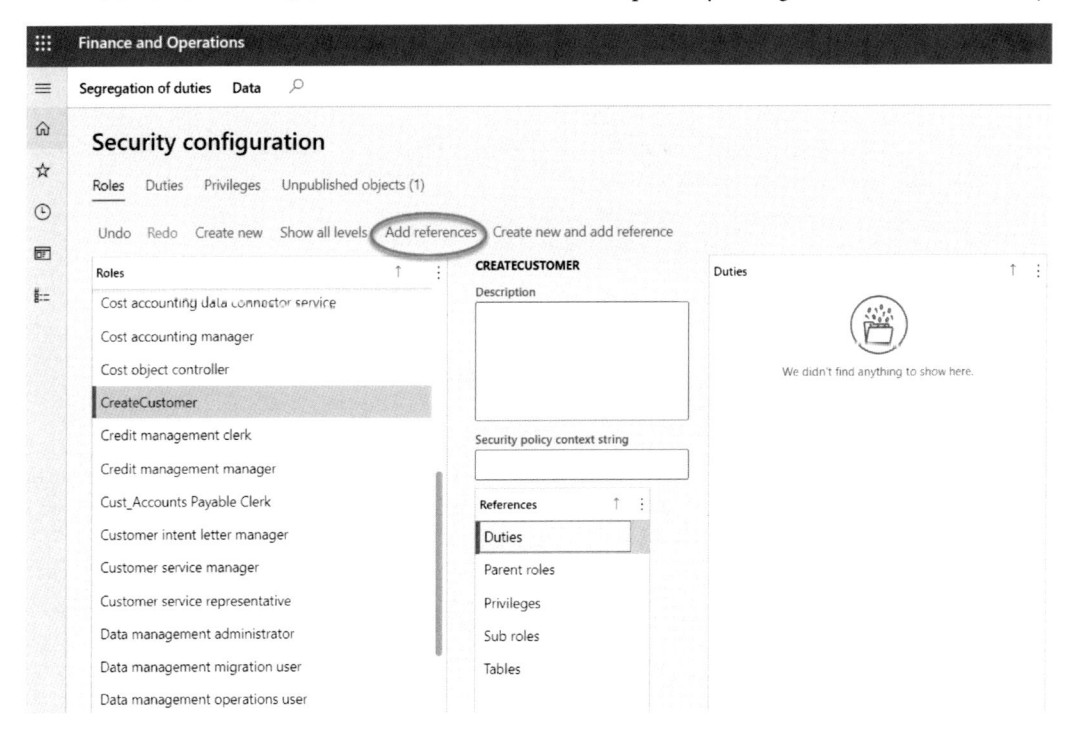

Figure 4.25: Add a reference to the new duty

72   Efficient Security Design

9. Now that we've completed the creation of the custom role, duty, and privilege, we must now publish all those objects so that we can move on to the next phase, where we will test out the new security configuration.

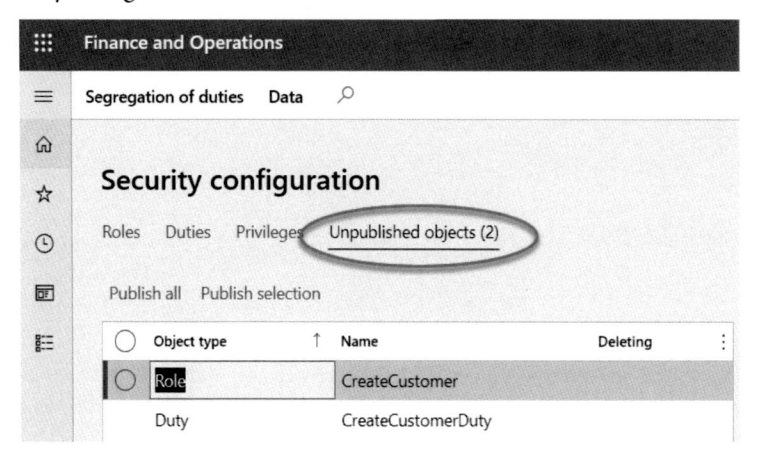

Figure 4.26: Publish new items

10. To add a new test user to the system, we'll first start by importing the user account. To complete this, click on the **Import users** button.

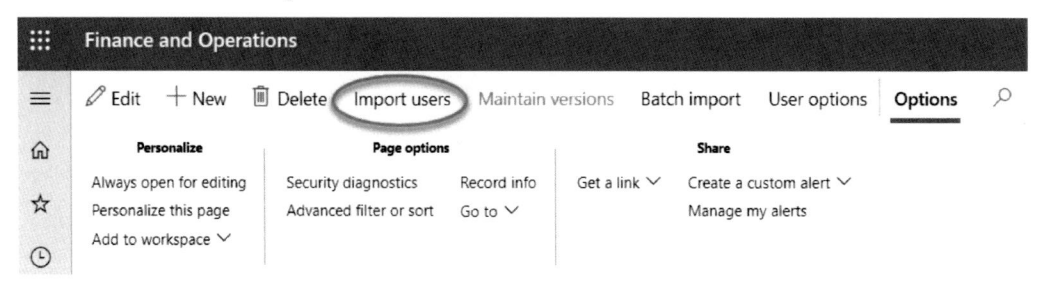

Figure 4.27: Import users

11. From the list of available users, select the user account you plan on testing the security role with. In this example, the account I'm using is called **D365 User Test**.

What does security look like in D365 F&SCM? | 73

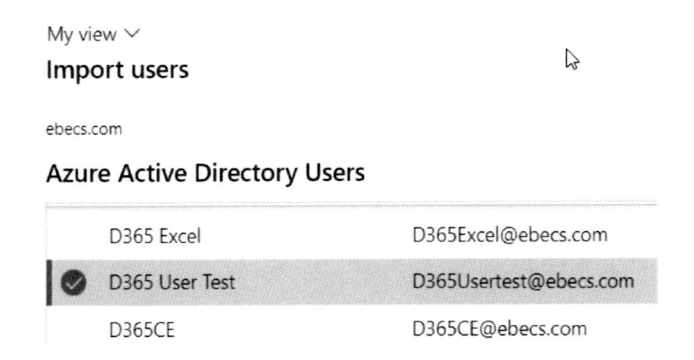

Figure 4.28: User options

12. Once the user has been imported, we'll need to add the security role. Click on the + **Assign roles** button.

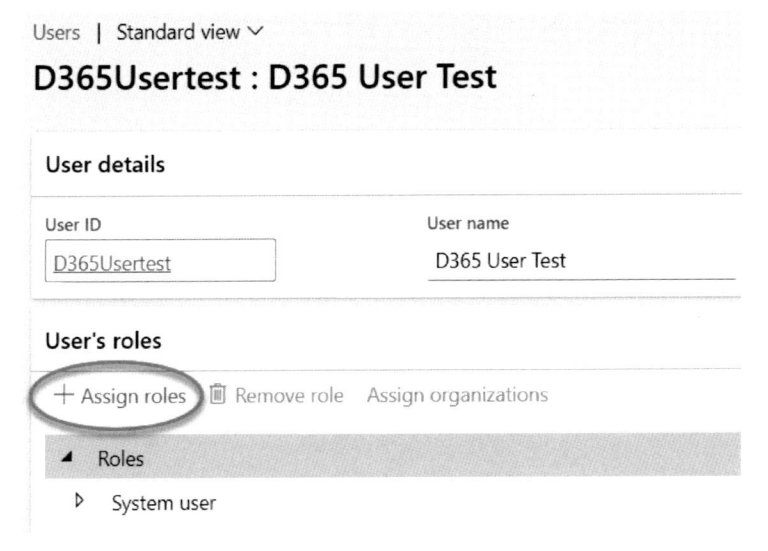

Figure 4.29: Assigning new user roles

13. Select the **CreateCustomer** custom role to add it to the user. We can now close the **User details** menu.

74 | Efficient Security Design

Assign roles to user

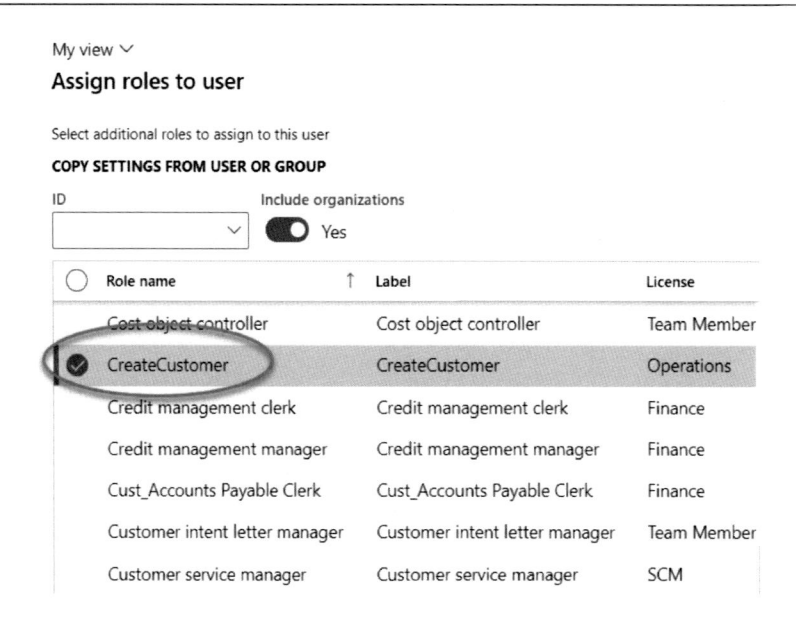

Select additional roles to assign to this user

COPY SETTINGS FROM USER OR GROUP

ID   Include organizations: Yes

Role name ↑	Label	License
Cost object controller	Cost object controller	Team Member
CreateCustomer	**CreateCustomer**	**Operations**
Credit management clerk	Credit management clerk	Finance
Credit management manager	Credit management manager	Finance
Cust_Accounts Payable Clerk	Cust_Accounts Payable Clerk	Finance
Customer intent letter manager	Customer intent letter manager	Team Member
Customer service manager	Customer service manager	SCM

Figure 4.30: Assign roles to users

14. The following screenshot shows an example of what the new security role would show for the test user.

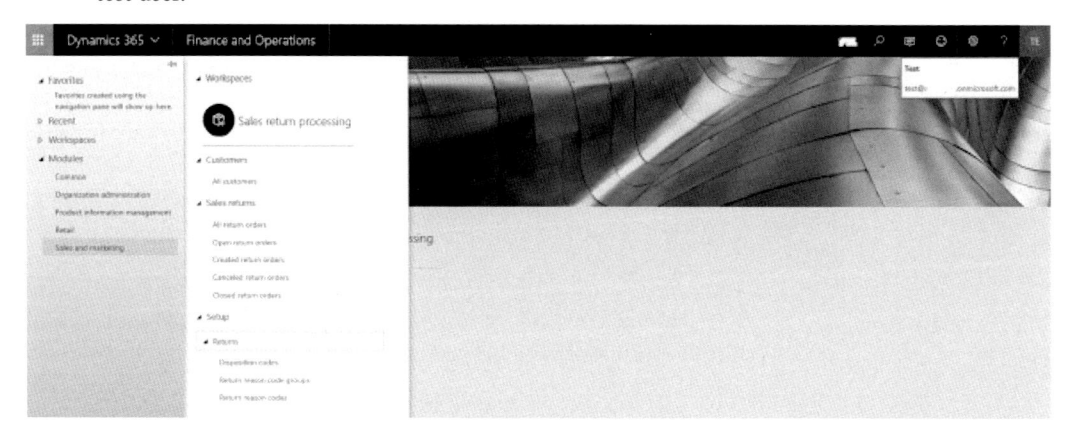

Figure 4.31: Trying a test user

Conclusion

As we've seen in this chapter, there is a lot to security. If you get good at it, you could be very popular with many companies. Hopefully, you now see and understand how important it is to be able to create custom security settings in D365 S&SCM. Being able to customize and configure security in the system makes it much easier to administer and easier for the users of the system.

In the next chapter, we're going to take an in-depth look into data integrations. Specifically, we're going to look at how to avoid errors when moving data into D365 F&SCM.

5
Planning for Successful Data Migration

In previous chapters, I've commented "This is the most important…" when it came to areas that can cause issues during a project, and I'm going to repeat that. Data is what makes the system run. Without data, the system is unusable.

When building a new system, much discussion, planning, and testing needs to be completed to make sure data is imported into the new system correctly. In this chapter, we'll discuss the major impacts and pitfalls related to data migration and data translation when moving into D365. We'll also look at tools and potential issues that can arise when moving data.

The main topics to learn about in this chapter are as follows:

- What is data migration?
- Data migration methodologies
- Data management
- Creating a migration strategy
- Data migration best practices
- Case studies

What is data migration?

One question that I get asked a lot from inexperienced solution architects is *"Why do I care what the data looks like? It's not my problem as a solution architect."* Well, that's not exactly true. As we've mentioned in a previous chapter, the solution architect is responsible for everything in the project, and data management/migration is one of the most important. I guess first off, we need to understand what data migration is. The simplest way to look at it is that data migration is the process of moving data from an existing system and importing it into D365.

And that data can come in many forms. It could be in an existing system, Excel spreadsheets, or flat files. Or even better, it might exist on paper in file cabinets (those projects are the ones where I want to cry). In any case, the data needs to be put into D365. But not all data. The only type of data that should be migrated is what is called **master data**. We'll get to that in a few minutes.

So, if we're going to continue to follow the *Success by Design* methodology, one of the first things we need to do is work with the client to determine where their data lives. If the client is migrating from an existing ERP system or finance system, then that should be where the majority of the data that we need to migrate lives. And again, it's not all data. The only data that needs to be migrated is "non-transactional" data.

Types of data

Quite often, the terms *master data* and *transactional data* are confusing. Knowing which is which is very important to data migration.

Master data defines all of the data that does not change often. The types of data that are included are customer records (i.e., customer number, name, address, etc.), release products, vendors, warehouses, and inventory layout. Moving forward, when we talk about data migration and data management, we'll be referring to master data.

Transactional data is data that is created because of some process, such as invoices, customer statements, purchase requisitions, and purchase orders. Transactional data will not be discussed as part of data migration. Transactional data should always be moved as a manual process. We'll discuss that as part of the best practices.

There are two other types of data that we will come across. **Historical data** is data that lives in various existing systems but is not current. This is data that is transactional but is used for current business activities. **Configuration data** is used to define parameters in the system. This is data that defines things such as number sequences, units of dimensions, tax codes, and the like. Master data is highly reliant on configuration data.

Data locations

As part of the *Success by Design* methodology, data migration and management are something that should be identified and started early in the *initiate* phase. The **solution architect** (**SA**) will work with the client to identify the following:

- Existing systems
- Master data in each of those systems
- Whether those legacy systems will continue to be used

Once the client and SA have identified the location of the data, they can start to organize data acquisition meetings as part of the *requirements-gathering* phase of the project.

Data management and migration is not a one-step process. Many projects fail because they do one of two things:

- First, they tend to think of data as something that you create daily, and old data doesn't matter too much. Because of this, they don't put enough thought into how data is recorded, where it's recorded, and what it's used for. This has a direct impact on reporting later. (We'll talk about reporting later in this chapter.)

- The second thing that happens is they wait until much later in the project to think about data. This is generally what happens because no one makes it their responsibility to work on data migration. As an SA, it's vital to identify data migration on day one of the project and sort out who is going to be responsible for the data. Generally, from the consultant side, you would use a technical architect to work on extracting the data, transforming it if necessary, and getting it moved into the new system. From the client side, you should have them identify someone that can be responsible for the testing of the data when it's in the new system. This would include how the reports use the data as well, so I would recommend someone who is from the client's BI team.

As mentioned, there are many different types of data that we will need to consider when doing a new implementation of D365. After we have identified the locations and type of data that exists, next, we need to figure out a methodology to move that data to the new system.

Data migration methodologies

Let's use an example of a company moving from a simple desktop accounting program to D365. All the data that they have in the existing software is only related to financial transactions. The version of their accounting software uses a localized database for all of the records and does not have a way to connect to external systems. All of the inventory they have in their warehouse is kept in a number of Excel spreadsheets. They also use the FedEx© online tool for calculating shipping costs when they have to ship items out to customers. They find that they are often retyping information into the online tool and are very inefficient.

The spreadsheets are often incorrect as well, due to the manual nature of how they have to be updated. Often, two or more people will be picking items for shipping. Once the first picker takes an item and the second goes to pick something, they will often find the inventory list doesn't match what's actually on the shelf.

Based on that information, the best method to move data is to put it into Excel and then migrate it into D365. But before we can do that, we need to make sure it's in the right format to be entered into D365. So, some data transformation must take place.

In another example, we have a company that is using an existing ERP system that is no longer supported and they are moving to a modern D365 system. This system has a locally-hosted MS SQL database. This type of migration is easier because we can connect data packages in D365 directly to the SQL server and extract the data that way.

These two examples show a couple of different methods that can be used to move data from an existing system to D365. Knowing where the data lives and what the data looks like directly determines what methods you'll use for the migration.

There are several other data management scenarios that can happen:

- **Environmental data**: If you have data that exists in one environment that needs to be copied to another environment, you'll run into this scenario when you're moving from a dev system to a testing system. This will happen frequently during the project.
- **Sharing data in the same system**: If you have a set of data that is to be used across multiple legal entities in the same installation, there are methods available to copy that data to each legal entity.
- **Blank implementations**: There will be times when you need to copy parameters from one environment to a new one. There will be no master data moved, just the parameters. Examples of this would include setting up new testing environments to facilitate testing of configurations and data.
- **Legacy data**: If you must move data from an existing AX environment to D365, there are methods used to migrate the data.

Different environments will also have different methodologies. If you're moving data from one Tier 1 to another Tier 1 environment, you'll most like use database copy/restore methods. If you're moving from Tier 1 to Tier 2, then you would use data packages. The following diagram shows some examples:

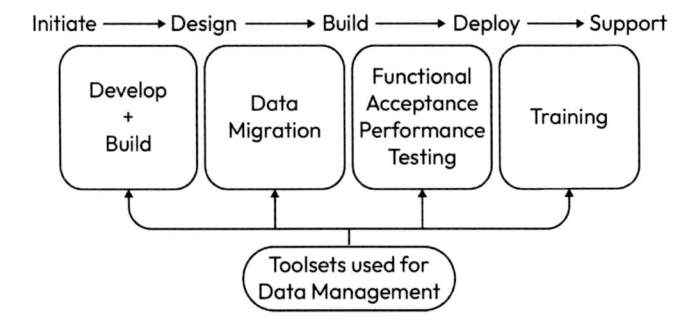

Figure 5.1: Methods of migration

Data management

To assist in the migration of data from different environments, we have several different toolsets at our disposal that make the process much easier. These toolsets can be broken down into three different types:

- **The data management framework**: This is a set of tools that are located on the main screen of the D365 F&SCM home page. This workspace contains all the functions needed to work with data packages.

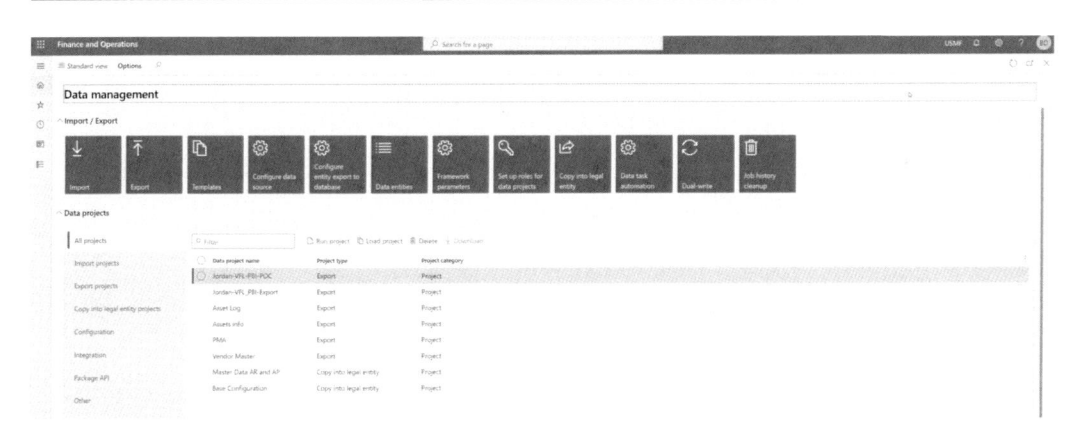

Figure 5.2: Data management workspace

- **Data sharing functions**: These tools are used to help migrate and synchronize data between different legal entities in the same company.
- **Standard database operations**: In this toolset, we use the standard database functions of backup/restore. We may also use these tools to do a data rollback, or a point-in-time recovery.

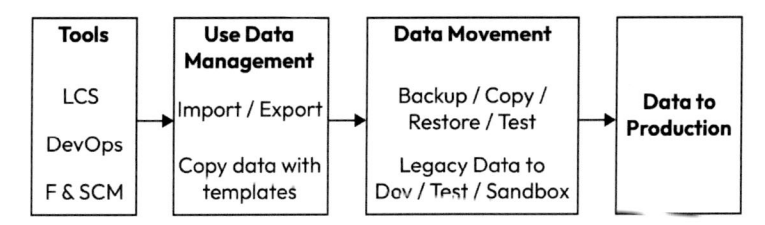

Figure 5.3: Data toolsets

Data management framework

The data management framework is a set of tools and procedures that are used to export, transform, validate, and import data between different environments. There are five different parts that make up the framework:

- **Data jobs**: A data job is a specific execution of a data project. Examples include uploading or exporting files from a system.
- **Data package**: This is a file that holds the contents of a data project, including the manifest of the jobs in the package.
- **Data project**: This holds the list of all the data entities in the jobs and all of the mappings for the jobs.

- **Data entities**: Data entities are user-defined values that are used to visualize data from multiple data tables. They generally represent something that is easy to understand, such as a customer or inventory item.
- **Job history**: The job history keeps track of the history of all staging and target jobs.

There are three different scenarios that support data entities. These are data migration, copying configurations from one system to another, and integrations.

Data entities

When moving data from one system to D365, we need to create data entities from the existing system that get the data formatted correctly in the new system. Data entities are an abstraction of the physical database tables. When looking at data, it might contain multiple fields of a database to represent a single item in the D365 table. If we look at an example of a vendor, the vendor entity might look something like this:

Vendor Entity
Vendor number
Vendor name
Primary address
Secondary address
Postal code
Primary phone number

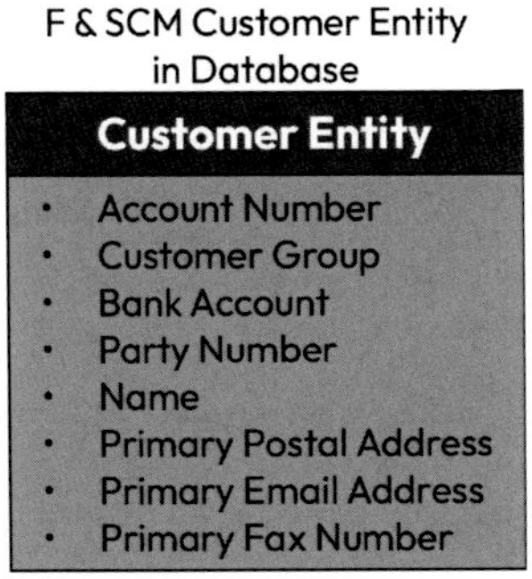

F & SCM Customer Entity in Database

Customer Entity
• Account Number
• Customer Group
• Bank Account
• Party Number
• Name
• Primary Postal Address
• Primary Email Address
• Primary Fax Number

Figure 5.4: Data entities

This is the way that we can conceptualize how the data in the database looks when moving to D365. This is also the method that is used to denormalize the database tables to a more concise data table.

Data mapping

The process of moving the data from one system to D365 needs to go through a mapping process. If you're moving from Dynamics AX, the mapping process will be relatively easy. But if you're moving from a legacy system, then the data types, fields, and aggregations may not match. In the data management workspace, we can use the Data Entities tool to view the mappings between systems. The following example shows an example of the data in the staging fields and how they map to the fields in the target system:

Figure 5.5: Mapping table

The tool also allows you to visually see how the mappings are configured:

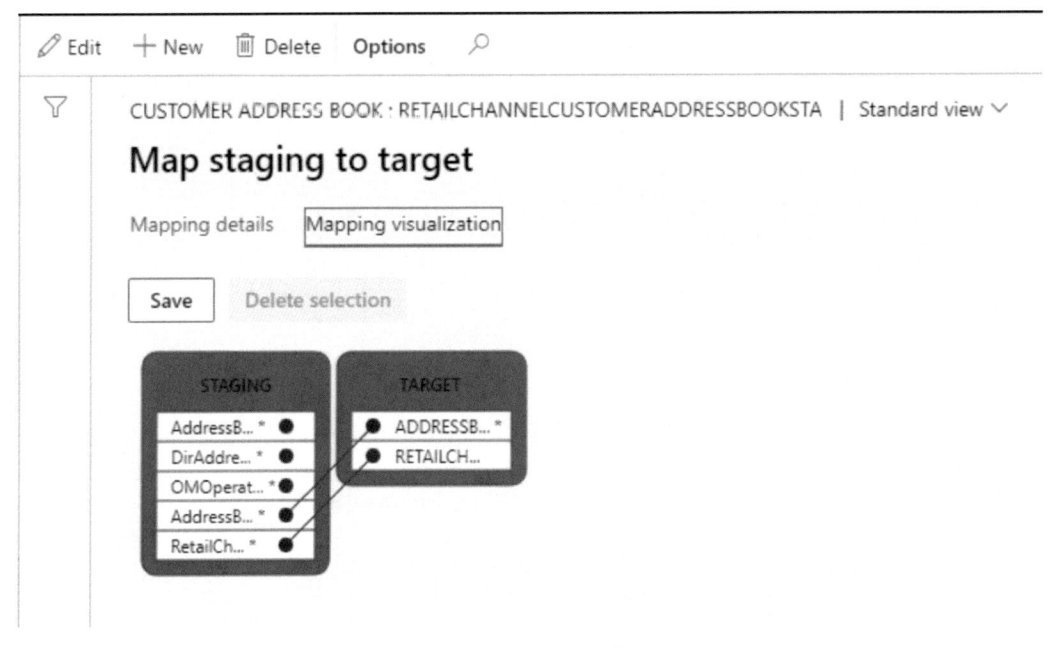

Figure 5.6: Mapping chart

Data tools

D365 has several different tools that are available for data management. In the next section, we'll look at some of the more important tools available.

D365 comes with a set of tools that assist with data migration. These include the following:

- **Data management workspace**: We previously discussed the workspace and what it can be used for.
- **Excel workbook designer**: The workbook designer is a tool that helps to design an export to Excel template that can be used with data fields. This allows you to create a table with the key fields needed for data to be exported to Excel. Once the fields have been created and the template design is ready, you need to publish the template to D365.
- **Office integration**: The Office integrations are made up of a number of tools, including the Excel Data Connector, which allows Excel workbooks to interact with OData services. There are also Document Management tools, which allow documents loaded as an attachment in D365 to be stored either in a flat file directory in Azure Storage (Blob Storage) or, preferably, in a SharePoint Online document library.

Another of the many tools is called **bring your own database** (**BYOD**). The BYOD tool allows an administrator to create their own database in Azure SQL. This database can be used to store one or more data entities from Finance and Supply Chain Management. BYOD is an option for when a client wants to keep an extended history of transactions from their existing systems. This way, they can have as much history as they want in the database and be able to shut down the legacy system.

Other uses for BYOD are when a client wants to export transactions from F&SCM into their own data warehouse, when batch transactions such as data copies need to be completed with other systems, and when using analytical tools that require a SQL connector to function.

To work with BYOD in your project, you need to use the **Configure entity export to database** tools from the **Data Management** workplace.

Creating a migration strategy

Now that we've looked at a few of the needs and tools for data management, let's change focus and look at how to create a data migration strategy that will be successfully executed during a project. We've also identified where the data lives, and what tools we plan on using. We need to break the migration strategy into three phases:

1. First, define what the migration strategy will be.
2. Second, create a cutover plan for go-live.
3. Third, determine how much and what data is to be kept as part of a data retention plan.

Prepare for data migration

As we get closer to the point where we can start to migrate data, having a detailed plan will simplify the life of both the SA and the client. There are several tasks that need to be completed so that we can accomplish both the migration of the data and also the client's business continuity.

> **Note**
> The processes involved in data cleanup and extraction are long. You will need to go through several iterations of the extraction, migration, and testing of the data. This is the reason we need to start this process right at the beginning of the project rather than waiting until later.

The tasks that we need to focus on include the following:

- Deciding on a strategy to import and export data
- Decide on tools to be used with Finance and Supply Chain apps
- If selected, set up BYOD
- Identify the data to be extracted for each source
- Create testing plans to validate the data
- Identify the data entities and make sure the field mappings are correct
- Execute several test migrations and validate the output
- Execute test scripts on the migrated data

After we've created and identified the primary strategy for the data migration, we next need to prepare for the actual data conversion. This part of the project involves activities related to data movement and transformations. During this phase, we'll need to organize the data in the legacy system and clean it up as much as we can to make the migration easier to manage. Some of this data cleanup will need to be completed outside of D365, including in multiple spreadsheets.

Also, because the data conversion is not going to be done as one single exercise, we may investigate using automation for some of the data tasks. Using automation will help to prevent human error during the conversion processes.

One major mistake that is done on a regular basis is that both the consultant and client wait too long into the project before they start to work on their migration strategy. As was mentioned previously in this chapter, this is something that needs to be started right at the very beginning of the project. If we wait until after the solution is created, we could potentially put the project at risk of not completing on time. Because there is a process that needs to be completed multiple times during the project, the sooner that is started, the better.

We also need to determine how we're going to test the data after it's been migrated, and create a validation checklist that should be followed. I recommend that this be completed by a BI specialist from the client.

Data import and export strategy

The data management framework defines how we are importing data into D365. It's up to the SA to determine the specifics of how the framework is used. We have several different integration patterns that we can use for F&SCM applications. The methods that we must migrate the data include OData, the Batch data API, custom services, external web services, and Excel.

OData is a data protocol that is used for creating and consuming data. OData uses **REST**, or **Representational State Transfer**, rules to complete **Create, Read, Update, and Delete** (**CRUD**) operations. OData is used over HTTP and HTTPS using **JavaScript Object Notation** (**JSON**). OData allows users to work with data by using RESTful web services. As it's based on a standard protocol, it is widely used in the market.

OData does have some limitations, the primary being that it only supports small data transfers. It's also not recommended as the protocol to use when connecting to Power BI reports.

The next scenario uses the **Batch data API**. Batch API is best used when you're working with very large sets of data that need to be transferred, as well as when these transfers happen on a recurring basis. Batch API supports several data formats and filters. You are also able to use XML and XSLT style sheets to format the data in the proper format.

A **custom service** will be used when you are required to use SOAP endpoints to connect the systems to migrate the data.

Lastly, we can use integrations between systems using Microsoft Excel. Excel integrations allow users to open data in a system in Excel, work with the data, modify it as needed, and then upload it back into the D365 system. It uses OData connectors to connect to data that is exposed in different systems, which allows you to pull data from a legacy system and import it into D365.

We also need to consider how the data is transferred across systems. The data can be processed in either synchronous or asynchronous methods. The method that is selected is based on which integration type you selected in the previous section. **Synchronous transfers** prevent data from being sent until the previous data set was received. **Asynchronous transfers** allow data to be sent in continuous streams without waiting for a confirmation of receipt before sending the next stream.

Validating data output

Early on in the project, it's recommended that you select a small amount of test data and run your migration project against it. Once you run that migration (you've completed the transformation of the data and mapped all of the fields), you need to analyze and validate that the data migration was successful.

This may need to be completed against each of the systems that you'll be pulling data from. The following chart shows the path to follow:

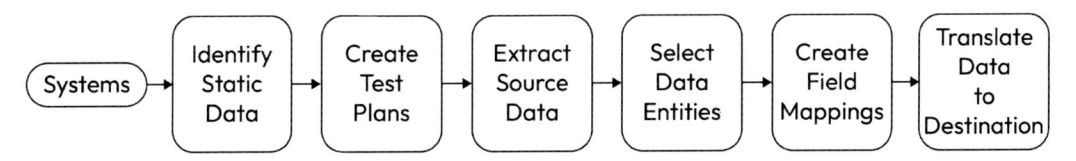

Systems → Identify Static Data → Create Test Plans → Extract Source Data → Select Data Entities → Create Field Mappings → Translate Data to Destination

Figure 5.7: Output validation path

Cutover plans

Now that we've completed a test migration and everything has been tested and validated, we now can move on to the cutover plan. The cutover plan is how we are going to complete the final migration to production. The data migration has to be included in the cutover plan. As with everything else we've mentioned, the cutover plan is something that needs to be identified and revisited throughout the project. The SA needs to keep this document up to date so that as the time comes for go-live, everyone knows what steps needed to be completed at go-live.

To allow the cutover to work smoothly, the following should be documented:

- All the data entities
- Any data dependencies
- The date and time the cutover is planned to be started
- Who will be responsible for completing the data migration (this should be completed by someone from the client)
- Backout plan in case something fails

As a part of the data management plan, you should develop a data retention plan. The data retention plan needs to be guided by how much data the company has and any regulatory requirements that the company might have to follow. The amount of storage that is used by D365 does not cost extra, but the amount of data in the database can have a negative impact on performance. I would recommend that if the company has a lot of historical data in its existing systems, I would create a subproject to create a BYOD in Azure to store all of its existing data. This accomplishes two things:

- It allows them to take all of the data from other systems and put it into one database system accessible for multiple activities, such as reporting
- It helps the company fulfill regulatory requirements

Depending on how much data the company creates on a yearly basis, I would recommend that they leave no more than 1 fiscal year's worth of active data in the system and export all the rest to the BYOD. You can create automated tasks in the data management workplace that can accomplish this for you.

Data migration best practices

We've talked a lot about some of the features of the data migration and management parts of the project. There are lots that we haven't talked about as well. But one thing that we need to discuss is Microsoft's best practices for data management. There are several of them, and we'll discuss each one, including my comments and recommendations for each one. These recommendations have been accumulated from my and fellow SAs' projects.

First and foremost, never ever use the production environment to test data migration. The data should be put into a backup system or database, if possible, and use that system to the data extraction parts of the migration tasks. Also, a Tier 2 system should be used for the majority of the development of the data packages. Once you've tested the data against backup and test environments and you've validated everything, when go-live comes, you can use the data packages against the production systems.

When preparing for the data migration, don't use the OData protocol for data transfer. You're better off using the Batch API due to the large amount of data that could be transferred. OData is limited to the number of items it can transfer at once, meaning the transfers will take far too long to complete successfully. Using the Batch API means that you'll be transferring larger amounts of data at once, but because it's run as a batch, it executes more efficiently. In my opinion, definitely use the Batch API.

One tool we haven't mentioned yet is **Dual-write**. Dual-write is a data integration tool that connects D365 F&SCM to D365 CE apps (Sales, Marketing, and Field Services). Dual-write should never be used as a data migration tool. It's designed to sync data between systems once they have been configured and put into production.

Dual-write will do an initial sync when the two systems are connected. However, if there is a large amount of master data or transactional data that needs to be replicated between F&SCM and the Dataverse, then you should migrate that data to the Dataverse and then connect Dual-write and complete the initial sync.

Other best practices follow standard IT processes. Always make sure you have a backup of the systems before you start doing data migration. Also, make sure you have a stable internet connection between your two sites. If not, then a data migration may overload your internet connection and the tasks will get corrupted.

Another best practice is that as part of the data migration planning sessions, you should plan out the systems that will be needed to complete the data migration testing. You need to plan for at least one Tier 2 environment. This environment should be separate from the main Tier 2 environment being used by the functional analysts, as it will need to be refreshed on a more regular basis. Every time you complete a test of the migration tasks, you will want to refresh the Tier 2 environment and prepare it for the next round of testing. As mentioned several times before, this process needs to be tested so much more than most of the other parts of the project. Once you've validated that everything is working as planned, you can then use this system to build and test reports.

Another best practice is that a Gold configuration environment should be set up. This environment has all the configuration, including all of the master and configuration data needed for go-live. This environment could be repurposed for the Tier 2 environment that was used for data migration testing. The important part of this environment is that it needs to have all of the users locked out except for admins and a few specifically identified core users. This will make the go-live and cutover processes run much more smoothly.

The next question that we'll talk about deals with what data to migrate. We've already discussed that we should be migrating configuration and master data and, based on requirements, how much historical data is required to fulfill any regulations. One type of data that seems to bring up a lot of discussion is transactional data.

Transactional data, as mentioned previously, is data that is entered daily and changes frequently. Because of that, it's not a good idea to migrate transactional data using data packages like you would master data. Why do I suggest this is not a great idea? Well primarily, it's because the data *does* change frequently. As an example, let's say that we have a vendor created in the system. Once you create the vendor record, the chances of it changing will be infrequent. At most, it might change once or twice after the record was initially changed. They may change where their business is located, so you would have to change the vendor's address. But the chances of this happening are rare. So, transferring that data using data packages is pretty safe.

But if you have created a purchase requisition from that vendor, there is a greater chance it will change. If the cutover happens in the system before the PR is converted to PO, then the prices, vendor, and delivery dates may change during the cutover timeframe, and then this record would be inaccurate. So, we want to avoid using any type of data package to migrate this type of data.

What I recommend as a part of the cutover timeframe is that a data outage is put in place. Usually, most organizations will do their cutover on a long weekend or during some time when they will have few people working in the system. This is the best time to do a data outage. This doesn't mean that the business stops processing things entirely, but it does mean that users no longer enter data into the existing systems.

All of those transactions, such as new purchases, new sales, and processing of invoices and customer statements, are completed after go-live. As a part of the cutover plan, you should include time for the manual entering of data that was created during the data outage. That will solve the problem of making sure the data is accurate. Also, it helps to make sure that the users are using the system properly and will work with it correctly in the future.

But we've missed all the open transactions in the system. There are two different ways we can deal with those. Depending on the cutover timeframe, we either can open the two systems side by side and manually enter the transactions into the new system, much like we did with the new transactions in the previous paragraph. Or the other way we can do the migration is to use Excel templates. If the existing system lets you extract data into Excel, you could move it to Excel and have it match the template needed to be imported into the new system.

By this point, you should have a completely migrated, live production system. Now, we can allow users to access the system and use it. Hopefully, everything you've completed during the project was successful and the users are happy with the new system.

Case studies

Before we end this chapter, let's look at a couple of projects I was involved in that were good and bad respectively. The good one worked well due to amazing planning and cooperation from the client. The second one didn't work out quite that way and was a major reason why the project went on much longer than planned.

Let's look at the successful one first. One of the first projects I worked on as an SA was with a client who had a small finance system in place and a manual system for everything else. Let's give a bit of background.

The company whose project I worked on was an international airport. After extensive searching, they decided on going with Dynamics as their ERP system. The company had approximately 300 employees who would be using the system. As was already mentioned, their finance system was an existing system that had been in place for several years. All their inventory and purchasing were completed in manual systems that were not included in their finance system, except for vendor information, such as name, address, and banking info.

The project was organized in such a way that the partner was well organized with what data needed to be transferred into the new system. Early on in the project, data that needed to be entered into the new system was clearly identified and data migration tasks were planned for throughout the project. The existing finance tool had the ability to export all information needed to be transferred into Dynamics into Excel, and then it could be transformed to work with Dynamics.

Because none of the non-financial information existed in that system, the client had the ability to populate Excel templates that were created as Dynamics templates and used to upload the information. This included inventory items, warehouse locations, and vendor information. For the go-live, a week-long outage was declared so no new transactions would be completed in the legacy system. All new transactions were recorded in Excel, and transactions that were to be completed, such as payments, were recorded in Excel and then entered into the new system.

In a later project, they implemented an asset management system. Because they didn't have any asset management system in place previously, they were starting from scratch. For this project, they used an extensive set of Excel spreadsheets to record all the assets in the business and used several months to collect this information. The data that was collected was successfully imported into the system using the Excel add-in.

The only failure of data in this project was the templates for the warehouse and inventory locations. When entering the data, an error was made on some inventory items where the values being entered were put into the wrong fields in the spreadsheet. This wasn't recognized until the following year when they did their year-end visual inventory count. Luckily, they still had the inventory upload sheets, and a correction to the data was made so that it was in the system correctly.

So overall, this project is a good example of what can happen when you plan data migrations properly.

The next project we're going to look at is a project where data planning didn't go very well.

In another project I was involved in, data was a secondary thought. In this project, I was a functional analyst and not the SA. The SA on the project was new and had no previous experience in discovery and project design. Unfortunately, there were no other individuals on the project who had enough previous experience to assist with the planning of the project.

It wasn't until the project was several months into the design that anyone mentioned anything about data and reporting. To make it equally challenging, the client wasn't really sure where all their data lived or what types of reports they were going to need in the new system. Because there was no identification of data management at the very beginning of the project, the project was at serious risk of not being completed on time. Also, there was a huge increase in the costs of the project, as new resources needed to be hired to work specifically on the data management problems.

The project was so disorganized that they didn't have an environment to load test data into, they didn't know how the data was going to be extracted from existing systems, whether or not it was compliant with D365, and how much it would need to be transformed before it could be loaded into D365.

The secondary issue was how the data would be loaded (or at least, what data was to be loaded) into D365. After looking at the data in the systems such as their warehouse application, the data team started to figure out how to transform the data into the correct formats that would work in D365.

As this moved along and they were starting to identify the data to be moved, they did a single successful data load into a test environment. After that data load, they assumed it was going to be correct and never looked at it anymore. They did continue looking at the different reports and were working to get all of the existing reports mapped to the new reports in D365.

As I mentioned, they only ran one successful test of the data load. When the project got to the last phase of user acceptance testing and they attempted to load the data, most of the templates didn't match the table values in the database. This caused a 3-month delay in testing, and ultimately, a delay for the go-live. This ended up costing the client almost $200,000 in consultant costs.

As we can see from the previous two examples, data migration is a major piece of all ERP projects. If it's not planned and managed properly throughout the life of the project, then it can have a major negative impact on the overall project.

So, what are the reports?

As I mentioned earlier, there are a number of different types of reports that exist in D365 S&SCM. The following is a list of the report types and the modules they belong to:

Module	Charts	Inquiry	List page	Power BI	SSRS	Total
Accounts payable		6			24	30
Accounts receivable		9	4		26	39
Asset management					8	8
Budgeting		9			4	13
Cash and bank management		8			13	21
Common		5	1			6
Cost accounting		4				4
Cost management		5			24	29
Credit and collections		3	2		10	15
Expense management					10	10
Fixed assets		1			19	20
General ledger		6			12	18
Human resources		4			40	44
Inventory management		12	3		34	49
Master planning		7				7
Organization administration	1	2			2	5
Payroll		6			4	10
Procurement and sourcing		3		1	23	27
Product information management		1			3	4
Production control	1	13		1	15	30
Project management and accounting		20			90	110
Questionnaire					5	5
Retail		15				15
Revenue recognition inquiry		1				1
Sales and marketing		7		1	20	28
Service management		1			4	5
System administration		8	1		6	15
Tax		6			15	21
Time and attendance		9			17	26
Transportation management		2				2
Warehouse management		8		1	12	21
Total Reports	2	181	11	4	440	638

Conclusion

Hopefully, after reading this chapter, you'll see how important data migration and management are to a project. If you don't look at data starting right from the beginning, it could very likely come back to delay you later on in the project.

In the next chapter, we'll take a good look at some of the licensing challenges that can occur in your project.

6
Licensing Challenges

Every project always has a challenge when it comes to how to purchase and assign user licenses. In all honesty, licensing is my least favorite topic to discuss, but as a **solutions architect** (**SA**), it's the one topic you cannot avoid. This chapter will discuss the following key topics:

- The types of licenses in D365 and how to assign them based on job type and security roles
- Licensing models
- Subscription types and licensing
- A licensing case study

Understanding the Microsoft licensing model

I've been working with Microsoft software in one form or another for over 30 years. I've been a **Microsoft Certified Technology Specialist** (**MCT**) for 25 years and have spoken at various different Microsoft conferences—from Ignite in 2020 to community conferences such as the *Scottish Summit©*. One of the most common questions I get is, "Can you please explain licensing to me?" The short answer is not easily. In fact, at a Microsoft conference in St. Louis many years ago, a gentleman brought his license agreement with him to the licensing booth and asked the ladies who were there whether they could explain it to him.

Unfortunately, they were not really license experts, and one of them saw me walking by and grabbed me to assist them. I spent three hours with the person going through the whole agreement he had and pointing out places where he could be saving money. Not everyone can get this amount of time from someone to help explain things to them. I'm going to say upfront, it's up to the SA, the deployment partner, and whoever is providing the actual licenses for D365 to make sure they fully understand the requirements prior to buying or selling the client their licenses.

Where can I get the licenses from?

Now that you've decided that D365 is the software platform for your organization, you next need to acquire licenses. There are several different ways to buy licenses. A volume license agreement with Microsoft is one of the ways to acquire licenses, and the other is from certified resellers. Most deployment partners are also certified resellers. The best value for money if you have a large number of users, let's say over 150, is to get a volume license agreement:

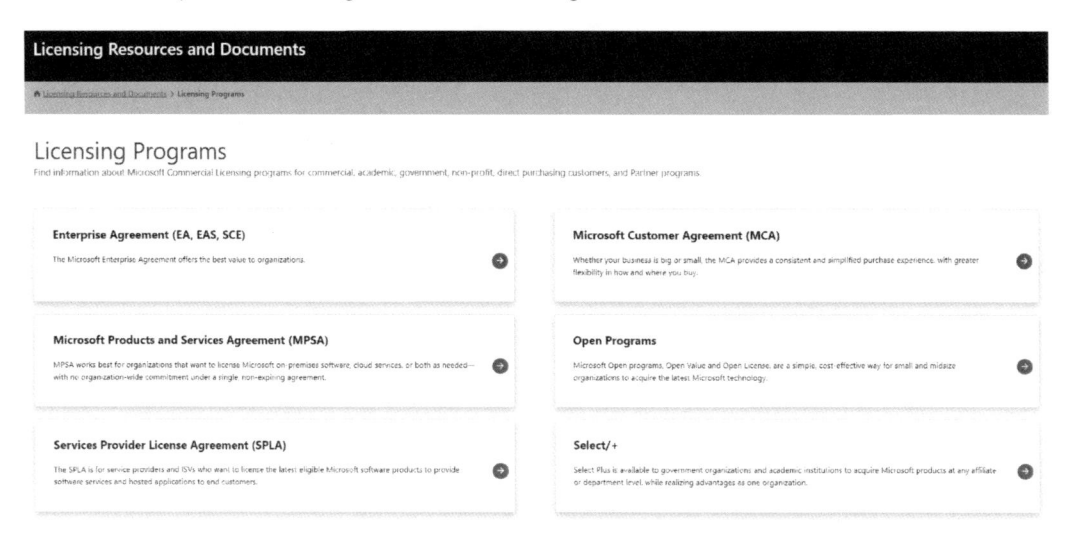

Figure 6.1: The Microsoft Licensing Programs website

Enterprise Agreements (EA) are best suited when you are licensing several different Microsoft products, including Office, Windows, SQL Server, and D365. These contracts are written to last for four or five years and include software version upgrades. When adding cloud applications, you will get a lower price for each user license. **Microsoft Products and Services Agreement (MPSA)** contracts work much like an EA, except it's used for individual products.

The third option that's available is pay-as-you-go metered licenses. Some applications, such as Dynamics 365 Fraud Protection, are licensed as pay-as-you-go and billed monthly. These products are part of the Azure tenant and are billed as an Azure application rather than a D365 application.

> **Note**
> Because you can buy many different types of licenses, it's strongly recommended that you don't mix and match the different license types. As an example, using a volume license for **D365 Finance** and a license acquired from a reseller partner for D365 **Supply Chain Management (SCM)** on the same tenant will lead to subscriptions that are incompatible. You should always use the same type of license across the same tenant.

Dynamics license types

As mentioned, the licenses for D365 are licensed by subscription, paid monthly. The license types fall into two different categories:

- **Assigned license**: These licenses are granted to a specific user or named user accounts and are generally referred to as Enterprise licenses. These license types can also be assigned to specific devices, such as handheld scanners, no matter whether the device is specifically assigned to a person or shared among many users.

- **Unassigned license**: This allows an administrator to grant a license to a user at the tenant level, no matter what type of device they connect with. Unassigned licenses can be granted to give a user complete access to an individual product, access to cross-applications (as an example, D365 Finance and Sales), and storage to increase capacity in the database.

Base versus attached licenses

Very often, a single user will need access to multiple Dynamics applications. Even though D365 Finance and SCM are "technically" a single product, it's licensed as two separate applications. Let's give a couple of examples of what I'm talking about. Let's say that a client needs to implement D365 Finance and SCM. They have 250 employees in total in the company, of which 16 work in the finance department and 25 in the procurement department.

Of the 16 in the finance department and the 25 in the procurement department, you will need to get 16 + 25 = 41 base licenses. Sixteen are Finance base licenses, and 25 are SCM base licenses. But of the 16 users in finance, 5 need to have access to the Procurement module in the system. These five users will need access to any **purchase orders** (**POs**) in the system so they can pay vendor invoices.

Instead of having to buy five base licenses and paying full price for those five licenses, you can buy five attached licenses. Those attached licenses give the users access to the modules they need access to at a discounted price. This is one way to save an organization a huge amount of money monthly.

The key to working with base and attached licenses is that they will only work with each other if the users belong to the same Azure tenant. If you're trying to access a resource in a different tenant, you'll be required to buy a full base license. This doesn't apply to legal entities, as those will all belong to the same Azure tenant.

Other licenses

You may be saying to yourself, "This is going to get really expensive!" And if you were only buying licenses based on the previous section, it could get expensive. But luckily, Microsoft has created a few other types of licenses that can help you save money but still give the users enough access to be able to get their job done:

- **Device licenses**: These are a type of license that are used for an individual D365 application. The advantage of this type of license is that you can have any users who are not specifically licensed for an application, able to use that application through a device. An example of this would be a warehouse worker who is a materials handler (i.e., someone who picks items from a shelf to deliver to a customer). By logging in and using the handheld scanner device, the users would get access to the SCM application.

- **Team or Team Member licenses**: These are a type of license assigned to a specific user but don't give user-specific access to a particular module. For example, you wouldn't be able to give a user a Team Member license if they were to execute the accountant role. Team Member licenses give a user the ability to do very basic tasks such as creating an expense report, filling out a purchase request, or viewing a report. If you have been assigned a Team Member license, you can view data that is created from one of the following applications: Finance, SCM, Commerce, Human Resources, Project Operations, Sales, Customer Service, and Field Service.

- **Operations license**: Operations licenses work much the same way as Team Member licenses but require a bit more access than what the Team license gives the user. This is a good choice when the user needs more access but not as much as a full user license would provide.

> **Note**
> When you're determining licenses, please remember that you can combine different license types. However, you must work on the assumption that if a user has a specific role in the system that falls into one of the default system roles, then they will need a full license, and that an attached or device license will not give them sufficient rights to work in the system.

The following chart shows you some of the applications where you have a Base application and a qualifying attached license:

D365 Base user license	Attached license per user				
	Commerce	Finance	HR	Sales	SCM
Commerce		X	X	X	X
Finance	X		X	X	X
HR	X	X		X	X
Sales	X	X	X		X
SCM	X	X	X	X	

Figure 6.2: License type chart

> **Note**
> D365 Human Resources as an app has been deprecated as a separate application. Instead, it has been rolled into D365 Finance and SCM. You can still get licenses for existing deployments, but new deployments are no longer available.

But I'm an administrator?

There is only one situation where a user will not require a user license. Any person who is added to D365 with the **system administrator** (**sys admin**) role does not require any type of license. This role gives administrators full access to all modules in D365 and all functions in Dynamics Lifecycle Services. Any user with a sys admin role would not do day-to-day work in D365 with their sys admin user account. They would still have a normal user account like every other user, which means they would most likely need a Team Member license.

How do we know what license to get?

No matter what type of licenses you eventually get for your organization, you will need to initially purchase 20 base licenses. It doesn't matter whether they are Finance or SCM modules; 20 is the number that's required.

There are a couple of different ways of determining the types of licenses required. Let's start off with Base licenses. Let's just look at what types of roles require a base license. One way is by going to a user account and adding a role to that user. When the role assignment popup opens, you'll be able to see what Base license type is required. The following screenshot shows an example of the roles and what license type is required:

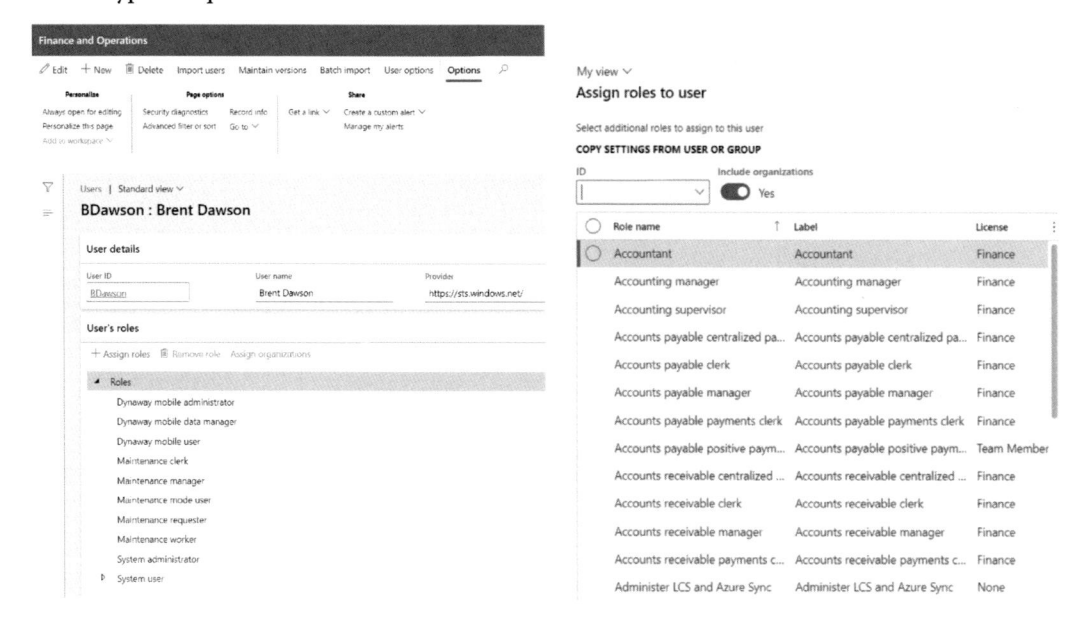

Figure 6.3: User admin menu

Plan out subscription requirements

As was previously mentioned, licensing is a complicated topic. If you don't get it right, it will cost the client a lot of money they weren't planning on spending, and it can impact an SA's reputation in the market. There are several tools that are available to SAs that can help you determine how many of each type of license will be needed for a deployment.

Dynamics 365 Licensing Guide

The Dynamics 365 Licensing Guide is the first place an SA can look to determine what types of licenses are needed for a deployment. From this guide, you can find out which security roles require what level of license. The following example shows some of the Finance roles, what the role does in the system, and the types of licenses that can be used to execute the role:

Role	Description	Finance (Base)	Ops-Activity	Team Members
Chief executive officer	Reviews financial and operational performance	X	X	
Budget contributor	Create, update, and approve departmental budget plans	X	X	X
Accounts payable positive payment clerk	Document accounts payable positive pay events	X	X	X

Figure 6.4: License comparisons

The Users page in System Administration

This page allows an SA to review the license requirements for each of the base user roles in D365. To view which license is required, open **System Administration | Configure Security**. Once in that location, select any role in the list, and the license type required will be listed on the very right-hand side of the table. The following screenshots show two different examples. The first shows an example of a Finance license, and the second shows an example of a Team Members license:

Figure 6.5: A role requiring a Finance license

Figure 6.6: A role requiring a Team Members license

> **Note**
> When looking at license types, the table will always display the largest license required for that security object.

Custom security

When creating custom security in D365 Finance and SCM, you need to know what the license requirements are for each of the roles, duties, and privileges you'll be working with. You can use the preceding tool to show which type of license you will need for that user to use the custom security and still be compliant with Microsoft's licensing requirements.

Subscription estimator

Another tool that can help with license requirements is the **Subscription estimator** tool located in Dynamics **Lifecycle Services**. This tool allows you to fill in a spreadsheet that contains a number of system requirements and then use that to create a license count for a deployment. The following screenshot shows where the tool can be accessed from:

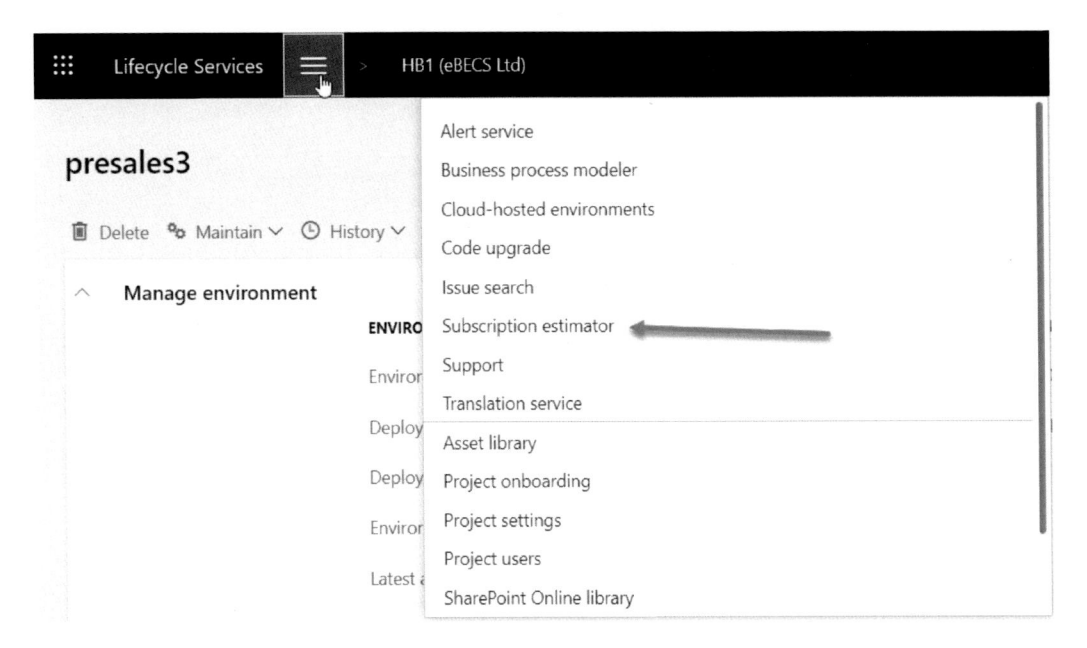

Figure 6.7: Access to the Subscription estimator from Lifecycle Services

Once in **Subscription estimator**, you must download a sample usage profile. Once that Excel file has been downloaded, you can enter some values, including an estimate of different types of transactions, how many legal entities are going to be deployed, and several other questions. Once you've entered in all that information (not all of the fields are required to be entered, but most can't be left blank, you need to enter 0), you can download the Excel file from this location:

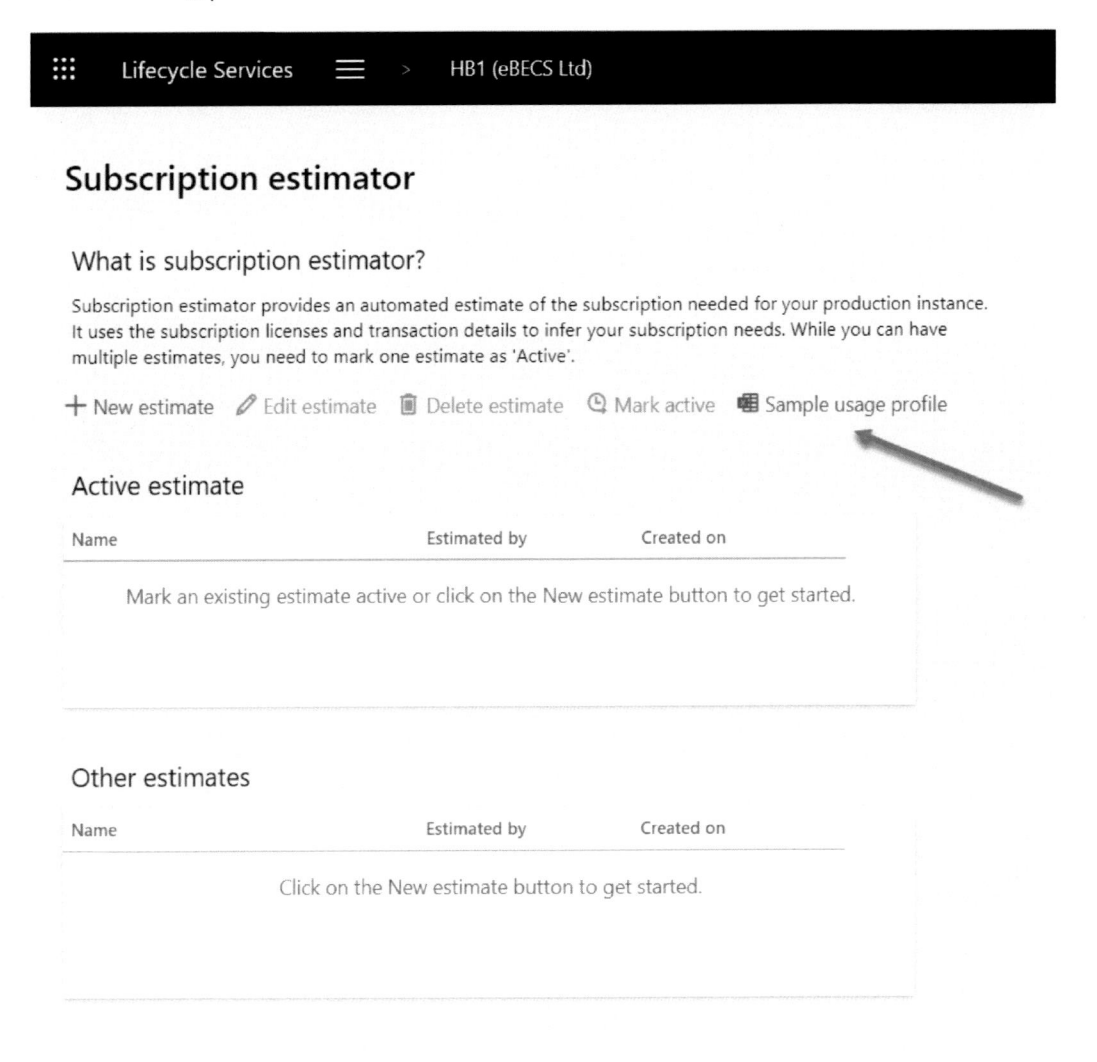

Figure 6.8: Download the sample usage profile Excel file

Once you've entered all the information, you will need to upload the Excel file into the estimator. Once that's been completed, it will take a few minutes to calculate the estimate. Please be patient. The estimate (the one you just loaded) will show up under **Other estimates**. If this is the one you wish to use, you will set it to be the **Active estimate** option.

To view the results, select the correct estimate from the **Other estimates** list, and below it, you will see the specifications. In the following screenshot, you can see that for the demo data I used in my Excel file, I will need 185 Enterprise user licenses (either Finance or SCM) and 75 Team Member licenses. This will be the closest estimate you can come up with for the number of license types.

> **Note**
> If you set up the environment with the number of licenses given here, but you decide to purchase more licenses prior to go-live, you'll need to inform the Microsoft FastTrack team so that they can be allocated in the production environment properly.

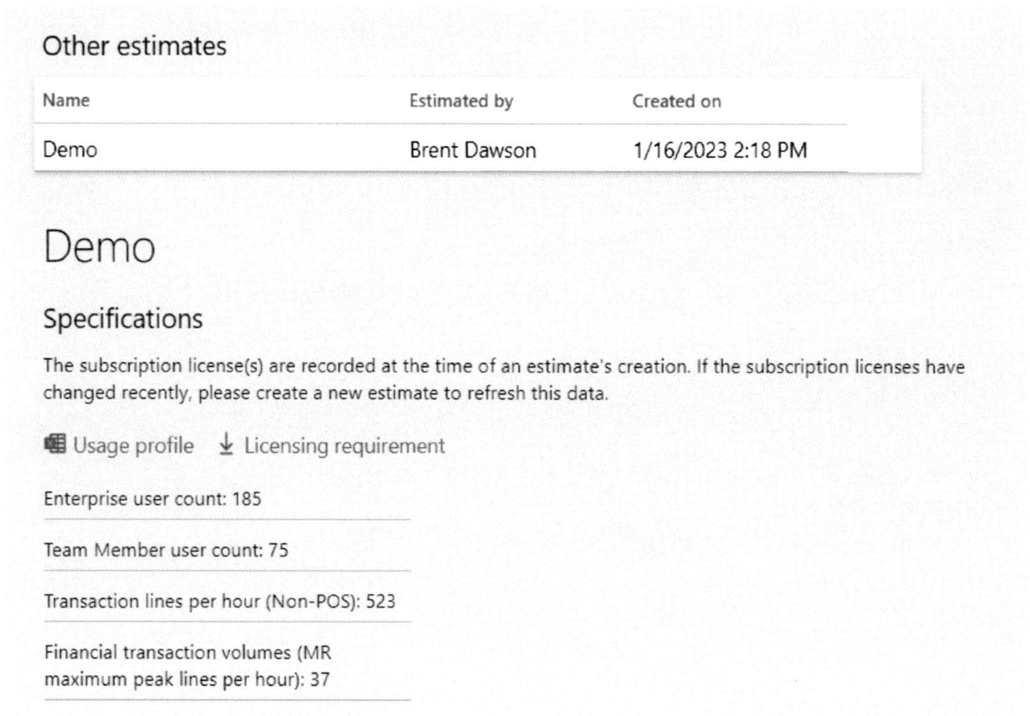

Other estimates

Name	Estimated by	Created on
Demo	Brent Dawson	1/16/2023 2:18 PM

Demo

Specifications

The subscription license(s) are recorded at the time of an estimate's creation. If the subscription licenses have changed recently, please create a new estimate to refresh this data.

Usage profile   Licensing requirement

Enterprise user count: 185

Team Member user count: 75

Transaction lines per hour (Non-POS): 523

Financial transaction volumes (MR maximum peak lines per hour): 37

Figure 6.9: An example of license counts based on a subscription estimate

ISV, External, and other license types

Now that we have discussed licensing in D365 Finance and SCM, we need to review other types of potential licenses that will be used in the system. First off, we have **Independent Software Vendor (ISV)** licenses. When we are looking at integrating an ISV into D365, we will also need to understand how the licensing for that ISV will work. Each ISV is different, but generally, they use two types of licenses. First, they have a system license, which will license the use of the ISV in D365. Basically, this means you can install it and turn it on in the system. The second license will normally be a per-user license. Depending on the ISV, they implement both types of licenses for a deployment to be compliant.

We also need to have a view of how many licenses will be needed if we allow external users to have access to D365. Generally, external users will not require a license. These types of users are treated like a system's internal users. Access is given through either the Vendor portal or the Customer portal, which are provided as part of the D365 installation.

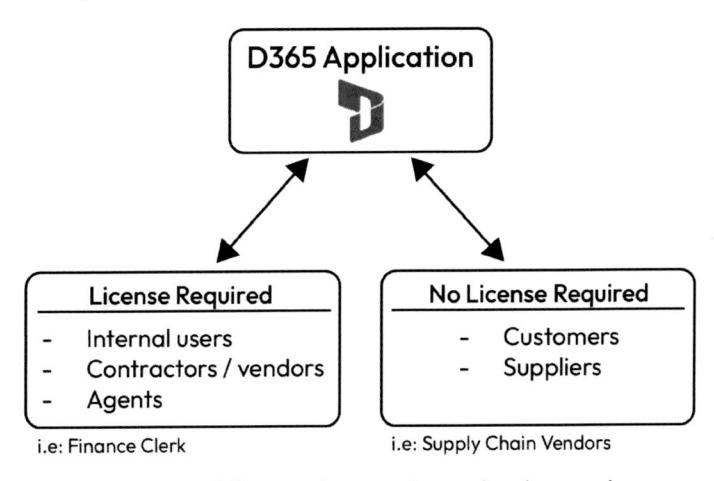

Figure 6.10: The differences between internal and external users

There is one specific tool that is included as part of the D365 SCM install, called **Asset Management**, which has a unique license requirement. When you purchase the licenses for SCM, you are licensed for up to 100 assets. If you go over that amount, you will need to pay for each set of assets above the 100 limit. Also, there are other features that you can add for Asset management, including a mobile app, a planning board, an electronic signature tool, and an analytics module. Each of those items has separate license costs that are paid to Dynaway (the original creator of the Asset Management module in D365).

Multiplexing

The concept of multiplexing is a licensing method used when a user takes advantage of either hardware or software that uses pooled connections or indirect access to information. Multiplexing does not reduce the overall number of licenses required for the different applications that a company will use. Instead, what it does is simplify how users are connected to information. Multiplexing is a set of rules that are used to prevent a client from purchasing fewer licenses than they would normally purchase.

For example, an organization takes advantage of multiplexing when using dual-write. If a company installs D365 Sales and D365 Finance and SCM, the company must license both of those applications

106　Licensing Challenges

as normal. However, if a person is primarily a Sales user, they can use Dual write to access information in Finance and SCM without having to have a Finance and SCM license. This is because the data they are trying to access does not reside in the Dataverse database that Sales is connected to. Honestly, an entire book could be written on just this subject alone. (That might be my next book.)

Assigning licenses

Now that we have determined and acquired the licenses required for a deployment, we need to assign those licenses to the users. The assignment of the different types of licenses is completed in the M365 Admin portal. Here, we see all the licenses that have been purchased and can assign whichever license is required to the individual users. In the following screenshot, we can see an example of how to assign a license to a user:

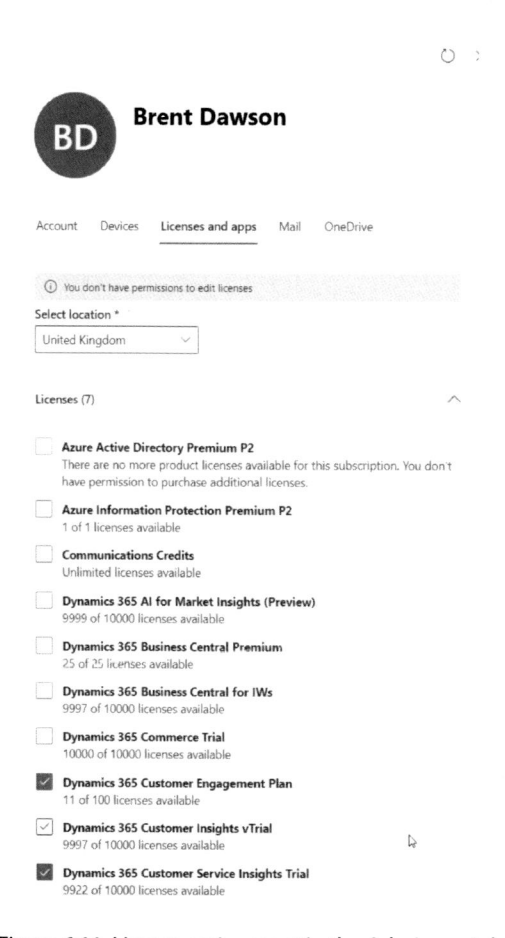

Figure 6.11: License assignment in the Admin portal

License reporting

Lastly, let's look at some of the reports that are available in the system to help us make sure we are compliant with Microsoft for the licenses we've assigned. When you go to the **System Administrator** module, you will find a section called **Inquires | License**. In that section you will find two reports:

- **User License Counts**: The **User License Counts** report shows you what licenses are assigned to what users. *Figure 6.12* shows the **User License Counts** report parameters:

User License Counts

Parameters

Date for Named User License User Co...
1/17/2023

Show list of users per access license ...
Yes

Destination

⇄ Change

Screen

Records to include

▽ Filter

USER COUNT BY ACCESS LICENSE TYPE TABLE

Named user license type
Finance

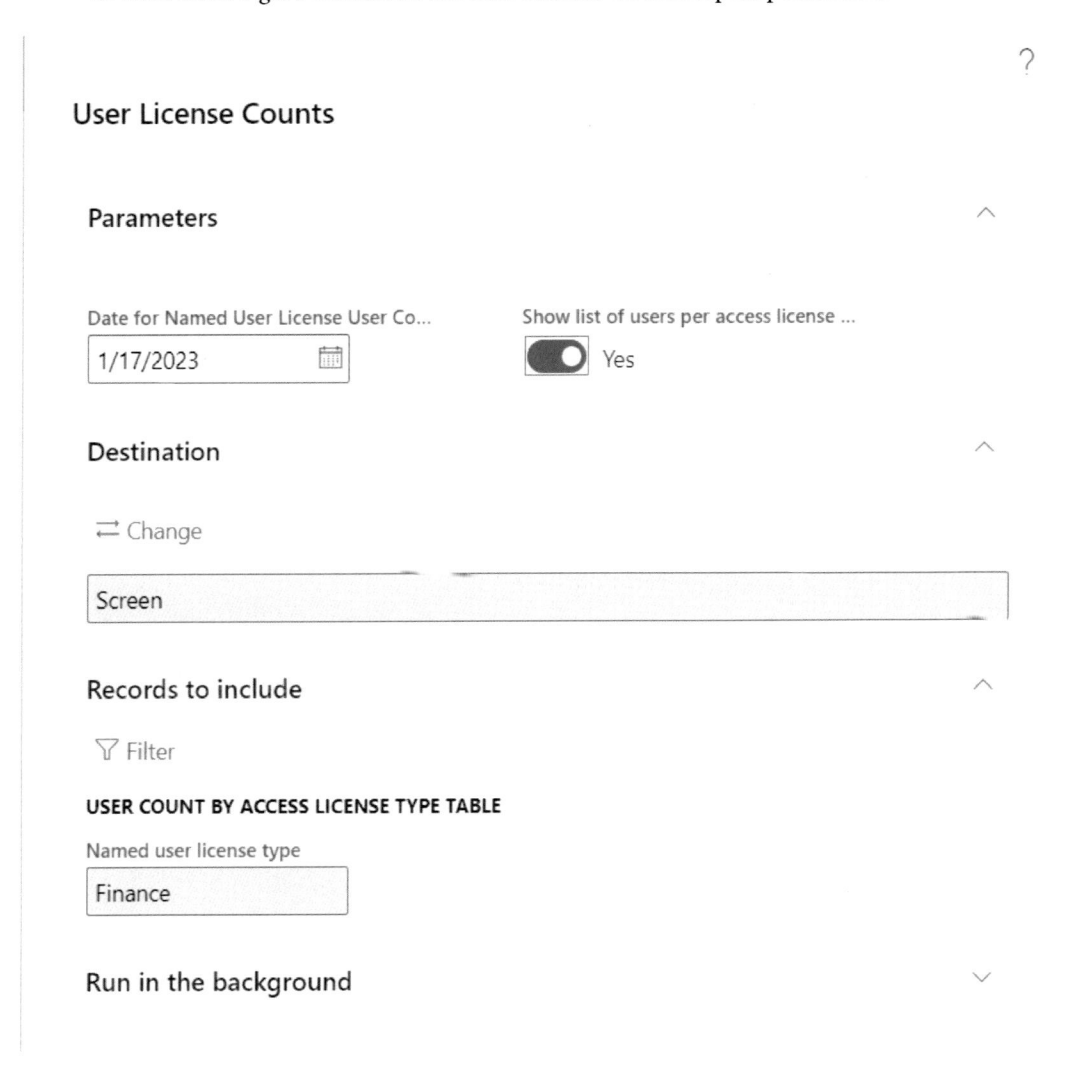

Run in the background

Figure 6.12: The User License Counts parameters dialog

The following screenshot is an example of a completed report:

Finance and Operations User Count Report
Excluding device users

Page 1 of 29
1/17/2023
1:52 PM

ebecs.com

Results Valid Date	4/29/2021
Access License Type	**Access License Type**
Activity	25

Alias	Network domain	User name
IngaPSUS@contosoax7.onmicrosoft.com	https://sts.windows.net/	IngaPSUS

Security Role	Access License Type
Employee	Team Members
Manager	Team Members
System user	Team Members
Purchasing manager	Operations

Alias	Network domain	User name
AprilPSUS@contosoax7.onmicrosoft.com	https://sts.windows.net/	AprilPSUS

Security Role	Access License Type
Employee	Team Members
Accounts payable payments clerk	Operations
System user	Team Members
Accounts payable clerk	Operations
Accounts payable manager	Operations

Alias	Network domain	User name
SaraPSUS@contosoax7.onmicrosoft.com	https://sts.windows.net/	SaraPSUS

Security Role	Access License Type
Chief financial officer	Activity
Employee	Team Members
Manager	Team Members
System user	Team Members

IMPORTANT - Compliance Guidance

This report does not account for non-authenticated users who may be accessing the server. It is the customer's responsibility to license every user accessing the server in accordance with the license terms. Some users could be considered "External Users" which do not require Client Access Licenses. Please refer to the Microsoft Dynamics 365 Enterprise edition Licensing Guide located here: https://www.microsoft.com/en-us/dynamics365/pricing for further guidance.

Disclaimer

This report is for informational purposes and is current as of the date and time printed above. You may copy and use this document for your internal, reference purposes. You may not modify any information in this report. Any change to this report renders it invalid immediately. This report is provided "as-is." MICROSOFT MAKES NO WARRANTIES, EXPRESS OR IMPLIED, WITH RESPECT TO THE INFORMATION PROVIDED IN THIS REPORT.

For more information on Dynamics 365 licensing, please visit https://www.microsoft.com/en-us/dynamics365/pricing.

Figure 6.13: Finance and Operations User Count Report

- **User License Counts History**: This report shows the number of different licenses used between certain search dates. The following is an example of what the report shows:

Dynamics 365 for Finance and Operations User Count History Report

Excluding device users
Application version: 7.0.6651.92

Page 1 of 1
2/15/2023
7:59 PM

From date: 4/29/2021
To date: 12/31/2154

Actual users count

From date:	To date:	Operations Licenses	Team Members Licenses	Activity Licenses
4/29/2021	12/31/2154	32	41	25

Figure 6.14: The User Count History Report output

Security configuration diagnostics

Another important tool that can assist license counts is the D365 **Security diagnostics** tool for task recordings. This feature in D365 Finance and SCM allows administrators to analyze the security requirements for a specific task or process. By generating an Excel file with detailed information about the necessary security roles, duties, and privileges for a recorded task, administrators can ensure that users have the appropriate level of access to perform their job functions while maintaining compliance with organizational security policies.

The process involves creating a task recording, capturing the actions performed during the task, and then generating security diagnostics based on the recording. This helps identify gaps in security or areas where user access needs to be adjusted, ensuring that only authorized users can access sensitive data and perform critical operations within the system. This feature is particularly useful for troubleshooting access issues and designing **role-based access control** (**RBAC**) within D365 Finance and SCM environments.

From here, you'll be able to determine which license type is needed for the specific type of task you are trying to execute. This is especially handy after you have created custom security.

Real-world example

I've presented a lot of information in this chapter about licensing and how to properly determine the correct number of licenses needed for a compliant deployment. If you have followed what I've written, it should be relatively easy to calculate the correct number of licenses. But you need to make sure that you fully understand how decisions you make as an SA can have a direct impact on license numbers and types. The following example is based on a real-life scenario I came across.

As I mentioned, I live in the UK (so I'm going to be talking in **Great British Pounds (GBP)**). A government entity had hired a Microsoft partner to come in and help them get their new D365 Finance and SCM system in place. As a large partner, they had many people who we assigned to the project. During the discovery phase, the SA convinced the client that they were going to create too many purchase requisitions on a daily basis, so it would be best for each user to have the ability to create POs instead. This decision had many more impacts than they realized at the time.

Firstly, by giving everyone the ability to create POs directly, it allowed them to bypass any purchasing controls the organization had. All the business processes that controlled those were no longer valid, but a new process was not put in place to help control purchasing. As a result, several people could fill out a PO for the same item and send them to vendors. This caused a huge increase in spending and double or triple deliveries. It also made it difficult for staff in the **Accounts Payable (AP)** group to validate that items that were ordered were actually delivered. This led to a large amount of staff turnover.

The other major impact that this decision caused was an increase in license costs to the client. This one decision cost the client an extra £7,500 per month in license costs. When in discussion with the client's IT department, I discovered what had been deployed; they were incredibly surprised that they were spending too much on licenses on a monthly basis. I went in and set up Purchase Requisition business processes, simplified ordering, and changed their license types. That helped to drop their monthly costs by almost £8,000 per month.

As an SA, it's very important that you have a full understanding of what the client requires for the application, which business processes and modules are going to be used, and how to price and license those systems correctly.

Conclusion

As we've seen in this chapter, licensing is a major part of deployment. Without proper licensing, companies will potentially pay too much or even too little for the work they perform in the system. We saw how to create a license report and also how to make sure any third-party ISVs have been licensed as well.

At this point, we've looked at the issues that I believe to be the parts of a project that can cause an SA the most amount of stress. Hopefully, I've been able to help you prevent or reverse some decisions that may have caused you problems with your project. The next seven chapters will walk you through some of the areas that you should follow to help make your project a success.

Part 2: From Solution Design to Deployment – Practical Advice

In this part, you will walk through the components of a successful solution design based on Microsoft's Dynamics FastTrack. You'll learn what documents and tools are used as part of the Success by Design methods. We will present the best practices and examples of the major areas that make up Success by Design.

This part has the following chapters:

- *Chapter 7, How to Plan a D365 F&SCM Project*
- *Chapter 8, Learning the Client's Business*
- *Chapter 9, Collecting Project Requirements*
- *Chapter 10, ALM Tools and Applications*
- *Chapter 11, Human Change Management*
- *Chapter 12, Building a Blueprint Solution*
- *Chapter 13, Deploying the Project Solution*

7
How to Plan a D365 F&SCM Project

In the previous chapters, we took a good look at the different areas that can be a major challenge during our D365 projects. Starting in this chapter, we're now going to begin looking at the process of running a project from start to finish, following the *Success by Design* model. I'm not going to specifically talk about project management methodologies, such as Agile or Waterfall, as I prefer a combination of the two. We'll talk about that in the next section.

This chapter will discuss the following:

- Project management and its tools
- Starting a project
- Project structure and checklists

By the time we're done with this chapter of the book, we'll know how to successfully create a project team, prepare for client discoveries, and create a blueprint solution. To achieve this, we'll look at the different types of project requirements and resources that will be needed to get the work completed. I will use some examples that I've had to deal with over the years.

Project management

I've been doing this for many years, and I can honestly say that using straight Agile for an ERP project isn't a good way to manage a project. Because of the way that Agile completes its effort in sprints, you never really get the whole solution before you start to deploy. You only need to solution what you're going to complete in that sprint. So, as far as I'm concerned, Agile is out. Waterfall is much better for ERP projects because you know the entire solution prior to starting the deployment part of the project. The downside of this method is that you don't know how anything works until you get to the end of the project. That is not optimal, as you can't get on top of any issues that may pop up before you're ready to go live.

I prefer to go with a hybrid of waterfall and agile. The hybrid mixture works well because you get to bookend the project with waterfall methods, and in the middle of the project, you use agile iterations. As the following diagram shows, the beginning of the project where we do the research, strategy, documentation, and blueprint is completed using the waterfall methodology. The actual development, deployment, and unit testing are completed using agile iterations. Finally, user acceptance testing and go-live use the waterfall method. This works best, as it allows you to know where you're going in terms of the solution, and then you can take that solution and break it down into smaller chunks, allowing for better utilization of resources and documenting your work quicker.

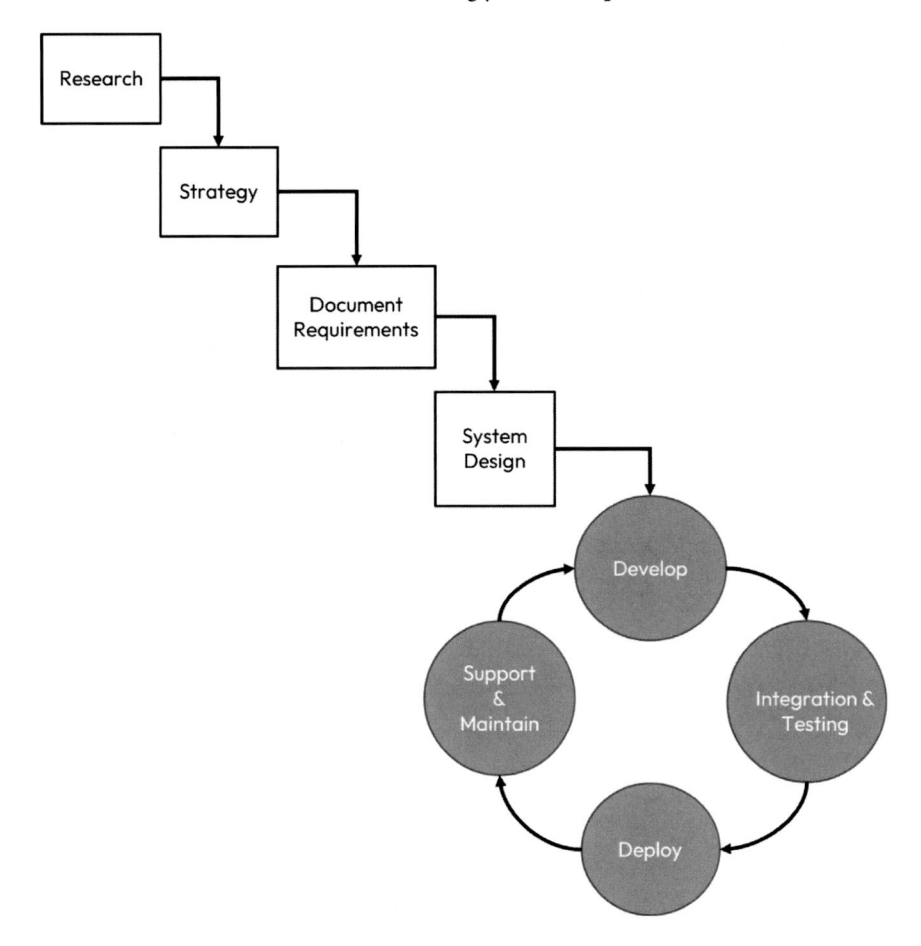

Figure 7.1: An Agile/Waterfall hybrid methodology

This is only one of the few things that need to happen at the very beginning of a project. This is something that should have been identified during pre-sales solutioning.

> **Note**
> You can talk to 10 people and get 10 different opinions, but I am a believer that whoever the SA is during the pre-sales stage of a project should be involved in the project delivery until at least the solution blueprint has been created. This way, you have a consistent view of the organization, its business processes, and how the solution should be designed. Also, the customer has a consistent person to deal with. If possible, try and be involved from pre-sales to blueprinting.

The project layout

Because we've agreed that the project will follow Success by Design, one of the first things we need to do is identify how we are going to approach the project. The project itself will be split into four different and distinct phases. The four phases and some of the tasks executed in each include the following:

Initiate	Implement	Prepare	Operate
Prepare to start	Design and build	Deploy	Go-live
Requirements	Coding	Testing	Live system health
Governance	Configuration	Go-live planning	Usage/statistics
Fit gap		Readiness	Maintenance
Customer project kickoff	Data modeling	Cutover planning	
	Performance		Post-go-live review
Solution review/signoff	Integrations	Go-live review	
	Data migration strategy		
	Security configuration		
	BI strategy		
	ALM		
	Testing		

Table 7.1: The Success by Design phases

For the rest of this chapter, we're going to focus on the **Initiate** phase. First off, how do we start from the beginning. If you're in an organization that has completed ERP projects for some time, you will most likely have a pre-defined set of documents and project structures you can use. However, we are not that lucky, so we're going to start building ours from scratch. That way, we get it the way we want it. If other people are nice to us, we might even share with them.

Project management tools

There are several different tools available to project managers to help control a project. These include Azure DevOps, Microsoft Project, and Dynamics 365 Project Operations. We will have a detailed discussion on these in *Chapter 10*.

Prepare to start

You are probably wondering, how do we prepare to start? That doesn't make much sense, but when you think about it, we can't actually start a project until we've prepared a few things. We need to prepare some documents that we can use during the different phases of the project. Also, we want to make sure we have identified the resources required, how we're going to track success, how we're progressing through the project, and who's going to be responsible for what.

Project team

Completing an ERP project takes a team. Now, I've been in this business a long time, and one of the phrases I used to hate was the term "team." I used to referee basketball, and to me, a team was the people on the court throwing the basketball around. But if you think about it, a project team is much like a basketball team. You have a coach, or the solution architect, and you have all the members of the project, which are the "team." The client's staff members, even though they really aren't, are the other team (we'll be nice to them, as they are paying the bill!), and finally, the referee is the project manager. They're going to keep us on the straight and narrow.

So, let's put the two teams together. The partner needs to provide the following types of people or resources:

- **Partner representative**: This is generally a salesperson or someone from a "success" team at the partner company. This is a very important position, as they will be the person who communicates on a regular basis with the client to make sure they feel like the project is proceeding successfully.
- **Project Manager (PM)**: This is self-explanatory. The PM is responsible for managing the time and budget for the project. Also, if the client has an internal PM, then both of them should be constantly communicating during the project.

> **Note**
>
> PMs come in various styles. Some PMs have no IT background. Other types have many years of experience in IT projects. Personally, the type of PM that I like has little or no experience in the ERP application. It doesn't matter if they have lots of IT project experience; I'd just prefer them to have very little ERP experience. That might sound weird, but there is a reason for this.
>
> In my experience, I've had PMs whose knowledge was limited, but they thought it was part of their job to help solution the project. I want the PM to keep track of time, make sure tasks are completed, and make sure we're well within the budget. As the SA, I don't tell them how to manage the project, and I don't want them to create the solution.

- **Solution architect**: You might be wondering why I listed the SA third and not first. As important as the SA is to a project, we must understand that ultimately, the PM is responsible for the delivery. So, in the hierarchy of the project, the SA will report to the PM.

- **Analysts**: Depending on the size of the project and the modules that will need to be deployed, the solution blueprint document will help to determine how many analysts will be required. In most cases, you will need a minimum of one financial analyst, one supply chain analyst, one manufacturing analyst, and a warehouse analyst. Many projects are sufficient in size that you may want to have more than one of each of the analyst roles. That way, the tasks can be split among multiple analysts and completed in less time.

- **Technical architect**: The role of the technical architect is to complete two separate tasks. First, they will work with the SA to organize the technical setup and configuration of the system. This includes setting up environments, managing the data migration, and helping with the day-to-day admin of the system.

- **Data analyst**: The data analyst is responsible for working with the technical architect to work on getting data transformed and imported into D365. They will also work with the BI analyst to make sure the data needed for reporting is working properly.

- **Developer**: The developer is integral to the project in a couple of different ways. First, they are responsible for editing all the report templates to fit with the client (things such as logos, report formats, and so on). They are also responsible for creating all customizations in D365 F&SCM and, finally, creating all the coding for any integrations needed to communicate with any other legacy application.

- **BI analyst**: We will need a data analyst to work with the client to set up data policies, reporting, and Power BI visualizations. This person will work hand in hand with the client's BI group.

- **ISV consultants**: If your project is going to be implementing one or more ISVs, you'll need to have a resource from that organization to assist in the entire program. This individual(s) should be present for the requirement sessions, development and deployment, and testing phases.

On the client side, we will require several resources as well. Again, depending on the size of the project, several people will be required.

- **Program manager**: Many organizations implement ERP systems as a part of a bigger business application replacement program. If there is a program manager, they will be the primary contact between the client and partner representative.

- **Project manager**: This is the client's internal PM. It's very rare that the client will not have their own PM. The two PMs will work together to keep the project on track. The partner PM will be responsible for managing the tasks of the partner, the client PM, and the **Subject-Matter Experts** (**SMEs**) from the client. Hopefully, they will get along well so that things go smoothly.

> **Note**
>
> I've been involved in projects where the PMs don't, for lack of a better term, stand each other. In one particular project, the partner went through three PMs before the client PM found someone they could work with. The shortest length of time that the partner PM was involved in was two hours. Whether you like it or not, the client PM is *always* right, if you catch my meaning.

- **SMEs**: The client SMEs are the people who answer questions during the requirement-gathering sessions, and they will help to create user stories for business processes that don't follow standard system configuration, create the testing scripts for use during all the testing sessions, and complete all the **User Acceptance Testing (UAT)** to validate that the solution fits the requirements.

> **Note**
>
> Depending on the length of the project, there may be a situation where you will need to backfill a resource due to sickness, vacation, or any other reason for leave. On the client side, they will need to make sure they have sufficient resources to work on the project.

The success of a project is directly related to the availability of the client resources. My opinion is that the client should dedicate their resources once the development and deployment phase of the project is done. They will be needed to test all the deployments completed by the analysts in each iteration of the project. If the resources are unavailable due to having to do their day job or some other reason, we can have several delays in the project, which may ultimately delay go-live and incur extra project costs. If possible, try and convince the client that they should backfill the project resources so that the backfill person does the SME's day job, allowing the SME to focus on the project.

Governance

Another task that we need to complete early on is how we govern the project. Governance is the framework we agree to follow. Part of this has already been completed as part of the pre-sales process, where we agreed to follow Success by Design and a hybrid project management method. One of the other outputs of this exercise is creating a success checklist. We need to have a list of successes that we can measure. This will help to get the project to a point where we can legitimately say, yes, the project fulfills our requirements.

The following is an example of some measures we can use to track success:

Architecture	Implementation	Governance
• Data migration • Data model • Functional design • Integrations • ISVs • Performance • Security	• Life cycle • Business continuity • Change management • Cutover • Fit/gap analysis • Rollout • Testing	• Schedule • Budget • Approach
Product	**Competency**	**Support**
• Customization replacement • Feature deprecation • Gaps • Bugs • Performance	• Customer • Partner	• Internal resource • External resource • Microsoft support

Table 7.2: Sample success measures

For each of these items, you assign a red, yellow, or green mark to let you know the status of each item. You can also add a black mark to show that an item is at risk.

Governance of a project will also need to include other areas as well. These can include, but are not limited to, the following:

- The goals of the project
- How the project will be organized
- The key areas of the project that can create risk
- The project plan

Project governance will also need to consider ISVs, potentially several partners involved in the project, and any governance the clients might already have. If you work with a larger client, they will often have their own internal governance models. As an example, at the airport where I worked, there was an engineering department. All the engineers were also PMs. When brought in to assist with projects, they followed a more engineering project management approach. It wasn't necessarily the best fit for an IT project, and it shows that some clients already have their own methods.

Framework

One of the outcomes that project governance will give us is a framework and the different techniques needed to make a project successful. We need to understand what the end goals of the project are and, once those have been defined, create a list of success matrix items to test against those goals. This is generally where the test plans come from. However, this also means we need to validate that those goals have been attained.

The plan that is created in this phase will be efficient in terms of how the project is driven (which tasks are completed and when), what the structure of the tasks is, and how the plan will be executed efficiently, on time, and, of course, within budget. However, it must also identify potential risks that can occur during the project. These risks can include things such as a lack of client resources, holidays and medical leave, weather, and system outages. This risk identification can help a project avoid common risk issues and allow the project team to anticipate them ahead of time.

Lastly, there must be some flexibility in the plan. Without flexibility, the project would be too rigid. You need to be able to move tasks around. Some tasks will take longer than planned due to one of the previously listed risks. Conversely, it's possible that some tasks will be completed in less time than previously thought. This can happen when creating things such as integrations.

Risks

Let's take a closer look at risks. I look at risks with the view that things can and probably will go wrong during the deployment of any ERP system. When looking at business applications, there are some specific types of risks that you should be concerned with. The types of issues can include the following:

- **Having project scope creep**: If the project doesn't have a detailed scope and what you need to deploy at the end, it will never, ever end.

> **Note**
> It often happens that people who plan a project have a set of goals that the project needs to accomplish. However, often, what is agreed to during the creation of the project doesn't always match up with what some of the SMEs or users want. Often, SMEs will have their own political agenda. This agenda may include wanting specific features or functionality included in the final product. If this happens, we get scope creep in the project, and this can have a very big negative impact on it. The other type of agenda may include resistance to a new tool or method to do something, so they will make the requirements so difficult that it makes it impossible to implement anything that will change the way they do it now. I've run into this in a couple of different projects, and it can literally bring a project to a stop.

- **Responsibility assignment**: You need to determine who is going to be responsible for what tasks during a project. If there is any type of disagreement or assignments are unclear, then there is a risk that tasks will be ignored or not completed because people either don't understand the assignment or don't think it's their responsibility and completely ignore it. This is where the PM or PMs need to get together and hash out who is responsible for what, ensuring that those individuals complete the tasks.

- **Little client involvement**: If the client and business users aren't engaged or fully involved in a project, then we have a massive risk. The people on the client side of the project need to be clearly identified, clearly made responsible for their expertise, and fully available when the project needs them.

> **Note**
>
> During a past project, I had a situation where the client didn't take seriously the amount of time that would be required by the SMEs from the company. Because of this, they expected that the people on the project would be doing their day-to-day job and also working on the project. They didn't backfill any of the staff. Due to this decision, it was mandated by the client that if we needed to have a meeting regarding anything to do with the project, we had to book meetings at least two weeks in advance. Needless to say, it was almost impossible to get a quick decision on anything if it involved more than two people. This one thing alone put the project at least a year behind schedule.

- **Technical deficit**: Many times, clients who install a business application will not have any experience implementing a system. As a good partner, you will need to guide the client along the implementation processes.

- **Go-live delays**: If you have issues that come up during a project, due to any of the issues listed previously, it can have a negative impact on go-live. As an example, if you don't recognize an integration that is needed before UAT, then this will delay the go-live because you'll need to scope, plan, develop, test, integrate, and test the new integration end to end. Obviously, go-live is going to be delayed.

- **Misunderstood expectations**: I know it shouldn't happen, but there are times when the expectations between the partner and client don't line up. Obviously, this is probably the most severe risk that can happen. If this does happen, my recommendation is to stop all work on the project and sit down and negotiate what the expectations are supposed to be. This might mean they need to reset the project, create a new statement of work, and possibly a new project budget.

> **Note**
>
> I was involved in a project where there were several assumptions made by the client that didn't exist in the project plan. The person who was the SA on the project didn't include items such as fixed assets, project accounting, and HR in the SOW. The client asked at what point in the project were we going to set the requirements and configure those models. The PM admitted to the client they were not in the scope of the project. Needless to say, the client was very (and I mean very) unhappy. Even in my role as a warehouse analyst, I had to ask why they were out of scope.
>
> To enable **Enterprise asset management (EAM)**, as an example, we need to have people hired for F&SCM as workers, with positions and jobs assigned to them. They also need to have a created project under which all EAM work orders are processed. This whole situation happened because of two reasons. First, the SA who created the project scope and pre-sales solution was junior and, due to lack of experience, didn't realize what importance those missing items meant to the project's success. Second, there wasn't a solution blueprint review to make sure that everything needed for the project was included. Even if you've been doing this for 25 years, it never hurts to validate the SOW from pre-sales before you start working on the project.

- **Disagreements between the stakeholders**: As mentioned in the previous note, there may be times when the client and the partner start pointing fingers at each other. If you can't resolve this situation early on, then it can lead to partners being fired or, worse yet, having lawsuits filed against them.

If a project doesn't have excellent governance, things will go wrong. Even if a project is completed and goes live, if you don't have an error-free delivery, there might be a feeling of a lack of confidence in the application. It may also create a feeling of dissatisfaction in the stakeholder that something isn't right with the system.

Project structure

How a project is structured is one of the ways that will help it run smoothly. The following items are generally used in most IT projects. Just knowing that these structures and processes are in place makes those who belong to the project or those that support it feel much more comfortable that those controls are in place and used to guide it.

Steering the project

Most projects will have a steering committee to help guide the project. They are there to reference, guide, and motivate the project team during the length of the project. The steering committee is usually made up of the executive project sponsor, senior company management, such as the director of IT, VP of finance, the program manager, both the client and partner PMs, and the project SA. There may be times when the committee will invite some members of the project to their meeting.

The committee should meet at least once a month, with the meeting topics including how the project is going, any major road or stumbling blocks, how the budget is doing, and whether or not any new major risks have popped up since the last meeting. If the steering committee doesn't take an interest in the project and is basically just there to fulfill their meeting requirements, plus there is very little interest in how the project is progressing, then the project can have major issues without any leadership from the top. The committee needs to believe that the PMs give them accurate and reliable information. If the committee is unengaged, then it really doesn't matter what the PMs tell them.

Project reports

One way that the steering committee is kept updated is through regular status reports produced by the PMs. It's also possible during the execution of a complex business application project that there could be multiple reports based on specific areas. Generally, these reports at the committee level should be made up of data that includes the following:

- Ways to prove that the data in the project status report is accurate
- Being able to answer whether the project is on track and budget
- What the major risks that can impact the go-live date are
- Whether there is anything that needs to be worked on by the steering committee to get back on track or prevent risks

> **Note**
>
> The information that the PMs get to put into the steering committee's status meetings comes from status reports that are generated by members of the project team. A few years ago, I was part of a project for an oil and gas services company as a Dynamics Administrator.
>
> We had to fill out weekly reports of what we had accomplished or, more precisely, in my case, what I had prevented other project team members from trying to break. The report format was just a simple template, with a couple of sentences stating what I completed and a few bullet points to highlight certain activities. After a few of these reports, I wanted to know if anyone actually read these reports, so I started putting in hypothetical questions, such as, "Where does the white in snow go when it melts?" and "If sour cream is already sour, why does it have an expiry date?" After a couple of weeks, the senior PM came to my desk with a rather serious look on his face, and asked me, "Where does the white in snow go when it melts?" That was my validation that someone actually read my reports.

Risks

Every project, regardless of whether it's an ERP project, an Azure project, or creating a new runway at an airport, has a risk register. Ideally, it's a central place where PMs and SAs can keep track of all of the risks during a project and give them a ranking. However, we want to make sure that we only enter items that are really risks. We don't want to record silly things such as items that don't reflect an actual project priority.

Stage gates

These are items that are milestone-driven. Milestones in a project plan are ways that you can look at what has been completed and determine whether it fulfills requirements. Usually, milestones occur between sprints in an Agile project methodology. If you're using a hybrid methodology, milestones can be entered periodically to show users how the project is currently going.

Change boards

Change boards are used specifically when you want to make a change to a project blueprint solution, or if you want to add new features. An example would be if you have a blueprint solution for a project but Microsoft releases a new feature or module that you want or need to use to make your solution better. The change board will evaluate the change, determine what time, effort, and cost it will have, and then it will make a recommendation of whether it should be done during the current project or until after go-live and implemented afterward.

Responsible, accountable, consulted, and informed

RACI is an acronym that stands for **Responsible, Accountable, Consulted, Informed**. A RACI chart (also known as a RACI matrix or RACI diagram) is a tool used to clarify and communicate the roles and responsibilities of individuals or groups involved in a project or business process.

These matrix roles include the following:

- **Responsible**: The person or people responsible for completing a task or making a decision
- **Accountable**: The person who is ultimately accountable for the task or decision, and who has the authority to make final decisions
- **Consulted**: People who need to be consulted or provide input on a task or decision but who are not ultimately responsible or accountable for it
- **Informed**: People who need to be kept informed of progress or decisions but who do not need to provide input or take action

A RACI chart typically includes a list of tasks or decisions, along with the roles and responsibilities associated with each one. The chart can help to clarify expectations, reduce confusion, and improve communication among team members or stakeholders.

The following screenshot shows an example of a RACI matrix template.

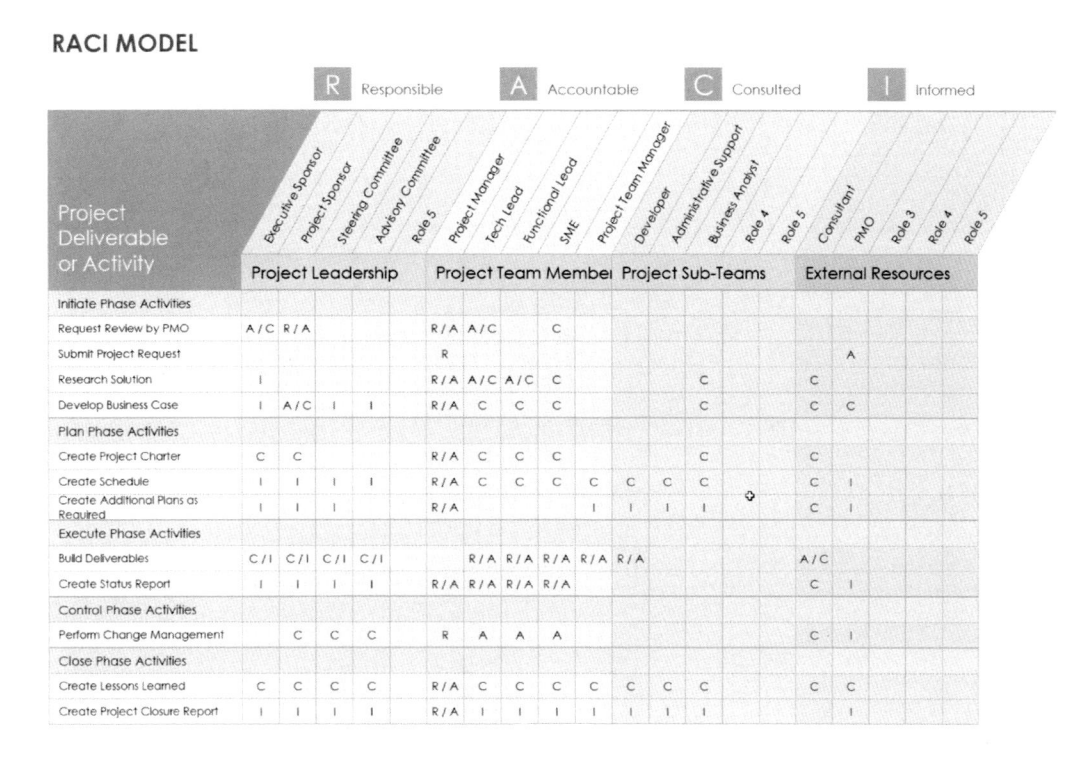

Figure 7.2: A RACI matrix

Business processes

One of the things that we need to identify during this part of the project is what business processes need to be included in it. As we create that list, we can also create a business process heat map. This heat map will help us keep track of which processes have been completed, which are in progress, and which are at risk. The following chart shows an example of a heat map.

A business process heat map example

Process design blocked or not started — Not completed — In progress — Testing — Completed

Figure 7.3: A business process heat map example

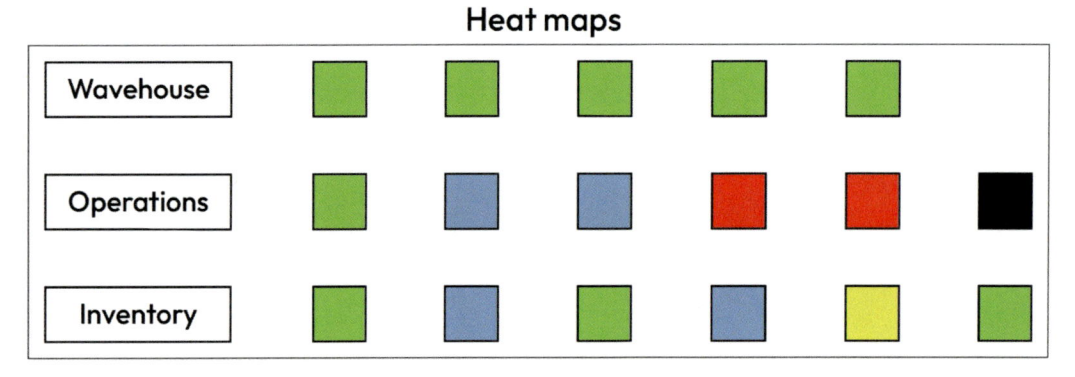

Heat maps

Figure 7.4: Heat maps

Project checklists

Lastly, one thing that can help a project move along successfully and make sure things are working well or are on track is to create a checklist. The checklist should contain the following:

Checklist	Items
Project goals	Make sure they are clear and able to be monitored throughout the project
	Map them properly to actions and measurable tasks
	Correctly translate them to project deliverables
	Make sure the goals are relevant to the appropriate stakeholders
Project organization and structure	Make sure the business and functional workstreams match
	Get strong executive sponsorship
	Enable and encourage cross-team collaboration
	Make sure the budget and resources are appropriately set for the length of the project
	Identify who is responsible for what during the project phases
	Identify and assign project roles and who owns what areas of the project
Project approach	Validate the way you want to use the methodology you've selected, make sure it works well with the business, and examine how the project constraints affect the project
Governance	Make sure there is a steering group and committee to oversee the project
	Make sure you set up and use a risk register
	Identify and add to the project plan milestones
	Make sure there is a change review board set up for the length of the project

Table 7.3 – Project Checklist

Conclusion

Now, at the end of this chapter, your head is probably spinning a lot. And to be honest, I've not really touched on all the issues in this chapter, but I think I touched on the ones that are the most important. You will find that there are many more things that you need to look at and keep in mind when putting your project together.

However, what you need to take from this is that project governance is so important to have a successful project. You need to deploy a product that fulfills all the requirements that are needed to make an application that all users are excited to start using daily.

In the next chapter, we're going to look at how we can find out about a client's business by interviewing the client and completing user requirement sessions. This will give us the requirements and a basis on which to create a solution blueprint.

8
Learning the Client's Business

A successful project is always about knowing what the client needs. Many times, clients are unaware of what it is that they need versus what they want. It's the job of the SA to work with the client to understand their needs and then create a solution based on that point of view.

In this chapter, we will look at how to create the solution blueprint for a project. We will also take as an example the project of a manufacturing company to see how to acquire requirements. In this chapter, we'll look at the following:

- Success by Design
- Business process optimization
- Fit-gap analysis
- Implementation tasks

Success by Design

Success by Design is a process improvement method that focuses on maximizing efficiency and effectiveness in a business. Here are some steps you can follow to get a client's business process using *Success by Design*:

1. **Conduct an initial assessment**: Begin by understanding the current state of the client's business processes. This may include reviewing documentation, observing operations, and interviewing stakeholders.
2. **Identify areas for improvement**: After the initial assessment, identify the areas where improvements can be made to maximize efficiency and effectiveness. This could be in the form of reducing waste, streamlining processes, or improving customer satisfaction.
3. **Develop a plan**: Based on the areas for improvement identified, develop a plan for making the necessary changes. This plan should include a timeline, resource requirements, and a detailed description of the process changes.

4. **Implement the plan**: Put the plan into action by making the necessary changes to the client's business processes. This could involve training employees, updating systems, or creating new procedures.
5. **Monitor progress**: Regularly monitor the progress of the changes and adjust as necessary. This will help ensure that the client's business processes continue to improve and meet the desired outcomes.
6. **Evaluate success**: Finally, evaluate the success of the changes made by comparing the current state to the original state. This will help determine whether the changes had the desired impact and identify areas where further improvements can be made.

By following these steps, you can effectively get the client's business processes using *Success by Design* and help the client achieve their desired outcomes.

The final goal of any business application improvement project is to replace inefficient applications with more modern, standardized applications. Also, we should implement a system that is more scalable to the organization.

Using *Success by Design* helps to produce a project that contains more consistent project phases and where communication between team members is clearer and flows better due to the types of tools used, such as Teams.

Where to start?

Every project needs a place to start before a solution can be created, and even before we can start asking people what their requirements are. My recommendation is to start with existing business processes. Sometimes this is easier said than done, but this is where you start.

But what happens if you are assigned to a project and the client doesn't have any documented business processes? That makes it a bit more challenging. In that case, if I were the SA during the pre-sales engagement, I would suggest recommending to the client that they do a *diagnostic*. I define a diagnostic as going in and looking at the current system they have and how a given person completes certain tasks. This way, you are not taking time out of the main project to get this information.

In fact, if you can sell an analysis and design phase, you can produce the business processes and start to work on the solution blueprint. Then, you can use this as the project's starting point.

> **Note**
> Later in this chapter and in a later one, we'll talk a bit about tools such as **Lifecycle Services** (**LCS**) for assisting with business processes.

If the client already has their processes documented, whether in a Word doc or as a chart/diagram, then you can at least get some information from the documents to do an analysis of what the client wants and needs in D365.

Let's speak the same language

I have never gone to an organization so different from every other company that even their basic business processes are different. I don't mean to be a jerk when I say it, but usually at the beginning of the project, I need to point out to the client that they are not any different from everyone else. All companies buy things, they must receive them, then they must store them, and finally pay the vendors' invoices. Most do the opposite as well. They buy things and then either sell those things, or make other things, store them in a warehouse, sell them, ship them, and collect payment for them.

Now, unless you must send an invoice to India to be pored over by a wise man in the mountains before you can submit it for payment, everyone does the same thing. If you do have to send it to India for examination, well, then you need to create a user story explaining the difference.

Every organization has a way of describing what they do and how they do it. Understanding that language is important so that you can create a solution that fits their requirements. It's been found that the best way to work on a D365 project is to stick with business language. The important thing to understand is that the language you're speaking is not just strictly technical language or terminology. You need to have an understanding of daily transactions and activities. Using this type of language means that you have less of a risk that the implementation team will get the requirements wrong. So, agree to a taxonomy that will be used during the project and stick to it. And try and do that right at the very start.

Here's an example: in Dynamics AX 2012, there was a feature called **Application Integration Framework**, which was used as a methodology to move data between AX and external applications. This was generally used in business-to-business and application-to-application integration scenarios – easy and straightforward to understand. But I worked at an international airport, and to the staff there, AIF meant something different. In the airline industry, AIF stands for Airport Improvement Fees.

So, if you're in a meeting and you're talking about setting up an integration between the airport and say, the bank, using an AIF, you better make sure that the two sides understand clearly what is meant when someone on the project team uses the term AIF. Otherwise, you could be having two different conversations at the same time.

> **Note**
> Another term that is in the D365 system is **Bill of Materials** (**BOM**) documents. Using the term BOM at an airport is usually not a great idea. We had to have a couple of project people stop using the term BOM and say the full name.

LCS BOM

To create a sample **BOM** from Dynamics **LCS**, you typically follow these steps:

1. Log in to Dynamics LCS using your credentials.
2. Navigate to the project for which you want to create a BOM.
3. Open the project and go to the **Business process modeler** section.
4. In **Business process modeler**, select the relevant business process or scenario for which you want to create the BOM.
5. Within the selected business process or scenario, locate the relevant task or activity that requires a BOM.
6. Click on the task or activity to open its details.
7. Look for the **BOM** tab or section within the task or activity details. Click on it to open the BOM editor.
8. In the BOM editor, you can add, modify, or delete items to create your BOM.
9. To add an item, click on the **Add** button and provide the necessary details such as item name, description, quantity, unit of measure, and so on.
10. To modify an item, select the item from the list and edit its details.
11. To delete an item, select the item from the list and click on the **Delete** button.
12. Repeat *step 8* as required to include all the necessary items in the BOM.
13. Once you have finalized the BOM, save your changes.
14. You can then export the BOM in various formats such as Excel, CSV, or PDF, depending on your requirements.

> **Note**
> The specific steps and options may vary slightly depending on the version of Dynamics Lifecycle Services you are using. It's always recommended to consult the product documentation or seek assistance from your system administrator for precise instructions.

Identifying the business processes

We are now speaking the same language. Let's move on to the next bit, which involves going over the business processes. Looking at what the company does now is vital to the solution being correct. But you also want to know where the company's processes are heading. Most organizations don't want to stagnate and are more than willing to adapt or change their processes to increase efficiency. If we look at expense management as an example, we know that expenses need to get approval and then be paid by the finance department. But if an organization builds out a multimillion-dollar system, they should take advantage of the new features in the system, likely including automation of the approval processes.

To identify the business process, it may be useful to start by looking at the overall goals and objectives of the organization. Once these have been identified, the next step is to break down the operations of the business into smaller, more manageable components and examine each component as a separate process. This can be done by analyzing the inputs, activities, outputs, and customers of each process.

For example, in a manufacturing company, the process of developing a new product might involve several smaller processes, such as research and development, product design, prototyping, testing, and production. Each of these smaller processes contribute to the overall success of the product development process and must be executed efficiently and effectively in order to achieve the desired outcome.

Once the processes have been identified and analyzed, the next step is to evaluate each process to determine its efficiency, effectiveness, and overall impact on the business. This information can then be used to make improvements to the processes, streamline operations, and increase overall success.

But just identifying the current business processes is only part of the process. It is true that the successful implementation of a project starts when you have a clear understanding of an organization's business models. This is known as the **Target Operation Model** (**TOM**). Out of this, you will start to understand the value that these processes create for the company, and how that data can be used to determine what types of products and services the company needs to create and how they will sell to potential customers.

Discovering how the processes drive the business model helps to highlight where the system needs to go so the company can adapt to future business demands. The implementation of new technologies can help an organization move to become more efficient. As mentioned previously, a company may want to implement technology to start using automation and save time in executing specific business processes. Other organizations may want to implement a modern supply-chain management ecosystem. And others still will want to implement efficiencies in their manufacturing.

This all sounds wonderful. If you go and watch or listen to several Microsoft seminars, you'd think that it was as easy as installing the software, and you're off to town. In reality, so many projects have the problem of letting the technology define what the processes will be. This is the wrong way to look at a project. You should let the technology be an enabler of what you want to do, not the reason why you want to change.

An organization also needs to be flexible enough to allow that technology to improve the business. A client who is so rigid in their thinking that the technology must bend to their current processes is wasting time and money.

> **Note**
> A previous project I was on had a group of people who didn't want to change, really, anything. When I asked the VP of IT why they were so set on things being done in certain ways, his response was the staff didn't adapt to change very well. After a few minutes of this, I asked him why they were even going through the very expensive process of changing systems if they were unwilling to adapt. After I said this, I was handed a bit of abuse and I decided I no longer wanted to do the project. I'm not willing to have to re-develop D365 just to make it work with people who don't want to change.

As companies mature and adapt to the new world, especially supply chains after COVID, understanding how processes need to change to handle that new world order is something that can make or break a project – and a company. Understanding the current state of the processes will assist you in creating an implementation capable of adapting just as much as the company will.

When a new business process is created, it allows for different parts of the business to adapt differently. Some parts of the company might want all shipments delivered to a central warehouse, while other parts might want deliveries shipped directly to production lines. Regardless of what the situation is, analysis of the business model, reengineering of processes, and implementation of strategies to set standards across the organization should all be considered as a part of the project definition.

Dynamics 365 F&SCM TOM

A Dynamics 365 **Finance and Supply Chain Management (F&SCM) TOM** is a framework that outlines the structure, processes, and principles for implementing and operating the Dynamics 365 F&SCM solution within an organization. It serves as a blueprint that defines how the solution will be utilized to achieve the desired business outcomes and optimize operational efficiency.

The TOM encompasses various components that collectively drive the successful deployment and adoption of Dynamics 365 F&SCM. These components include the following:

- **Organizational structure**: The TOM defines the roles and responsibilities within the organization, establishing clear ownership and accountability for different aspects of the F&SCM solution. It identifies key stakeholders, such as business process owners, system administrators, and end users, and determines their involvement throughout the implementation and ongoing operations.

- **Business processes**: The TOM outlines the core business processes that will be automated and improved using Dynamics 365 F&SCM. This involves mapping out the end-to-end workflows, such as procurement, inventory management, production planning, financial management, and sales order processing, and streamlining them for increased efficiency and effectiveness.

- **Data management**: The TOM addresses data governance and management practices for maintaining accurate, reliable, and secure data within the Dynamics 365 F&SCM solution. It establishes data standards, defines data ownership, and ensures proper data integration and synchronization across various systems and modules.

- **Technology architecture**: The TOM outlines the technical infrastructure required to support the Dynamics 365 F&SCM solution. It includes considerations for hardware, software, networking, and integration with other systems. The architecture is designed to provide scalability, performance, and security to meet the organization's needs.

- **Change management**: The TOM incorporates change management strategies to ensure a smooth transition to the Dynamics 365 F&SCM solution. It involves assessing the organization's readiness for change, developing communication plans, providing training and support, and actively managing resistance to ensure successful adoption by employees.

- **Performance measurement**: The TOM defines **key performance indicators** (**KPIs**) and metrics to measure the effectiveness and efficiency of the F&SCM solution. It establishes a framework for ongoing monitoring, reporting, and continuous improvement, enabling the organization to track its progress and make data-driven decisions.

- **Governance and compliance**: The TOM establishes governance structures and processes to oversee the implementation and operation of Dynamics 365 F&SCM. It ensures compliance with regulatory requirements, internal policies, and industry standards, while also promoting transparency, accountability, and risk management.

By following the Dynamics 365 F&SCM TOM, organizations can align their business processes, technology infrastructure, and people effectively. This facilitates the successful implementation and utilization of the solution, driving operational excellence, increased productivity, and improved decision-making capabilities.

Why understand the TOM?

Understanding the customer's business model is imperative to project success for several reasons:

- **Alignment of project objectives**: The customer's business model defines how its organization operates, generates revenue, and delivers value to its own customers. By understanding the organization's business model, you can align the project objectives with its overall strategy, goals, and **KPIs**. This alignment ensures that the project outcomes contribute directly to the customer's success and addresses their specific needs.

- **Tailoring solutions to customer requirements**: Each business model is unique, with its own set of processes, resources, and constraints. By understanding the customer's business model, you gain insights into their specific requirements, pain points, and areas for improvement. This knowledge allows you to tailor the project solutions to their needs, offering relevant features, functionality, and benefits. This customization increases the chances of project success and customer satisfaction.

- **Identifying dependencies and risks**: A deep understanding of the customer's business model helps you identify dependencies and potential risks associated with the project. You can determine how the project interacts with existing processes, systems, and stakeholders within the organization. This awareness enables you to anticipate challenges, plan for contingencies, and mitigate risks effectively. By proactively addressing these factors, you enhance the project's chances of success and minimize disruptions.

- **Facilitating effective communication and collaboration**: When you understand the customer's business model, you can speak their language and communicate effectively with key stakeholders. This shared understanding builds trust, credibility, and rapport, facilitating collaboration throughout the project lifecycle. It enables you to engage in meaningful discussions, clarify requirements, and gather feedback in a way that resonates with the customer's business context. Effective communication leads to better decision-making, efficient problem-solving, and ultimately, project success.

- **Maximizing value creation**: Projects are initiated to create value for the customer's business. By comprehending their business model, you can identify areas where the project can generate the most significant value and impact. This understanding enables you to prioritize project activities, allocate resources effectively, and focus on delivering outcomes that align with the customer's strategic objectives. By maximizing value creation, you enhance the overall success and **return on investment** (**ROI**) of the project.

In summary, understanding the customer's business model is essential for project success. It ensures the alignment of project objectives with the customer's strategy, allowing you to tailor solutions to their specific requirements, identify dependencies and risks, facilitate effective communication and collaboration, and maximize value creation. By incorporating this understanding into your project planning and execution, you increase the likelihood of meeting customer expectations, achieving project goals, and delivering successful outcomes.

Business process optimization

One of the first tasks that needs to happen during the initiate phase of the project is mapping out all the business processes. Business process mapping represents all the steps that happen throughout a process. Baseline business processes are referred to as *as-is processes*. These could be legacy processes or newly defined ones. Many organizations will go through a business process modification project prior to implementing an ERP system. One of the more popular methods is called the **Five Diamond Method**.

The Five Diamond Method is a framework for explorative business process management that helps organizations identify and optimize their processes. The five steps of the Five Diamond Method are as follows:

1. **Discover**: In this step, the organization's processes are analyzed to identify areas for improvement. This includes identifying processes that are redundant, inefficient, or outdated, and determining the root cause of any problems.

2. **Define**: In this step, the organization defines its desired state for each process, including the scope, objectives, and desired outcomes. This step also involves creating a detailed process map to clearly define each step in the process.

3. **Design**: In this step, the organization creates a design for the optimized process. This includes identifying the tools, technology, and resources needed to support the new process, as well as determining the roles and responsibilities of each team member involved in the process.

4. **Deploy**: In this step, the organization implements the optimized process, including training team members, testing the process, and making any necessary changes to ensure its success.

5. **Monitor and optimize**: In this final step, the organization continuously monitors and optimizes the process to ensure it is running efficiently and effectively. This includes regularly reviewing the process and making improvements as required to ensure it remains aligned with the organization's goals and objectives.

By following the Five Diamond Method, organizations can effectively identify and optimize their processes, resulting in improved efficiency, reduced costs, and increased productivity.

We do need to remember that as-is business process mapping doesn't give you the step-by-step solution but rather outlines how the whole solution should be defined. The goal of mapping the as-is business process definition in **D365 F&SCM** is to understand and document the current state of a company's operations. This mapping process allows companies to identify areas for improvement and make informed decisions about how to optimize their processes using the capabilities of D365 F&SCM.

By mapping the as-is business process, a company can do the following:

- Gain a clear understanding of how their operations are currently functioning
- Identify bottlenecks, inefficiencies, and areas for improvement
- Create a roadmap for implementing D365 F&SCM to optimize their processes
- Ensure that the implementation of D365 F&SCM aligns with the company's goals and objectives

Having business processes mapped early can provide significant value to an organization in several ways:

- **Improved clarity and understanding**: Mapping processes clearly defines the steps involved in each process, making it easier for everyone involved to understand what needs to be done and why. This can lead to improved communication and collaboration between team members.

- **Increased efficiency**: By mapping processes early, organizations can identify inefficiencies and areas for improvement. This can help organizations streamline their operations, reducing the time and resources required to complete tasks and increasing overall efficiency.

- **Better decision-making**: Having a clear understanding of processes and the data involved in each step can help organizations make informed decisions about their operations. This can lead to improved performance and increased profitability.

- **Improved risk management**: Mapping processes can help organizations identify potential risks and take steps to mitigate them. This can help organizations avoid unexpected problems and minimize their impact on the business.

- **Better alignment with goals and objectives**: Mapping processes can help organizations align their operations with their overall goals and objectives. This can help organizations prioritize their efforts and allocate resources effectively to achieve their desired outcomes.

Mapping business processes early provides organizations with a clear understanding of their operations, which can lead to improved efficiency, better decision-making, and increased alignment with their goals and objectives.

One example of a company that wanted to move its business processes from brick-and-mortar to e-commerce is the retail giant, Walmart. Walmart has been a traditional brick-and-mortar retailer for decades but in recent years, it has shifted its focus to e-commerce. The organization realized that with the increasing trend of online shopping, it was important for it to have a strong online presence.

Walmart has invested heavily in its e-commerce platform, making it easier for customers to shop online and receive their orders quickly. Additionally, it has experimented with new delivery options such as in-store pickup, same-day delivery, and curbside pickup to make shopping more convenient for its customers.

By moving its business processes to e-commerce, Walmart is not only making shopping more convenient for its customers, but also reducing the costs associated with maintaining brick-and-mortar stores. It is now able to reach a larger customer base and offer a wider range of products and services to its customers. In conclusion, Walmart's move to e-commerce has been a strategic decision aimed at improving its business and staying ahead of the competition in the rapidly changing retail landscape.

When reviewing new process diagrams, it's important to consider the following factors:

- **Clarity and simplicity**: The diagram should be easy to understand and follow, using clear and concise symbols, labels, and flow lines.
- **Accuracy**: The diagram should accurately reflect the steps involved in the process, in the correct sequence and interconnection.
- **Completeness**: The diagram should include all relevant steps in the process, without leaving out any important details.
- **Relevance**: The diagram should only include information that is relevant to the process being diagrammed, avoiding unnecessary details.
- **Consistency**: The symbols, labels, and flow lines used in the diagram should be consistent throughout, creating a clear and uniform visual representation.
- **Scalability**: The diagram should be able to accommodate changes or growth in the process, allowing for future modifications as needed.
- **Usability**: The diagram should be usable by all relevant stakeholders, including those who may not have technical expertise in the process.
- **Compliance**: The diagram should be in compliance with relevant industry standards, regulations, and best practices.

- **Communication**: The diagram should effectively communicate the process to all relevant stakeholders, promoting understanding and collaboration.

By considering these factors, you can ensure that the process diagram is accurate, effective, and easy to understand for all relevant stakeholders.

Next, let's take a look at how to model a solution based on client requirements.

Solution modeling

Digital transformation has a significant impact on the creation of business processes. It enables organizations to streamline and automate many manual tasks, leading to increased efficiency, improved accuracy, and reduced costs. Here are some ways in which digital transformation affects the creation of business processes:

- **Improved data collection and analysis**: Digital tools and technologies make it easier to collect, store, and analyze data. This can help organizations identify areas for improvement in their business processes, making them more efficient and effective.
- **Automation**: Digital transformation makes it possible to automate many manual tasks, freeing up employees to focus on higher-value tasks. This can lead to increased productivity, improved accuracy, and reduced costs.
- **Improved customer experience**: Digital tools and technologies can be used to create a seamless and personalized customer experience, leading to increased customer satisfaction and loyalty.
- **Increased collaboration and communication**: Digital transformation makes it possible for employees to collaborate and communicate more easily, regardless of location. This can lead to improved teamwork and increased innovation.
- **Flexibility and scalability**: Digital business processes can be easily scaled up or down as needed, providing organizations with greater flexibility to respond to changing business requirements.

Some tools and applications that have only been created within the last 5 or 6 years include cloud processing, Internet of Things, data lakes, machine learning, artificial intelligence, process automation, and virtual reality. All of these tools and technologies have a direct impact on how a company will plan to transform its business.

Fit-gap analysis

A fit-gap analysis is a process used in project management and business analysis to assess the differences between the requirements of a new system or solution and the capabilities of an existing system. The purpose of a fit-gap analysis is to identify the gap or differences between what is desired and what is currently available.

The analysis involves comparing the business requirements for a particular project or solution with the functionality of existing systems or solutions. This allows organizations to identify areas where they need to make changes to their existing systems or develop new solutions to meet their requirements. A fit-gap analysis can also help organizations to prioritize the changes that need to be made and determine the resources required to make those changes.

The process typically involves four main steps:

- Identifying the business requirements
- Assessing the capabilities of existing systems
- Identifying the gap or differences between the two
- Developing a plan to address the gap

The output of a fit-gap analysis can be used to inform decision-making around system selection, development, and implementation.

A fit-gap analysis for **D365 F&SCM** can be completed using a combination of tools and techniques, including the following:

- **Business process mapping**: This involves creating a visual representation of the current business processes and the desired processes. This can help to identify areas where the current system may not meet the requirements and where changes need to be made.
- **Requirements gathering**: This involves working with stakeholders to understand their specific needs and requirements for the new system. This information can be compared with the capabilities of D365 F&SCM.
- **Gap analysis worksheet**: This is a tool that can be used to document the gaps between the business requirements and the capabilities of the current system. The worksheet can include columns for the business requirement, the current system capability, and any gap or difference between the two.
- **System demonstrations**: This involves demonstrating the functionality of D365 F&SCM to stakeholders to help them understand the capabilities of the system and identify areas where it may not meet their requirements.
- **User acceptance testing**: This is a testing process that involves putting the system through a series of tests to ensure that it meets the requirements of the stakeholders. This can also help to identify any gaps or areas where changes need to be made.
- **Project management software**: This can be used to manage the fit-gap analysis process, track progress, and document the results.
- **Stakeholder communication**: This involves regular communication with stakeholders to ensure that they are aware of the progress of the fit-gap analysis and any changes that are being made to the system.

One of the important things to get out of this is that if you stick to the out-of-the-box functionality, you should have fewer issues during the deployment. The gap analysis is what we use to get the differences between the way the client does things and the way the system does it. This is exactly why doing the fit-gap analysis is vital.

The following diagram shows a standard process for purchasing products to be used in-house. This is also known as procure to pay.

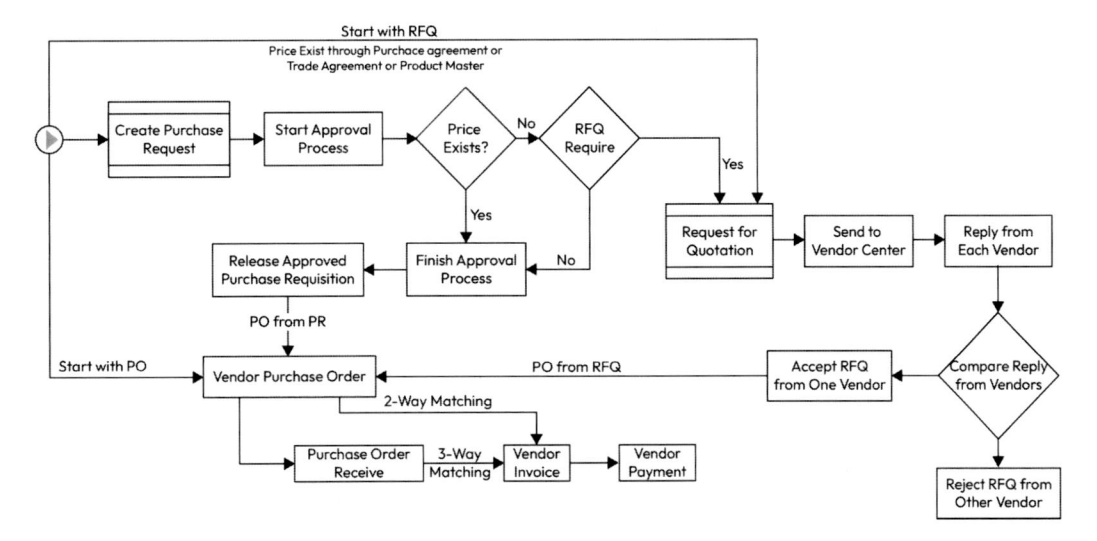

Figure 8.1: Purchasing workflow

If the company's needs are different to the OOB process, let's say that they need to have some invoice scanning done, then that will need to be added to the process.

LCS tools

Dynamics Lifecycle Services (LCS) provides several business process tools to help organizations manage and maintain their D365 F&SCM solutions, including the following:

- **Business process modeler (BPM)**: BPM is a tool in LCS that provides a visual interface for designing, modeling, and automating business processes in D365 F&SCM. With BPM, users can create workflows, define business rules, manage business events, and automate tasks, all within a single, integrated platform.

- **Process Library**: The Process Library is a centralized repository of pre-configured business processes, which can be imported and used as a starting point for creating custom processes. The Process Library includes best practices, common use cases, and industry-specific processes for various business areas, such as procurement, sales, and inventory management.

- **Process Configuration**: The Process Configuration tool provides a visual interface for managing and maintaining the configuration of business processes in D365 F&SCM. With this tool, users can view the status of their processes, identify areas for improvement, and make changes to their processes as needed.
- **Process Documentation**: The Process Documentation tool provides a visual representation of business processes, including the steps involved and the data flow between them. This tool helps organizations understand and document their business processes, making it easier to maintain and update them over time.

These tools in LCS work together to help organizations manage and maintain their D365 F&SCM solutions, ensuring that their business processes are optimized, up to date, and aligned with their changing business needs.

Business process modeler (BPM)

Dynamics 365 **BPM** is a tool in D365 F&SCM that provides a visual interface for designing, modeling, and automating business processes. With BPM, users can create workflows, define business rules, manage business events, and automate tasks, all within a single, integrated platform.

BPM provides a visual representation of a business process, making it easy to understand and manage. Users can easily drag and drop different elements, such as conditions, actions, and tasks, to create a workflow. Business rules can be defined to control the flow of data, and business events can be triggered to initiate workflows and business rules.

One of the key benefits of BPM is that it allows organizations to streamline and automate their business processes, reducing manual errors and improving efficiency. BPM also provides an intuitive and user-friendly interface, making it easy for users to create and manage workflows, business rules, and other components of their business processes.

D365 F&SCM provides several components to work with BPM. These include the following, all of which can be created and managed using BPM:

- **Workflows**: Workflows are used to automate business processes in D365 F&SCM
- **Business rules**: Business rules are used to define the conditions and actions that should be taken when a specific event occurs in the system
- **Business events**: Business events are used to trigger workflows and business rules in D365 F&SCM
- **Process tasks**: Process tasks are used to automate tasks in D365 F&SCM
- **Forms**: Forms are used to display information in a user-friendly format

- **Reports**: Reports are used to display information in a structured format.
- **Integrations**: Integrations are used to connect D365 F&SCM with other systems.

These components work together to help organizations automate and streamline their business processes in D365 F&SCM. To use Business process modeler, you'll need to have an active Dynamics 365 subscription.

The following are some of the tools that can be used with D365 Business process modeler:

- **Power Automate**: Power Automate can be used to automate tasks and create workflows to streamline business processes. It can also be integrated with Business process modeler to trigger events and execute tasks within the business process.
- **Dynamics 365 apps**: Business process modeler is designed to work with other Dynamics 365 applications, such as Sales, Customer Service, and Marketing. These apps can be used to create customer relationships, manage customer interactions, and automate business processes.
- **Microsoft Power Platform**: Microsoft Power Platform is a suite of tools that includes Power Apps, Power BI, and Power Automate. It can be used to create custom business applications, analyze data, and automate workflows.
- **Microsoft Visio**: Microsoft Visio can be used to create detailed process flow diagrams that can be imported into Business process modeler. This can be useful for creating complex process maps or for visualizing data in a way that is more conducive to your organization.
- **Azure DevOps**: Azure DevOps can be used to manage software development projects, including the development of custom applications and integrations with other systems. It can also be used to manage the deployment and testing of applications and workflows that are built using Business process modeler.

Implementation of requirements

The D365 F&SCM process-centric implementation lifecycle involves several phases, including the following:

- **Assessment and planning**: In this phase, the current business processes are analyzed and the goals for the D365 F&SCM implementation are defined. A project plan is developed that outlines the timeline, budget, and resources required for the project.
- **Requirements gathering**: In this phase, the requirements for the D365 F&SCM implementation are gathered from stakeholders and documented. These requirements will serve as the basis for the design and configuration of the solution.
- **Solution design**: In this phase, the solution design is developed based on the requirements gathered. The design will include the process flows, data structure, and customizations required to meet the business requirements.

- **Configuration and testing**: In this phase, the solution is configured and tested to ensure that it meets the business requirements. This phase also includes the development of test cases and test plans to validate the solution.
- **Data migration**: In this phase, the data from the current systems is migrated to the D365 F&SCM solution. This process includes data cleansing, data validation, and data mapping.
- **User acceptance testing**: In this phase, the solution is tested by end users to ensure that it meets their requirements and expectations. Feedback from the users is collected and incorporated into the solution as needed.
- **Deployment and go-live**: In this phase, the solution is deployed to the production environment and becomes the new system of record for the organization. The solution is monitored to ensure that it is functioning as expected and that any issues are resolved quickly.
- **Ongoing support and maintenance**: In this phase, the solution is supported and maintained to ensure that it continues to meet the needs of the organization. This includes addressing any issues that arise and making any necessary updates or improvements to the solution.

This implementation lifecycle provides a structured approach to implementing D365 F&SCM and helps to ensure that the solution meets the needs of the organization and is delivered on time and within budget.

The implementation of the blueprint solution is basically the delivery of all the business processes that have been defined during the requirements-gathering meetings. The delivery phase will potentially need to modify some of the requirements as the configuration might not exactly match the system. This is a very common occurrence that shouldn't be of any concern. Things will change; that's why we're in this business.

Case study

As I mentioned previously, I've been involved in many different projects over the years. Most projects have been straightforward when it comes to getting business requirements. As I've said, business processes are mostly the same across just about every company. When looking at finance and purchasing modules in the system, each deployment is pretty much the same. There may be some slight differences, but for the most part, things will all be the same.

The biggest changes usually arise when it comes to manufacturing or asset management. One example from a previous project occurred when trying to figure out what a company did for its manufacturing processes. It was a difficult project to work on because the client was very steadfast that they wanted their existing business processes to be exactly the same in D365. Because of this, a whole lot of customization needed to be completed so that things would work as they wanted.

One strong example of this was in terms of the terminology to be used. Generally, when you are producing items based on a **BOM**, you use discrete manufacturing processes. When I had this discussion with the CIO, he was concerned that it wouldn't fit how they worked. It didn't show how they did things, and the most difficult part of this project was the absolute resistance to change. Also, the warehouse that was attached to the assembly lines was included in their current warehouse management system. The materials handlers would put items wherever there was sufficient space in the warehouse. This made it difficult to find items and get them to the proper places for assembly.

During discovery, I proposed that we create a different warehouse for each assembly line, a finished goods transfer warehouse, and a quarantine location. As part of this, I suggested that we label the shelves for specific items that were used on a daily basis and re-organize the shelves so that items used most were moved closest to the lines. This was roundly shot down as the warehouse manager in the production facilities didn't want to go through the effort of counting the items they had on the shelves already and moving all the items around. They wanted to create one big warehouse for everything, and not specifically label where the products were put. They left it up to the materials handlers to log where on the shelves they put the items.

In this case, the client got their way. It was a very difficult process to get the system to work the way they wanted, and I left the project prior to it being completed. As an SA, sometimes you just have to accept that, while you are right and your recommendations follow the best practices, you won't be able to convince the client otherwise. Just take your lumps and move on, and hopefully, it won't negatively impact your reputation as an SA.

Conclusion

In this chapter, we saw how we can acquire requirements from the client needed to create a solution blueprint. We also looked at different ways to determine what the system will do compared to the client's requirements. In the next chapter, we'll look at how to identify and convince a client when their requirements don't fit into the out-of-the-box system.

9
Collecting Project Requirements

A good solution architect will have the political skills required to work with clients in how they accomplish a requirement. Sometimes clients will expect that the system will do something that it's not designed to do. Sometimes, it's through negotiation with the client that the **solution architect** (**SA**) can get them to adjust their expectations and, possibly, change their business processes to best fit the system. This chapter will talk about how to get the client to work with the architect to create a viable solution that will get the project to a successful end.

As we've moved through this book, one of the things I've hopefully impressed on you is that the SA has a big role in the project's successful outcome. Since we have discussed more technical aspects of the role of the SA, in this chapter, we're going to focus more on the non-technical aspects of the role. This is where personality and political skills come into play.

It's important to realize that every partner has a method they use to collect requirements. Some use group meetings while others use surveys. In the end, this exercise is critical so the partner has a clear understanding of what the client's requirements are and can therefore provide the best recommendations for the project to be successful.

By the end of this chapter, you'll be prepared to complete tasks such as the following:

- Listening to a client's requirements
- Out-of-the-box versus customization
- Negotiate changes to client requirements
- What does the solution blueprint document contain?

Where do we start?

According to a Chinese proverb, *a journey starts with a single step*. In our case, our journey starts with a single destination. That single destination is what the solution will provide. But we must be sure about what the solution will provide before we can get to that destination. We can't fail; there is too much time and money riding on what we plan to produce. In the last chapter, we talked about how to come up with a solution once we understand a company's business processes. Now, we need to take that understanding and produce a design that fulfills those requirements.

The best place to start with this understanding is by completing a playback of the business processes. Some organizations call it **Simulation 0** or **Sim 0**. Basically, the point of this presentation is so the partner has a full understanding of what the client's requirements are. This also allows the SA to show how the system does specific business processes out of the box. From here, you can figure out what is different from out-of-the-box to the customer requirement.

Why out of the box?

Microsoft's philosophy when it comes to Dynamics 365 is to provide an out-of-the-box solution that can be easily configured and customized to meet the unique needs of each customer. They understand that every business has unique requirements, and they have designed Dynamics 365 to be flexible and adaptable to those needs.

In particular, Microsoft aims to provide a solution that is all of the following:

- **Comprehensive**: Dynamics 365 provides a full suite of integrated business applications that cover all the key functional areas of an organization, including sales, marketing, finance, operations, customer service, and more.

- **Easy to deploy**: Dynamics 365 is designed to be easy to deploy, with minimal IT involvement required. It can be accessed through the cloud, allowing for easy access from anywhere and on any device.

- **Configurable**: Dynamics 365 can be easily configured to meet the specific needs of a business. This includes customizing forms, fields, and workflows to match the unique requirements of an organization.

- **Customizable**: For businesses with more complex requirements, Dynamics 365 can be customized using Microsoft's Power Platform. This allows businesses to build custom applications that integrate with Dynamics 365 and extend its functionality.

- **Scalable**: Dynamics 365 is designed to scale as businesses grow. It can handle many users and can be easily expanded to meet changing business needs.

Microsoft's philosophy is to provide a flexible and adaptable out-of-the-box solution that can be easily configured and customized to meet the unique needs of each customer. If we can keep the solution as close to out-of-the-box as possible, then we reduce the chances that any modifications made through customizing the system won't be broken by future updates that Microsoft will make to the system.

It should be pointed out, at this point, what is referred to as a *customization*. Here, we go back to taxonomy again, but in the system, we create customizations and personalization. **Personalization** is how an individual person sees the system. Personalization includes settings such as screen color and what columns are shown on screens in the system. **Customization**, on the other hand, is a modification of the system code that runs D365. Customizations are completed in the system to add extra functionality that it doesn't have out of the box.

Let's talk a bit about development

We need to talk about development and how development works in D365 F&SCM. As mentioned, customizations are modifications that are made to the out-of-the-box functionality. An example of customization would be the addition of a new column to a form and table that lets a client add extra data to the customer record. In previous versions of AX, a developer would be able to go into the underlying code base, change the structure of the code, compile it, and then ultimately, deploy it to a production environment.

It was relatively simple to complete, due to each installation being local and not shared by other organizations. In D365, on the other hand, we don't have that advantage. If we want to create a customization, we must go through a bit more effort. First, D365 is a shared application, accessed as a **Software as a Service** (**SaaS**) application. With everyone sharing the base code for D365, no one user has the ability to change the code for their purposes.

Basically, the concept is that if everyone shares the code base, then no one will be too far out from the current revision number. Microsoft will only allow a company to be *n-1* in terms of its current version. If Microsoft allowed individual companies to modify the base code, then every user of the system would get that modification, which may not match what they need to use. So, Microsoft restricts access to the code base and the database that the system runs on. In order to let customers create customizations, Microsoft has implemented a coding technique called **extensions**.

Extensions are a way to customize and extend the functionality of the standard application without modifying the core code. These extensions provide a way to create new functionality or modify existing functionality in a controlled and upgradable way. With extensions, developers can add new fields, tables, forms, reports, and business logic to the application, and can also modify or replace existing objects.

Extensions are developed using Microsoft's X++ programming language, which is an extension of the Java language. X++ is designed specifically for code development with D365 and allows developers to create and modify objects using declarative syntax and code snippets.

Once the extensions have been developed and tested, they can be deployed to a D365 environment, either as a separate package or as a part of a solution. **Packages** are self-contained units that can be installed and uninstalled independently, while **solutions** are collections of related packages that are deployed together as a single unit.

Understanding the differences

We've listened to the client; we've figured out what the business processes are that they have, and now we've created examples in the demo environment to show what the system can do.

Note that, at this point, we're using the demo environment from a deployment with the Contoso demo data. Depending on what the customer wants or needs, you could create a new legal entity and then use that as the basis of what you will build going forward. Make sure that you emphasize to the client that this is only a demonstration of what the SA thinks the company's business processes are.

After we do the demo, the client says that the app doesn't really work the way they want it to. So, we can do another activity to better understand what they have that is part of the system and what isn't. This activity is called a **fit/gap analysis**. A fit/gap analysis is a process used in D365 to determine the degree to which a company's business processes align with the capabilities of the D365 software.

The analysis involves identifying the business processes of the company and comparing them to the features and functionalities provided by D365. The objective is to identify any gaps or differences between the company's business processes and the software's capabilities.

The fit/gap analysis is typically conducted during the implementation phase of a D365 project. The analysis helps the implementation team to understand the extent of customization or configuration required to meet the company's needs.

Once the gaps are identified, the implementation team can work with the company to determine the best course of action to address them. This may involve customizing the software, changing the company's business processes, or a combination of both.

The fit/gap analysis is an important part of the implementation process because it helps ensure that the D365 software meets the company's needs and supports its business processes. It can also help identify areas where the company may need additional training or support to use the software effectively.

What tools are available?

D365 provides several tools and applications that can be used to complete a fit/gap analysis. These tools are included in the *Lifecycle Services* site, DevOps, and in D365 itself. The following list explains some of the tools and templates available:

- **Requirement gathering templates**: These are pre-built templates that help to capture requirements from the business users. They can be customized to fit the specific needs of the organization. These templates are available on the *Lifecycle Services* website, within the project site. You can also get these from the *Success by Design* website.
- **Process mapping tools**: These are used to document the current business processes and map them to the D365 system. This helps to identify the gaps between the current processes and the system's capabilities. These tools include the **Business Process Modeler** (**BPM**) that is in Lifecycle Services and Azure DevOps. Another tool that is used to help create business

processes is Task Manager. Task Manager is a process recording tool that you run from within D365, and it records all mouse clicks and keystrokes. From these recordings, you can upload the process into the BPM tools.

- **Use case diagrams**: Use case diagrams help to visualize the system's requirements from the user's perspective. They help to identify the different scenarios that need to be tested in the system. These diagrams can be created using Microsoft Visio. Most of these types of diagrams are generally created as swimlane diagrams.

- **Excel spreadsheets**: Excel spreadsheets are commonly used to capture and organize the requirements and features of the system. They can be customized to fit the needs of the organization and can be easily shared and updated. We'll look at this in a bit more detail later in this chapter when we talk about user stories.

- **Gap analysis templates**: Gap analysis templates help to document the gaps between the current business processes and the system's capabilities. They help to identify the areas where customization or configuration is required.

The following figure is an example of a fit/gap analysis template that can be used to record a business process:

Reference No	Requirements	Category	Priority	System/Application	SSIS (KWS)	MuleSoft	Logic App	Data Factory	Work Around	Notes
1	Integration should supports Batch Integration	Business	Medium	System A	•	•	•	•		
2	Integration should supports Reel Time Integration	Business	High	System A	•	•	•			Supports only the application has webhook functionality built
3	Connect data both Cloud and On-Prem	Business	High	System D	•		•	•		
4	Send Summary Email Notification once Integration Complete	Technical/Business	Medium	System B	•	•	•	•		
5	Scale on demand	Technical	Medium	All		•	•	•		

Figure 9.1: Fit/gap template

- **Business process modeling tools**: These tools help to create visual representations of the business processes and can be used to identify areas where the system can be optimized.

The choice of tool(s) depends on the organization's specific needs and the complexity of the project. It is important to select the right tools and use them effectively to ensure a successful fit/gap analysis in D365.

Another tool that is used, mostly successfully, is an Excel spreadsheet called a **Requirements Traceability Matrix** (**RTM**). This matrix is used as a way to coordinate all of the requirements from the client and put them into a format that is usable by the partner to create the correct output.

The RTM collects and displays the following key information:

- **Requirement ID**: Unique identifier for each requirement
- **Requirement Description**: A brief explanation of what the requirement entails
- **Source**: The source of the requirement, which can be a person, a document, a piece of legislation, and so on

- **Priority**: The importance or urgency of the requirement
- **Rationale**: The reason why the requirement is needed
- **Use Cases**: The situations in which the requirement would be applied
- **Test Cases**: The tests designed to validate whether the requirement has been fulfilled
- **Status**: The progress of the requirement, whether it's still being developed, has been met, or has been dropped
- **Associated Components**: The parts of the system that are impacted by the requirement
- **Verification Method**: The method by which the requirement is verified
- **Traceability**: The links to related requirements

By collecting and organizing all this information, an RTM helps ensure that all project requirements are defined, implemented, tested, and satisfied. It also helps to manage changes to the requirements and to track their impact on the project.

Another way that you can collect information about the differences between default business processes and specific processes of the client is to use an agile project management technique called **user stories**. User stories are a technique used in agile project management to capture requirements from the perspective of the end user. They are brief, concise, and informal descriptions of a feature or functionality of the software being developed.

A user story typically follows this format:

"As a [user], I want to [action], so that [benefit]."

For example, *"As a customer, I want to be able to easily search for products on the website, so that I can quickly find what I'm looking for."*

The user story is written from the user's perspective and focuses on the user's needs and objectives. It is intentionally brief and open-ended, allowing for flexibility and collaboration in the development process.

User stories are used to facilitate communication and collaboration between the development team and the stakeholders, such as product owners and customers. They help ensure that the development team is working on the features and functionalities that are most important to the end users and provide a clear understanding of the requirements for each feature. In agile project management, user stories are often used in conjunction with other techniques, such as backlog grooming, sprint planning, and retrospectives, to ensure that the project stays on track and meets the needs of the users.

> **What not to do**
>
> I was once involved in a project where the partner had decided that they would be creating a solution for the client but using only user stories. First of all, this is a really bad idea. It's a bad idea because we can't tell the client what the overall solution is if we don't have that documented before the project really kicks off. If I was a client, I would want to know what I'm going to be delivered when the project is completed.
>
> Using just user stories as the solution, I don't get a detailed and finalized plan. The user stories tend to change during the project. Even though user stories can play an important role in determining which business processes are not out of the box, they can't be the only tool used to build out the solution.

So, in review, acquiring business processes is a critical first step when implementing a D365 system. The goal is to identify and document existing business processes to determine how they will be managed and automated within the D365 system. The best methodology for acquiring business processes and turning them into a solution blueprint for a D365 project involves the following steps:

1. **Conduct a thorough analysis of the business**: The first step is to understand the current state of the business by conducting an analysis of the current business processes and identifying pain points and areas for improvement.

2. **Identify key stakeholders**: Identify key stakeholders who will be involved in the D365 project, including business process owners, subject matter experts, and IT personnel.

3. **Develop a process inventory**: Develop a comprehensive inventory of all business processes, including those that are core to the business, those that are support functions, and those that are non-essential.

4. **Map processes to D365 modules**: Once the processes have been identified, map them to the corresponding D365 modules that will manage and automate them.

5. **Document the solution blueprint**: Document the solution blueprint that outlines the D365 modules that will be used to manage each business process, the business rules, and any customizations or enhancements that need to be made to the D365 system.

6. **Validate the solution blueprint**: Validate the solution blueprint with key stakeholders to ensure that it accurately reflects the business processes and the requirements of the organization.

7. **Implement the D365 system**: Finally, implement the D365 system and monitor its performance to ensure that it is meeting the business requirements and delivering the expected benefits.

By following these steps, organizations can ensure that they acquire business processes in a systematic manner and turn them into a solution blueprint that meets the requirements of the business. This will help to ensure the success of the D365 project and ensure that the organization can achieve its goals and objectives.

Okay, so what's next?

We have the business processes written down and planned out. Now, we must make sure that they can be completed in D365 as the client requires. We did the fit/gap analysis and we know what will and won't work by default, but the client is insistent that the system works exactly the way their current business process works. What do we do now? There are two different ways to approach this:

- First, we can try to better understand why they are so set on a specific process
- Second, we can try to convince them that our way is better

Let's listen to the client

Now, you might be thinking *"I'm the SA! I'm the expert in this system. What does the client know about anything? That's why they hired me!"* Frankly, if that is the attitude that you go in with, you've already failed. You have to go in with an open mind and be flexible enough to realize that their business might have a very valid reason for why they do things. So, let's listen and find out. But how do we listen to get the best of the conversation?

Active listening

Active listening is a skill that you will need to master. This means going beyond the words the person is speaking and trying to understand the meaning and intent behind those words. You can't listen to a client and respond without considering only what they've just said. So, let's take a look at some of the ways we can participate in active listening and some ways we can become an expert at it.

Active listening is a communication skill that involves listening with full attention and engaging with the speaker in a way that conveys empathy, understanding, and respect. It requires focusing on the speaker's words, tone of voice, body language, and emotions, while also giving verbal and non-verbal feedback to indicate that you are present and paying attention.

Active listening is more than just hearing the words that the speaker is saying. It involves a deep level of engagement that goes beyond the surface level of conversation. Active listeners seek to understand the underlying message, emotions, and needs behind what the speaker is saying. They do this in the following ways:

- **Paying attention**: Active listeners focus their attention on the speaker and avoid getting distracted. They maintain eye contact, avoid interrupting the speaker, and give their full attention to the conversation. This also shows that you have respect for the speaker, which will help to make them more comfortable in the conversation.
- **Clarifying and paraphrasing**: Active listeners seek to clarify and summarize what the speaker is saying, to ensure that they have understood the message correctly. They may paraphrase what the speaker has said, ask clarifying questions, or summarize the key points to show that they are following the conversation.

- **Responding appropriately**: Active listeners respond in a way that shows empathy, understanding, and respect for the speaker. They may offer words of encouragement, express appreciation, or provide emotional support as needed. Again, if the client feels like you respect their point of view, then they will feel more willing to accept your comments in reply.
- **Non-verbal cues**: Active listeners pay attention to the speaker's body language, facial expressions, and tone of voice to understand their emotions and needs. They use their own non-verbal cues, such as nodding, smiling, and maintaining eye contact, to convey their engagement and understanding.
- **Avoiding judgment**: Active listeners avoid passing judgment or jumping to conclusions about what the speaker is saying. They remain open-minded, respectful, and non-judgmental, even if they disagree with the speaker's perspective. Basically, keep quiet until the speaker has finished, but as mentioned earlier, don't just be polite and let them finish speaking only to give your opinion without considering what they have just said.

Active listening is a crucial communication skill that involves engaging with the speaker in a way that conveys empathy, understanding, and respect. It requires paying full attention, clarifying, and summarizing the message, responding appropriately, using non-verbal cues, and avoiding judgment. By practicing active listening, you can improve your communication skills, build stronger relationships, and enhance your overall well-being.

What can I do to get better at active listening? Active listening techniques are methods used to improve the quality of communication and demonstrate a deeper level of understanding and empathy to the speaker. Here are some active listening techniques:

- **Pay attention**: Give the speaker your full attention and maintain eye contact
- **Avoid interruptions**: Let the speaker finish talking before you respond or interrupt
- **Paraphrase**: Restate what the speaker said in your own words to show that you understand
- **Reflect feelings**: Reflect on the speaker's emotions and respond accordingly
- **Ask open-ended questions**: Ask questions that encourage the speaker to share more information
- **Summarize**: Summarize the key points the speaker made to show that you were listening and you understand what was said
- **Non-verbal communication**: Use non-verbal cues such as nodding, facial expressions, and body language to show that you are actively listening
- **Avoid distractions**: Remove any distractions that could take your attention away from the conversation, such as your phone or computer
- **Empathy**: Show empathy and understanding for the speaker's situation and feelings
- **Respond appropriately**: Respond appropriately to the speaker's communication, whether it is positive or negative

An example of active listening would be "*That is a complicated process. I'd like to walk through the steps of the process to better understand how we can implement this.*" This shows that you understand that what they are talking about is complicated, and asking for them to assist you in understanding the process shows you need their help in solving the problem.

Active listening is an important skill to have in the workplace. It helps you better understand problems and collaborate to solve problems. As a bonus, it also shows that you are patient, which is an invaluable skill in the workplace.

Using diagrams

If there is one application that is part of the Microsoft Office Suite that I'm not a complete fan of, it's PowerPoint. For some reason, in the last few years, PowerPoint has become the tool of choice when drawing diagrams. Personally, I love using Visio for drawing diagrams. I can't draw with any accuracy. In fact, I can't even draw stick people to look like stick people (I can write, but I can't draw… well, I hope I can write). If you don't have access to Visio, then drawing in PowerPoint will have to do.

One of the drawbacks of PowerPoint is that it has all sorts of bells and whistles built into it. People like to make the graphics move and fade. And quite often, users put too much text on their slides, in too small a font, causing the slides' consumers to spend too much time trying to read what's on the slide rather than understanding the message it's trying to convey.

So, if we're going to draw diagrams to help communicate what we want the client to understand, we must make it very simple. Simple graphics, simple colors, and specific text will make your message clear. If you are clear, you have a better chance of getting the client to agree with your method to get the business processes into the system. If you can diagram out how the process could be modified to fit how the system works, you may just convince the client to modify their processes.

Another method to help show that your way might be better is by creating a **Proof of Concept** (**POC**). The POC can be created to show the client how the system could handle the process based on out-of-the-box functions. But a POC could also be helpful to discover how the system can be modified to fit the process. You may discover, during the creation of the POC, that it won't be as hard to make the system work with the process the client doesn't want to modify.

Where are we?

As we've seen, there are several methods that the SA can use to help them persuade a client that how they do things may not necessarily be the best way to approach the problem. But those techniques will only work if you have a good working relationship with the client. You both need to be able to trust each other. The client needs to trust that you have their best interests in mind when making recommendations, and not what is technically easy for the project team. And, as the SA, you need to be able to trust that the client is being honest with you in what they determine to be unchangeable business processes.

When trying to get a client and an architect to agree to a change in a business process that the client doesn't currently use in their business, it's important to approach the situation with a clear plan of action. Here are some steps you can take to increase the likelihood of agreement:

1. **Start by identifying the benefits**: It's important to clearly outline the benefits of the proposed change to the client. This could be increased efficiency, improved productivity, cost savings, or any other tangible benefits that the client may be interested in.

2. **Understand the client's current process**: To effectively persuade the client to adopt a new business process, you need to understand their current process. This will help you identify potential pain points or inefficiencies that the new process can address.

3. **Provide evidence**: Provide data and case studies to support the proposed change. This will help the client see that the new process has been effective in other businesses and industries.

4. **Address concerns**: Be prepared to address any concerns or objections that the client may have. This could include addressing potential risks, addressing concerns about the learning curve associated with the new process, and addressing any potential resistance to change.

5. **Collaborate**: Work with the architect to find a solution that meets the needs of both the client and the business. This may involve adapting the proposed change to better suit the client's needs or finding a compromise that works for everyone.

6. **Communicate effectively**: Throughout the process, communicate clearly and frequently with the client. This will help build trust and ensure that everyone is on the same page.

The key to getting a client and an architect to agree to a change in a business process is to understand the client's needs and concerns, provide evidence of the benefits of the proposed change, and work collaboratively to find a solution that works for everyone involved.

> **Case study**
>
> A few years ago, I was part of a project where the client had an existing ERP system that had to be heavily customized to be able to support their processes. This manufacturing company had several different processes that were kind of odd. As an example, they had a business process that said when new items were manufactured, they would go to a warehouse and be stored there until they were ordered, picked, and shipped to a customer.
>
> This setup allowed for new orders to automatically reserve inventory in the warehouse, in a first in, first out structure. Generally, that was acceptable, except they had certain buyers who had a requirement that all the products they ordered had to be delivered in one delivery to their warehouse. Those orders generally were in the 100s of items.
>
> Now, this was an issue because D365 will only allow you to set the warehouse to automatically reserve a product when a sales order is confirmed. If we enabled auto reservations, then any order that came after this customer's couldn't be fulfilled until this order was picked.
>
> So, for example, if there were only 100 items in the warehouse, and the order was for 175, and the manufacturing lines could only produce 5 a day, that means that any order that was placed after theirs couldn't be fulfilled for approximately 16 days. They could potentially end up with a few canceled orders because they were unable to fulfill those orders in a timely fashion, even though there was sufficient stock in the warehouse to fill orders under the 100 items. The client didn't accept that the system had this particular limitation, and we had to create a POC to show them that it was an either/or choice.
>
> Luckily, the client that had the specific purchasing requirement was contacted by the sales team and agreed to change their requirement, allowing the project to continue without issue. This is the type of issue that can arise many times during a project, and in this particular case, a POC was the best method to show the client that their requirements were not available in the system. We got lucky this time, but next time, it could be much different.

Create the solution blueprint

By this point, we should know everything that is required to put together the solution blueprint. We know the requirements; we should know most of the processes that will need to be modified. Further fit/gap analysis will need to be executed during the implementation phase of the project so that the analyst can communicate to the developer and the SA what will need to be modified or created, in order for the system to work the way the client wants it to.

We need to understand exactly what the solution blueprint is and how it should be structured, and also what information it should contain.

A solution blueprint is a comprehensive document or plan that outlines the details of a proposed solution to a particular problem or challenge. It typically includes a description of the problem or opportunity, an overview of the proposed solution, the resources required to implement the solution, a timeline for implementation, and a list of key stakeholders and their roles and responsibilities.

A solution blueprint can be used to communicate the proposed solution to stakeholders, including project sponsors, team members, and other stakeholders, to ensure everyone understands what needs to be done and what outcomes are expected. It can also serve as a reference document throughout the implementation process, helping to ensure that the project stays on track and that all key elements of the solution are properly executed.

In the case of a D365 implementation, a solution blueprint may be in the form of an architecture document, which outlines the technical specifications and requirements for a software application. This document may include diagrams, flowcharts, and other visual aids to help illustrate the proposed solution.

The purpose of a solution blueprint in *Success by Design* is to provide a clear and comprehensive roadmap that guides individuals, teams, or organizations toward achieving their desired outcomes.

A well-designed solution blueprint can help ensure that all stakeholders have a shared understanding of the problem being solved, the objectives to be achieved, and the steps required to get there. This can help to minimize confusion, misunderstandings, and wasted effort or resources. Additionally, a solution blueprint can help to identify potential obstacles or risks that may arise along the way and enable stakeholders to plan for these contingencies in advance.

The blueprint should contain only enough information to give a high-level description of the architecture to help someone understand what the project will produce. In this document, the SA will have identified any gaps, challenges, and inconsistencies that will be written into the solution, and produced a plan to remediate those items.

The first workshop that will need to be completed in the project, as a complete implementation team, will be the solution blueprint workshop. The entire team will review the blueprint, comment on it, and make recommendations on how it can be improved and agreed upon for the client. This is also going to be a living document, so it needs to be placed in a central location where all of the members of the implementation team can read it and potentially make edits to it.

> **Note**
>
> Even though it would be nice to allow all the members of the implementation team to make edits to the solution blueprint, it's not a great idea. As we've discussed, sometimes, project members have their own political agendas and may take the opportunity to modify the document. So, I recommend that *only* the SA and the PMs (both the client and the project's PM), should be given the ability to edit the document. If you place it on a SharePoint site or in Teams, you can restrict who has *View* and who has *Edit* capabilities on the document.

The solution blueprint is an important document, but it's not a novel. Even though there will be many sections to it, it shouldn't be too long. That, of course, makes it a bit of a challenge to know just how much data should actually be in the document. The correct level of detail is important. As the project progresses, you will have the opportunity to create many more detailed documents, including Functional Design Documents and Technical Design Documents. Those documents allow for the amount of detail required to describe and build out processes.

This document should also not contain great detail when it comes to describing the business processes. This document will also not contain anything to do with discussing various ISV solutions, how training will be completed, and any documentation around training or anything to do with code reviews or system features. Again, all this information will be placed in other documents that come out of the various workshops later in the project.

One important item that should be included in this document is anything to do with licensing. You need to make sure that the solution will fit within the licensing that has been purchased during the sales phase of the project, and will also allow you to determine that a further purchase of licenses will be needed to be properly compliant with Microsoft.

A *Success by Design* solution blueprint should include the following types of information:

- Clearly state the objectives that the solution aims to achieve. These objectives should be specific, measurable, achievable, relevant, and time-bound.

- List the requirements that the solution should meet. These requirements may include functional requirements, technical requirements, and user requirements. Keep these requirements at a high level.

- Provide a detailed design of the solution. This design should include the overall architecture, data flow, user interface design, and any other design elements that are relevant to the solution.

> **Note**
> Even though the user interface is predefined, this could include items such as custom workspaces, images, Power BI embedded reports, screen colors, and custom navigation.

- Describe how the solution will be implemented. This may include the technology stack, programming languages, deployment strategy, and any other relevant information.

- Outline the testing strategy for the solution. This should include the types of tests that will be conducted, the testing approach, and the expected outcomes.

- Provide a timeline for the solution. This should include the estimated start and end dates for each phase of the project, as well as any milestones that need to be achieved. The following figure shows an example of the high-level project timeline:

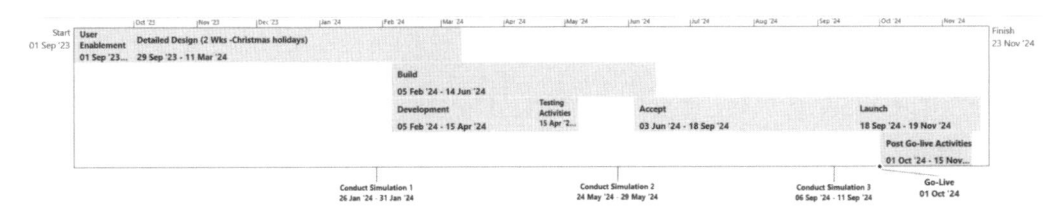

Figure 9.2: High-level project timeline

- Detail the budget for the solution. This should include the estimated costs for development, testing, implementation, and ongoing maintenance. The following example shows what a budget might look like for a project:

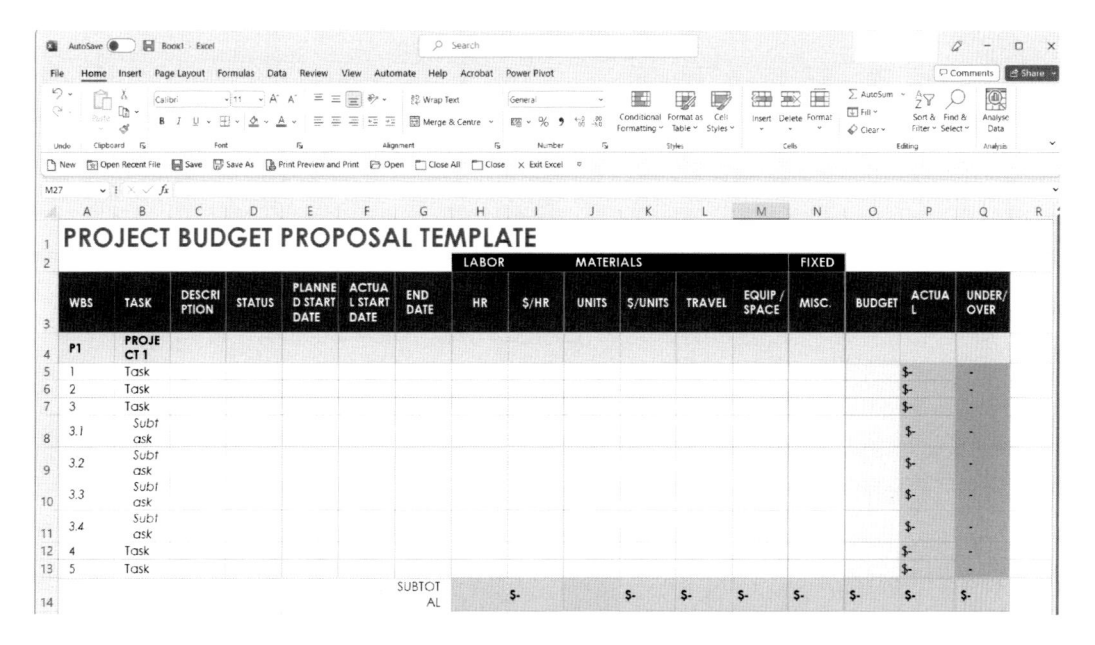

Figure 9.3: Project budget proposal

- Identify any risks associated with the solution. This may include technical risks, business risks, or other types of risks that may impact the success of the solution. The Risk Register document will be a living document that will need to be updated regularly, not only to add items to the register but also to remove items that have been dealt with. This will be an important document to use when you're meeting with the project governance board.

- Identify the stakeholders who will be involved in the solution. This may include business owners, end users, developers, project managers, and other stakeholders who have an interest in the success of the solution.

- Describe the support strategy for the solution. This should include the expected level of support that will be provided, the channels through which support will be provided, and any other relevant information.

- Summarize the scope of the solution. This is an important item because it helps the project stay on track and does not allow for any project scope creep to rear its head. Scope creep needs to be tightly controlled by the SA and PM.

- Identify change management and escalation paths. You need to specify how change management will be implemented in the project, how that change management will be used, who will make change design decisions, and what type of turnaround the change board will work with. You should also specify how to escalate issues that happen during the project. If you specify this here, then project team members know what the process is to escalate issues to the appropriate design and decision maker.

The document should also contain information about the components that will make up the solution. You need to include the following:

- The D365 applications that will be included (this might include Finance, Supply Chain Management, or any of the CE applications).
- Any Power Platform components that will be used, including Power Apps, Power BI, Dataverse, Power Automate, and Power Virtual Agents.
- Any connections and configurations for apps included in Azure Active Directory.
- Connections to Microsoft 365 applications including SharePoint Online, Microsoft Teams, Microsoft Word and Excel, and Outlook.
- Any legacy applications that will have integrations created to allow for data transfer.
- Any ISV solutions you will include in the overall solution. Note: don't do a comparison of ISVs, but only add the ones that you have identified as being an absolute addition to the solution.
- The document management solution the project will use to house all the project documents. This could be Teams, SharePoint Online, or any other document-handling system. I would recommend keeping all the documentation in DevOps.
- Printing needs to be laid out in the solution and should also be included in the document.
- All legal entities that will be created, and if necessary, any localizations that will be associated with those entities.

Another addition to the solution document would be swim lane diagrams of business processes. These provide a simple and visual way of understanding how the system will be configured to handle all the processes. The following is an example of such a diagram:

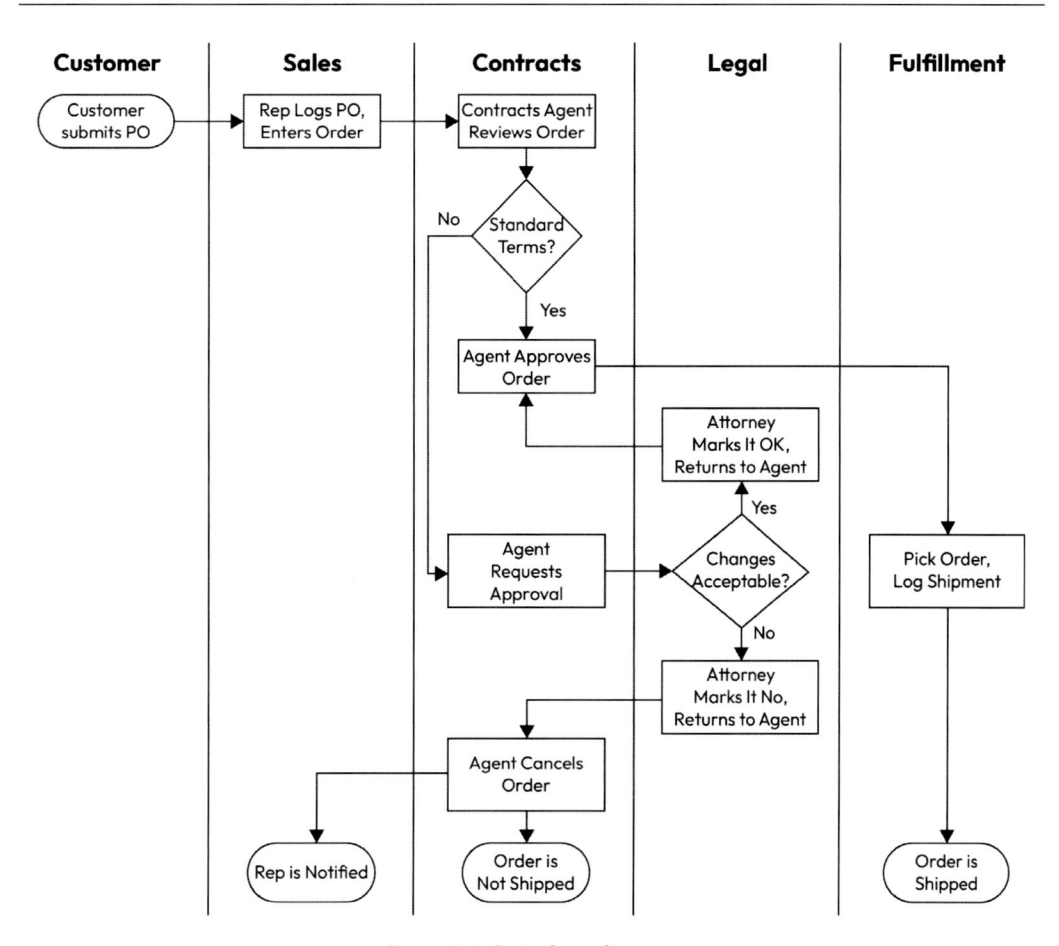

Figure 9.4: Swim lane diagram

Conclusion

This chapter has discussed, in detail, how important the communication process between the client and partner is to a successful project. The D365 deployment can only be done correctly if everyone is on board with the end goal the project will produce. Sometimes it will be easy to agree on the solution, and at other times, it might be more difficult. But being a well-rounded SA can help you navigate any differences between you and the client and still come up with a viable solution. Most importantly, understanding all of the end-to-end business processes, with their requirements, will allow this process to be easier.

It comes down to trust. Both sides must trust that each is doing its best. If you have that, then you've solved several of the problems ahead of time.

In the next chapter, we're going to look at the application life cycle and the tools available to help get the project across the finish line.

10
ALM Tools and Applications

A challenge that many projects experience is what tools should be used to help with code management, project management, testing, and deployment. In this chapter, we will look at the tools necessary to assist in successfully running and deploying a D365 project. We will look at the following tools:

- Azure DevOps
- Dynamics Lifecycle Services (LCS)
- Task Recorder
- The Regression suite automation tool (RSAT)
- Visual Studio

At the end of this chapter, I'll walk through the process of getting a DevOps project created for an ERP project.

Azure DevOps

Microsoft Azure DevOps is a set of cloud-based tools and services for software development teams that helps them plan, build, test, deploy, and monitor applications. It provides a comprehensive platform for managing the entire application life cycle, through project planning and tracking, code development and testing, and deployment and delivery.

Azure DevOps includes various tools such as Azure Boards for project planning and tracking, Azure Repos for source code management, Azure Artifacts for package management, and Azure Pipelines for **continuous integration and continuous delivery (CI/CD)** pipeline automation. These tools can be used independently or in combination to support the software development process.

The DevOps tool is the single best place to manage an ERP project. The four main roles that DevOps plays in the project include the following:

- **Source control management**: Azure DevOps offers a Git-based version control system that helps developers manage the source code of an ERP project. This ensures that all changes are tracked, and different versions can be easily compared and merged.

- **CI/CD**: Azure DevOps can be used to create pipelines that automate the build, test, and deployment process of an ERP project. This ensures that changes are automatically deployed to the development, testing, and production environments.
- **Project management**: Azure DevOps also includes tools for Agile project management such as boards, backlogs, and sprints. These tools help teams plan, track, and manage their work effectively.
- **Testing**: Azure DevOps offers various testing tools such as Azure Test Plans and Selenium that can be used to automate and manage different types of tests such as unit, integration, and regression tests.

Azure DevOps is the single location to manage the majority of project work. DevOps connects to D365, Visual Studio, and GitHub. First off, we need to get DevOps configured for our project. Once we're in the system, we'll need to create a new project. The following figure shows how to create a new project.

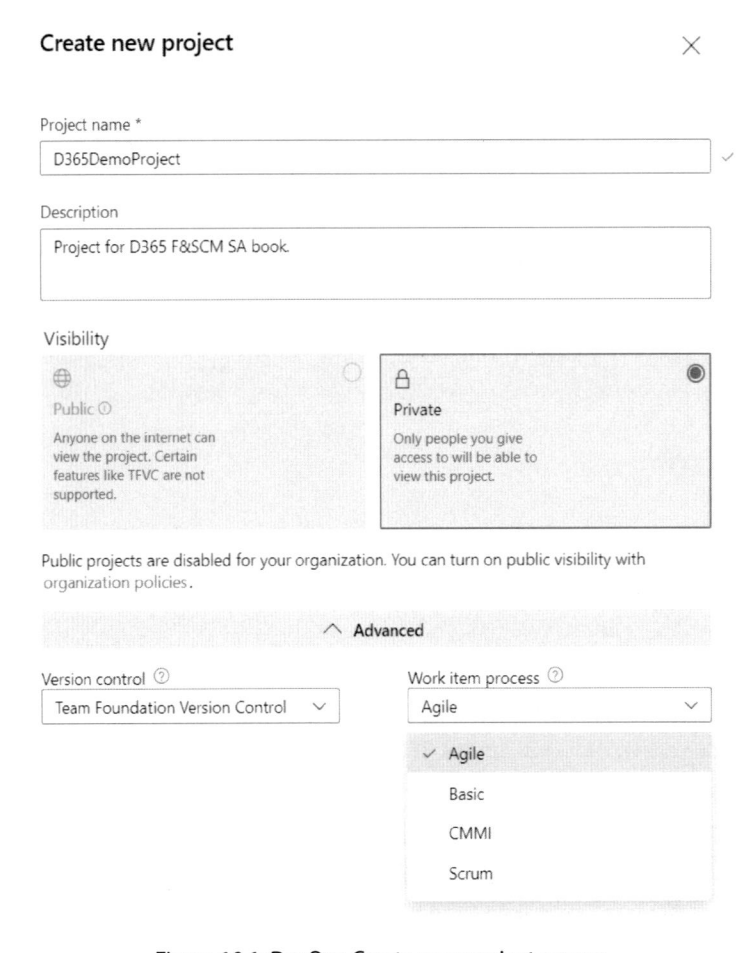

Figure 10.1: DevOps Create new project screen

We need to make sure that the new project is set to **Private**. We want to restrict who can access this information in the project. If you going to sell a solution that you create in D365, you could make that specific project a **Public** one, which people who purchase your solution can download from.

One thing I need to point out is the option to select the type of **Version control** and **Work item process**.

Version control

There is no one-size-fits-all answer to this question, as the choice of DevOps version control depends on several factors, including the specific needs and requirements of your D365 **Finance and Supply Chain Management** (**F&SCM**) projects, your team's expertise, and your preferred toolset.

That being said, there are a few popular options that you might consider when it comes to selecting the version control option:

- **Azure DevOps**: This is a popular choice for many D365 F&SCM projects, as it provides end-to-end DevOps capabilities, including version control, build and release management, testing, and more.
- **Git**: Git is a distributed version control system that is widely used in the industry, and it is well suited for collaborative development. You can use a cloud-based Git service such as GitHub or GitLab, or you can host your own Git repository on-premises.
- **Team Foundation Version Control** (**TFVC**): This is a centralized version control system that is integrated with Azure DevOps, and it provides features such as branching and merging. It is a good choice if you are already using Azure DevOps for other aspects of your project.

Ultimately, the choice of DevOps version control will depend on your specific needs and preferences. You may want to consider factors such as ease of use, collaboration features, integration with other DevOps tools, and cost when making your decision.

> **Note**
> TFVC has two different models that can be used for your project. The first is **Server** workspaces. These types of workspaces have a central location where developers check out code and files on their local computers. The second workspace, which is the most used workspace for D365 F&SCM projects, is a **Local** workspace.
>
> In this type of workspace, each dev and team member has a local copy of the latest version of the code from DevOps and works on their code base offline. Once the dev has created their code, and tested it locally, they check their changes back into the central code base. They will resolve any potential conflicts as required.

Release pipelines

Release pipelines use a CI/CD process to define and build release pipelines. The pipelines automate the building, testing, and deployment of the code changes, so you can quickly and safely deliver updates to a D365 F&SCM system. The SA isn't the one who specifically sets up the pipeline, but they do need to have the background knowledge of how the processes work, so they can advise any technical project resources as required.

The process of setting up a release pipeline in Azure DevOps uses the following steps:

- **Define your release process**: Start by defining the steps involved in your release process, including code reviews, testing, deployment, and post-deployment checks. Make sure everyone involved in the release process understands the process and their role in it.

- **Set up your DevOps environment**: Use a DevOps tool such as Azure DevOps or GitHub to set up your environment. This should include your source code repository, build and release pipelines, and any testing and deployment tools you need.

- **Create a build pipeline**: Your build pipeline should automatically compile your code, run any tests, and package your application into a deployable format.

- **Create a release pipeline**: Your release pipeline should automate the deployment of the application to your test and production environments. This should include any necessary configuration and database updates.

- **Test and validate your pipeline**: Before you release your pipeline, test it thoroughly to make sure it's working as expected. You can use tools such as Selenium or TestComplete to automate your testing.

- **Deploy your pipeline**: Once your pipeline is tested and validated, deploy it to your production environment. Monitor your application closely after the release to ensure everything is working correctly.

- **Continuously improve**: Finally, continue to improve your release process by collecting feedback from your team and customers. Use this feedback to identify areas for improvement and make changes to your process as needed.

Remember that every organization's release process will be different, so it's essential to tailor your process to meet your specific needs.

Project management

Azure DevOps can be used as a project management tool for a Dynamics 365 F&SCM project, helping to streamline the development and deployment process and improve overall project efficiency. Here are some key ways in which DevOps can be used in a D365 F&SCM project:

- **CI/CD**: DevOps can automate the build, testing, and deployment process, reducing the time and effort required for manual tasks. By using tools such as Azure DevOps, developers can set up automated pipelines that build, test, and deploy changes to the D365 F&SCM system, ensuring that updates are delivered quickly and reliably.
- **Infrastructure as Code (IaC)**: DevOps encourages the use of IaC to manage infrastructure resources such as servers, databases, and networks as code. This allows developers to automate the provisioning and management of infrastructure resources, reducing the risk of errors and inconsistencies in the environment.
- **Agile Project Management**: DevOps is closely aligned with Agile methodologies, which focus on iterative development and continuous improvement. By adopting Agile practices such as sprint planning, backlog prioritization, and daily stand-up meetings, teams can work together more efficiently and deliver higher-quality software.
- **Monitoring and feedback**: DevOps provides tools for monitoring the performance of the D365 F&SCM system and collecting feedback from users. By analyzing metrics such as the application response time, error rates, and user behavior, teams can identify areas for improvement and make data-driven decisions about future development efforts.

As was mentioned previously, organizations can choose from one of three different types of project management for a D365 project: Agile, Waterfall, or Hybrid. As Azure DevOps is built to support Agile by default, I want to point out a few things that the tool will do when using this methodology. Here are some ways in which Agile project management can be applied in a DevOps context for D365 F&SCM projects:

- **Sprint planning**: In Agile, development work is typically organized into sprints, which are short periods of time (usually two to four weeks) during which a team focuses on delivering a specific set of features or improvements. In D365 F&SCM projects, sprint planning sessions can be used to prioritize work, set goals for the upcoming sprint, and assign tasks to team members.
- **Backlog management**: The product backlog is a prioritized list of features or improvements that need to be made to the D365 F&SCM system. In Agile, the backlog is managed collaboratively by the team and the product owner, who is responsible for ensuring that the most valuable items are prioritized. In a DevOps context, the backlog can be integrated into tools such as Azure DevOps, allowing teams to manage work items and track progress more easily.
- **Daily stand-up meetings**: Daily stand-up meetings are short (usually 15 minutes or less) meetings in which team members share progress updates, discuss any blockers, or challenges they are facing, and plan their work for the upcoming day. These meetings can help teams stay aligned and ensure that everyone is working towards the same goals.

- **CI/CD**: As mentioned earlier, DevOps promotes the use of automation to streamline the software development and deployment process. In an Agile context, this means setting up automated pipelines that can build, test, and deploy changes to the D365 F&SCM system quickly and reliably.
- **User feedback and retrospectives**: Agile emphasizes the importance of collecting feedback from users and stakeholders to inform future development efforts. In a DevOps context, teams can use tools such as Azure Application Insights to collect telemetry data on how users are interacting with the D365 F&SCM system. Additionally, Agile teams typically hold regular retrospectives to reflect on what went well and what could be improved in the previous sprint, allowing them to continuously improve their processes.

Testing

One of the other roles that DevOps is especially good at, is testing. Testing can fall under two different types:

- First, we have manual testing scripts. The testing scripts are created while the requirements-gathering sessions are completed. The point of the script is that you need to have some metrics to execute and make sure the business process is executed correctly.
- Second, we have automated testing scripts. The testing scripts that are created as part of the manual testing process, can also be used to automate the testing. We'll discuss that later in this chapter with RSAT.

In a DevOps environment for D365 F&SCM projects, managing test scripts involves the following key steps:

- **Planning and defining test cases**: Work with the business and development teams to identify and define test cases that cover all aspects of the solution. This includes functional, integration, performance, and security testing.
- **Creating test scripts**: Develop automated test scripts for each test case using a suitable testing framework such as Selenium or Microsoft's own Testing Tools. Make sure to include both positive and negative test scenarios.
- **Storing test scripts**: Store the test scripts in a version control system such as Git. This allows for easy access to previous versions and collaboration between team members.
- **Running tests**: Automate the execution of the test scripts using a CI tool such as Azure DevOps or Jenkins. This ensures that all tests are run consistently and regularly.
- **Analyzing results**: Review the results of each test run and identify any failures. Investigate the cause of the failures and update the test scripts as needed.
- **Retesting**: Once the test scripts have been updated, rerun the tests to ensure that the issues have been resolved.

- **Reporting results**: Share the results of the tests with the stakeholders, including the business and development teams. This helps to identify areas that require further improvement.

Besides managing test scripts, DevOps has several tools that can be used to help test various parts of a D365 F&SCM deployment. Here is a list of tools that can be utilized:

- **Visual Studio Test Professional**: This is a testing tool that can be used for manual and automated testing of D365 F&SCM applications. It offers features such as test case management, test execution, and reporting.
- **Microsoft Test Manager**: This is a tool that can be used for test planning, test case management, and test execution. It integrates with Visual Studio and Azure DevOps to provide a complete end-to-end testing solution.
- **Selenium**: Selenium is an open source testing tool that can be used for automatically testing web applications. It can be used to test the user interface of D365 F&SCM applications.
- **JMeter**: JMeter is an open source tool that can be used for load-testing web applications. It can be used to test the performance of D365 F&SCM applications under heavy loads.
- **Postman**: Postman is a tool that can be used for testing APIs. It can be used to test the APIs that are exposed by D365 F&SCM applications.
- **Coded UI Test**: Coded UI Test is a testing tool that can be used for automatically testing user interfaces. It can be used to test the user interface of D365 F&SCM applications.
- **Appium**: Appium is an open source tool that can be used for automated testing of mobile applications. It can be used to test mobile applications that are developed using D365 F&SCM.
- **SpecFlow**: SpecFlow is a testing tool that can be used for **behavior-driven development (BDD)**. It enables collaboration between business stakeholders, developers, and testers by using a common language to define and automate tests. SpecFlow integrates with Visual Studio and Azure DevOps.
- **TestComplete**: TestComplete is a testing tool that can be used for automated testing of desktop, web, and mobile applications. It offers features such as test recording, test scripting, and test execution. TestComplete integrates with Visual Studio and Azure DevOps.
- **LoadRunner**: LoadRunner is a testing tool that can be used for load-testing web and mobile applications. It can be used to simulate thousands of concurrent users and measure the performance of D365 F&SCM applications under heavy loads.
- **SoapUI**: SoapUI is a testing tool that can be used for functional and performance testing of SOAP and REST APIs. It can be used to test the APIs that are exposed by D365 F&SCM applications.
- **Robot Framework**: Robot Framework is a testing tool that can be used for automated testing of web, desktop, and mobile applications. It offers features such as test case creation, test execution, and reporting. Robot Framework integrates with Visual Studio and Azure DevOps.

- **Apache JMeter**: Apache JMeter is an open source testing tool that can be used for load-testing web applications. It can be used to test the performance of D365 F&SCM applications under heavy loads.
- **Telerik Test Studio**: Telerik Test Studio is a testing tool that can be used for automated testing of web, desktop, and mobile applications. It offers features such as test recording, test scripting, and test execution. Telerik Test Studio integrates with Visual Studio and Azure DevOps.

As with any testing tool, the selection of a tool depends on the specific requirements of the project and the skills of the testing team.

Next, let's take a look at the features that we need to use for a D365 environment using Dynamics LCS.

Dynamics LCS

Dynamics LCS plays a crucial role in a Dynamics 365 F&SCM project. LCS is a cloud-based service that helps customers manage the application life cycle of their Dynamics 365 deployments, including implementation, maintenance, and upgrades.

Some of the key roles of LCS in a D365 F&SCM project include the following:

- **Project management**: LCS provides a project management framework that allows project managers to plan, track, and collaborate on project tasks and timelines. This framework includes features such as task management, issue tracking, and status reporting.
- **Environment management**: LCS allows users to provision and manage environments for development, testing, and production. This includes the ability to create and configure environments, manage users and security, and monitor performance.
- **Implementation**: LCS provides tools and resources for implementing D365 F&SCM, including project templates, best practices, and guidance on configuration and customization.
- **Upgrade management**: LCS helps customers manage the upgrade process for their D365 F&SCM deployments. This includes providing tools for testing and validating upgrades, as well as guidance on how to prepare for upgrades.
- **Support and issue maintenance**: LCS provides tools for monitoring and troubleshooting issues in D365 F&SCM deployments. This includes the ability to track incidents and service requests, as well as access to a knowledge base of common issues and solutions.

LCS is an essential tool for managing the application life cycle of a D365 F&SCM project. It provides a centralized platform for project management, environment management, implementation, upgrade management, and support and maintenance, helping customers to streamline their deployments and ensure successful outcomes.

Environments

The major role of the LCS tool is the creation and management of D365 F&SCM environments. Microsoft Dynamics 365 F&SCM environments that are created and managed from LCS can be classified into several types:

- **Sandbox**: This type of environment is typically used for development, testing, and training purposes. It is isolated from the production environment and can be refreshed with the latest data from the production environment.

- **OneBox**: This is a single-environment deployment that combines all the components of the D365 F&SCM application stack, including the database, application server, and web server. It is used for testing and development purposes and can also be used for demonstrations and training.

- **Tier-1 Production**: This is the primary production environment that hosts the live instance of a D365 F&SCM application. It is typically deployed in a multi-server configuration and is designed to handle large volumes of data and transactions.

- **Tier-2 Production**: This is a secondary production environment that provides backup and disaster recovery capabilities for the Tier-1 environment. It is typically deployed in a geographically separate data center to ensure high availability and data redundancy.

- **Cloud-hosted environments**: These are D365 F&SCM environments that are hosted in the cloud, such as Azure. They provide scalability, flexibility, and cost-effectiveness, as they eliminate the need for on-premises infrastructure and reduce maintenance costs.

When you create your subscription, you will get three environments: one Tier-1 environment for development, one Tier-2 environment for the sandbox, which is used primarily for testing, and one Tier-2 to Tier-5 for the production server. It's usual during the project itself for there to be multiple Tier 1 VMs and multiple Tier 2 servers for testing and training.

Next, let's look at some tools that can be useful in many ways during a project – first, a business process recorder, which can be used to help configure security, and a way to write documentation.

Task Recorder

Another tool that is incredibly useful is called **Task Recorder**. Task Recorder is a tool that can be found in many software applications, such as Microsoft Dynamics 365, Microsoft Office, and other business software offerings. Its primary purpose is to capture a sequence of actions performed by a user on a software application and convert them into an automated script that can be replayed later.

Task Recorder is particularly useful for automating tasks that are time-consuming or repetitive, as it can significantly reduce the amount of manual effort required. This tool can also be helpful in testing software applications, as it allows testers to easily repeat complex test scenarios without having to manually repeat each step every time.

In addition, Task Recorder can be used to create training materials for new employees or users of a software application. By recording a series of steps, a user can create a step-by-step guide that can be used to train others on how to use the software effectively.

The way Task Recorder works is relatively simple. When a user initiates a task, Task Recorder starts recording every action that the user performs in the application. This includes things such as clicking on buttons, entering data, navigating between screens, and so on. As the user completes the task, Task Recorder captures all these actions and saves them as a macro or script.

Once the recording is complete, the user can then replay the macro or script at any time. This allows them to automate the same task or process with just a few clicks, rather than having to manually perform each step every time.

Task Recorder is particularly useful in scenarios where users need to perform repetitive or complex tasks. For example, if an employee needs to generate a specific type of report every week, they can use Task Recorder to record the steps they take to generate the report and then automate the process. This can save a significant amount of time and reduce the risk of errors or inconsistencies in the report.

Task Recorder can also be used to create training materials for new users of a software application. By recording a series of steps, an experienced user can create a step-by-step guide that can be used to train others on how to use the application effectively.

Task Recorder for security configuration

While Task Recorder is not specifically designed for security configuration, it can be used to assist with this task.

Here are some ways Task Recorder can be used to assist with security configuration:

- **Recording security setup steps**: Task Recorder can be used to record the steps required to set up security roles, permissions, and access levels. This recording can be used as a reference to ensure that all necessary steps are completed and that the setup is consistent across multiple users and roles.

- **Generating user guides**: The recordings created by Task Recorder can be converted into user guides that provide step-by-step instructions for performing specific security-related tasks. These guides can be used by end users to understand how to perform tasks such as updating their passwords or requesting access to additional resources.

- **Identifying security vulnerabilities**: By reviewing the recordings created by Task Recorder, security analysts can identify potential vulnerabilities in the system. For example, they may notice that certain roles have more permissions than necessary or that some users have access to sensitive data that they shouldn't have.

Task Recorder can be a valuable tool for assisting with security configuration. Recording and documenting the steps required for specific security-related tasks can help ensure that security is set up correctly and consistently across the system.

Here's an example of how Task Recorder can be used to assist with security configuration.

Let's say you are responsible for setting up security roles and permissions for a new Dynamics 365 implementation. You want to ensure that all necessary steps are documented and that the setup is consistent across multiple roles and users:

1. Start by launching Task Recorder from within Dynamics 365.
2. Click on **New Recording** and give your recording a name such as `Security Role Setup`.
3. In Dynamics 365, navigate to the **Security Roles** area and begin recording your actions as you set up a new role. This might include steps such as the following:

    A. Creating a new security role

    B. Defining the role's name and description

    C. Setting up access levels and permissions for the role

    D. Assigning users to the role

4. Once you have completed the recording, you can review the steps and make any necessary edits or annotations.
5. You can then save the recording and share it with other team members involved in the security configuration process.
6. By using this recording as a reference, you can ensure that all necessary steps are completed and that the setup is consistent across multiple roles and users.
7. If any changes need to be made to the security setup in the future, you can refer to the recording to ensure that the changes are made correctly and consistently.

Using Task Recorder to document security setup steps can save time and reduce errors when configuring security roles and permissions within Dynamics 365.

Task Recorder in D365 F&SCM can be used for various purposes other than documentation and security configuration, such as the following:

- **Training**: Task Recorder can be used to create training materials for end users. By recording the steps to complete a task, a trainer can easily create step-by-step guides or videos that can be used to train new users.
- **Testing**: Task Recorder can be used to create test scripts for system testing or user acceptance testing. By recording the steps to complete a test scenario, testers can easily execute and repeat the test case.

- **Process improvement**: Task Recorder can be used to identify and document process improvements. By recording the steps to complete a process, users can identify inefficiencies or areas for improvement and share those with the appropriate teams.
- **Data migration**: Task Recorder can be used to create data migration templates. By recording the steps to complete a data import/export, users can create templates that can be used to migrate data from one system to another.
- **System configuration**: Task Recorder can be used to configure system settings. By recording the steps to configure a setting, users can create templates, which can be used to apply the same configuration to multiple environments.

Task Recorder is a versatile tool that can be used for various purposes in D365 F&SCM beyond just documentation and security configuration.

RSAT

RSAT is a testing tool that allows users to create and run automated tests to validate business processes and scenarios in D365 F&SCM.

With RSAT, users can create test cases and scenarios that simulate real-world business scenarios in D365 F&SCM. These tests can then be executed automatically, reducing the time and effort required for testing and increasing the efficiency of the testing process.

RSAT includes a set of predefined test cases, as well as the ability to create custom tests. It also includes features for recording and replaying user interactions, data-driven testing, and the ability to schedule and manage test runs.

Overall, RSAT is a powerful tool that can help users ensure the quality and reliability of their D365 F&SCM implementations by automating the testing process and reducing the risk of errors and issues.

Here's an example of how RSAT can be used in Dynamics 365 F&SCM.

Let's say you're an organization that uses D365 F&SCM for your financial management. You have recently customized the system to include a new payment method for vendor payments, and you want to ensure that this new feature is working as expected.

To test this new payment method, you can use RSAT to create a test scenario that simulates the vendor payment process using the new payment method. You can specify the input data, such as the vendor details, payment amount, and payment method, and the expected output, such as the payment confirmation and the update of the vendor's payment history.

Once the test scenario is created, you can run it using RSAT. RSAT will automate the entire process, from entering the data to validating the output, and report any discrepancies or errors that may occur. You can then review the results and make any necessary adjustments to the payment method configuration or the test scenario.

By using RSAT, you can ensure that your new payment method is working correctly and that it does not affect other parts of the system. This helps to minimize the risk of errors and issues and ensure the quality and reliability of your D365 F&SCM implementation.

Let's say you want to test the creation of a new customer account in D365 F&SCM using RSAT. Here are the steps you can follow:

1. **Launch the RSAT tool**: First, launch the RSAT tool in D365 F&SCM by navigating to the **Regression Suite Automation Tool** workspace.

2. **Create a new test scenario**: Next, create a new test scenario by clicking on the **New** button and selecting **Test Scenario** from the drop-down menu. Enter a name for the test scenario, such as `Create Customer Account`.

3. **Define the test steps**: In the test scenario, define the steps that are required to create a new customer account. For example, you can specify that the user should navigate to the **Customers** workspace, click on the **New** button, and fill in the required fields, such as the customer name, address, and contact details.

4. **Set the expected results**: After defining the test steps, set the expected results for each step. For example, you can specify that the customer account should be created successfully and that the customer details should be displayed in the **Customers** workspace.

5. **Run the test**: Once the test scenario is defined, run the test by clicking on the **Run** button. RSAT will execute the test steps and compare the actual results with the expected results. If there are any discrepancies or errors, RSAT will highlight them in the test report.

6. **Review the test report**: After the test is completed, review the test report to identify any issues or errors. If necessary, make any changes to the customer account creation process and re-run the test.

By using RSAT in this way, you can automate the testing process and ensure that the customer account creation process is working as expected. This can help to minimize the risk of errors and ensure the quality and reliability of your D365 F&SCM implementation.

Visual Studio

Visual Studio is an **integrated development environment** (IDE) that is commonly used to develop and customize D365 F&SCM solutions.

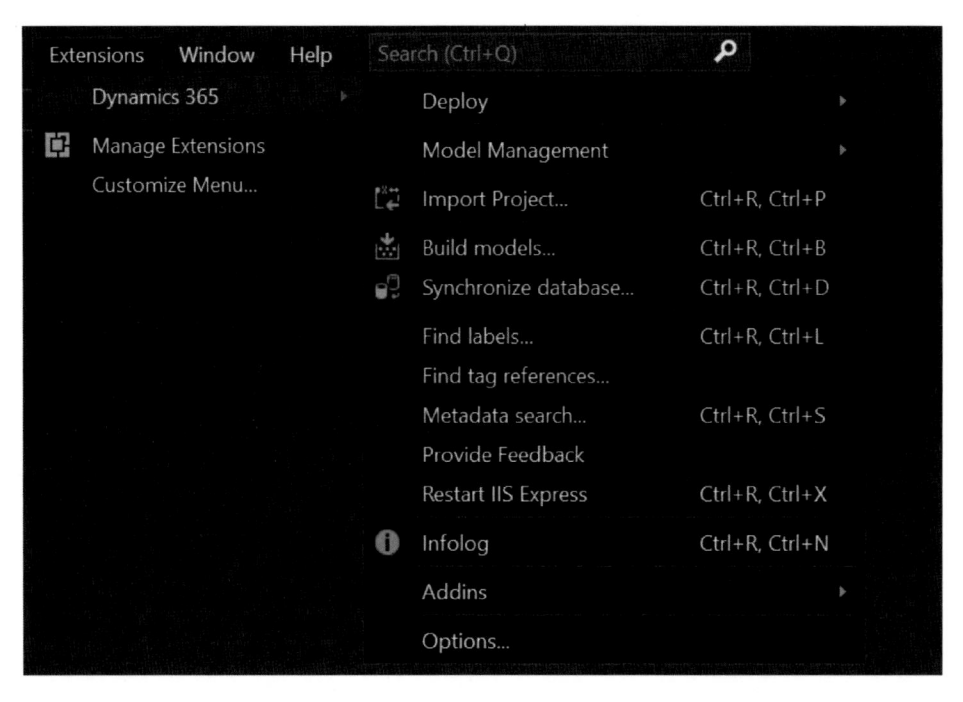

Figure 10.2: D365 F&SCM Visual Studio extensions

Visual Studio provides a range of tools that enable developers to write, debug, and deploy custom code and extensions for D365 F&SCM. Some of the key features and capabilities of Visual Studio that are relevant to D365 F&SCM development include the following:

- **Code editor and debugger**: Visual Studio provides a powerful code editor with features such as syntax highlighting, code completion, and debugging capabilities that make it easy to write and debug custom code for D365 F&SCM.
- **Dynamics 365 Finance and Operations tools**: Visual Studio includes a set of tools specifically designed for D365 F&SCM development, such as the Dynamics 365 Finance and Operations project templates, which provide a starting point for creating customizations and extensions.
- **Extensions development**: Visual Studio provides support for developing extensions, which are a key feature of D365 F&SCM. Extensions can be used to add new functionality or modify existing functionality in D365 F&SCM without modifying the core code.
- **Integration with source control**: Visual Studio integrates with popular source control systems such as Git and provides tools for managing source code repositories and tracking changes.

Visual Studio plays a critical role in D365 F&SCM development by providing developers with the tools and features needed to create, test, and deploy customizations and extensions for the platform.

Here's an example of how Visual Studio can be used to create simple customization for D365 F&SCM.

A company wants to add a new custom field to the Customer table in D365 F&SCM. They want to create a field called `Preferred Language` that will store the customer's preferred language.

To create this customization using Visual Studio, the following steps can be taken:

1. Open Visual Studio and create a new Dynamics 365 Finance and Operations project.
2. Add a new table extension for the `Customer` table.
3. Add a new field to the table extension and name it `PreferredLanguage`.
4. Set the data type of the new field to `String`.
5. Save the changes to the table extension.
6. Build and deploy the customization to the development environment.
7. Test the customization by creating a new customer record and verifying that the **Preferred Language** field is visible and can be populated with data.

By using Visual Studio to create this customization, developers can leverage the powerful code editor and debugging tools to write high-quality code that integrates seamlessly with D365 F&SCM. They can also use Visual Studio to manage the source code for customization and collaborate with other developers on the project. Overall, Visual Studio is an essential tool for any D365 F&SCM developer looking to create customizations and extensions for the platform.

When you open Visual Studio as an Administrator, you'll be able to view the AOT for the connected D365 instance.

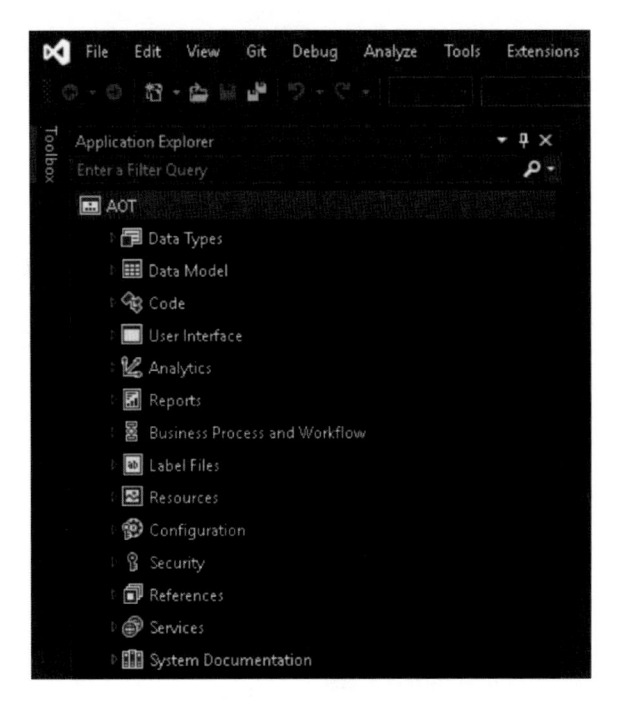

Figure 10.3: Visual Studio view of the AOT

DevOps examples

To show you how to work with some of the tools, we're going to show how to create a D365 F&SCM project in DevOps, and how to create a test script.

Creating a project

This is an example of how to create a new D365 F&SCM project in DevOps and prepare it for a developer:

1. Open your DevOps project and go to the **Projects** tab.

DevOps examples   181

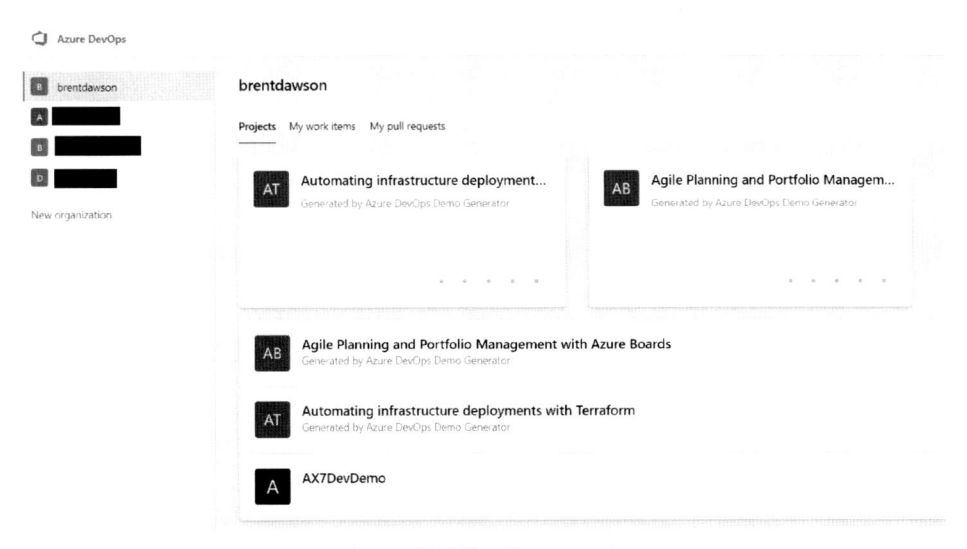

Figure 10.4: DevOps projects

2. Click on the **New project** button in the top left-hand corner.
3. Give your project a name and click **Create**:

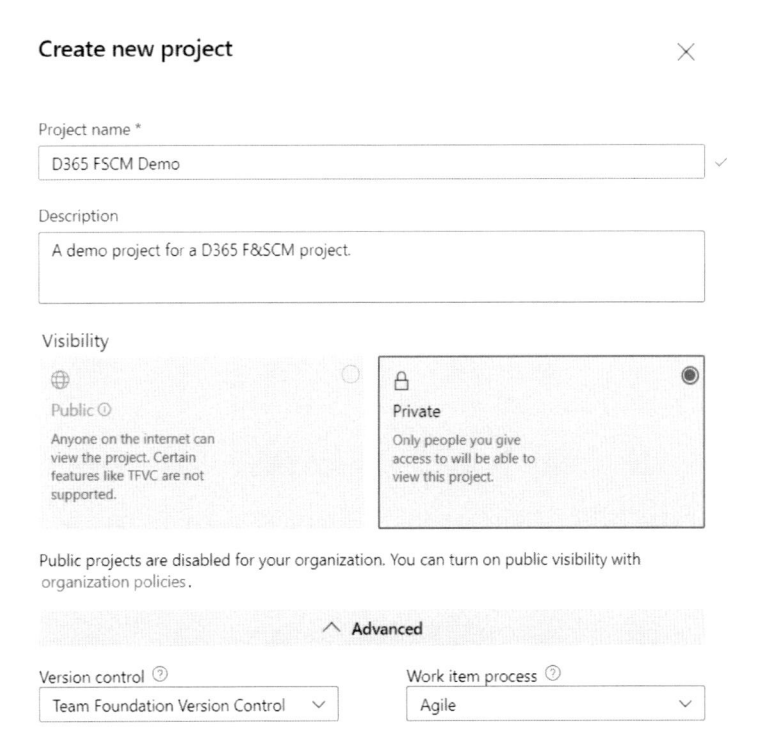

Figure 10.5: Create a new project

4. Once the project is created, go to the **Boards** tab and select **Backlogs**.

Figure 10.6: Backlogs board in DevOps

5. Click on the **New Work Item** button to create a new User Story. Enter a name.

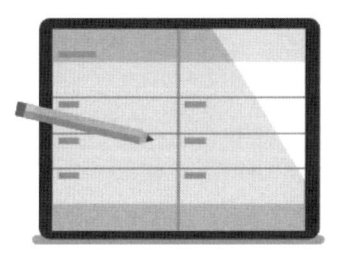

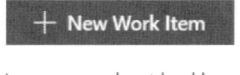

Figure 10.7: Create a new work item

6. Add any relevant attachments or links to the User Story item.

Figure 10.8: User Story information

7. Assign the User Story to the developer who will be working on it.
8. Add any additional tasks or subtasks to the User Story as needed.
9. Once the User Story is complete, move it to the **Active** state.
10. Create a new branch in the source control repository for the project.
11. Clone the repository to the developer's local machine.
12. Install the necessary software and dependencies for the project on the developer's machine
13. Open the project in the development environment and begin working on the backlog item.

By following these steps, you can create a new D365 F&SCM project in DevOps and prepare it for a developer to start working on it.

Another example of a task that DevOps is very good at is managing testing scripts. To set up a test script in Azure DevOps for Dynamics 365 F&SCM projects, you can follow these general steps:

1. Create a new project in Azure DevOps or use an existing one.
2. Create a new test plan or test suite in Azure DevOps to organize your test cases.
3. Create test cases for your D365 F&SCM project in Azure DevOps. You can create test cases manually or import them from Excel or other tools.
4. Associate your test cases with your D365 F&SCM project. You can do this by specifying the relevant D365 F&SCM configuration and data requirements in the test case steps.

5. Create a test plan or test suite in Azure DevOps that includes the test cases you created.

6. Set up your test environment for D365 F&SCM testing. This may involve configuring test data, test users, and other resources in your D365 F&SCM environment.

7. Configure your test settings in Azure DevOps. For D365 F&SCM projects, you may need to specify the target environment, URL, and authentication details.

8. Run your test script in Azure DevOps. This will execute the test cases in your test plan or test suite and generate test results and reports.

Note that the specific steps for setting up a test script in Azure DevOps for D365 F&SCM projects may vary depending on your project requirements and configuration. It's also important to ensure that your test scripts are designed to test the specific functionality and scenarios in your D365 F&SCM project and that they are maintained and updated as your project evolves.

The following figure shows what tasks can be completed in Test hub.

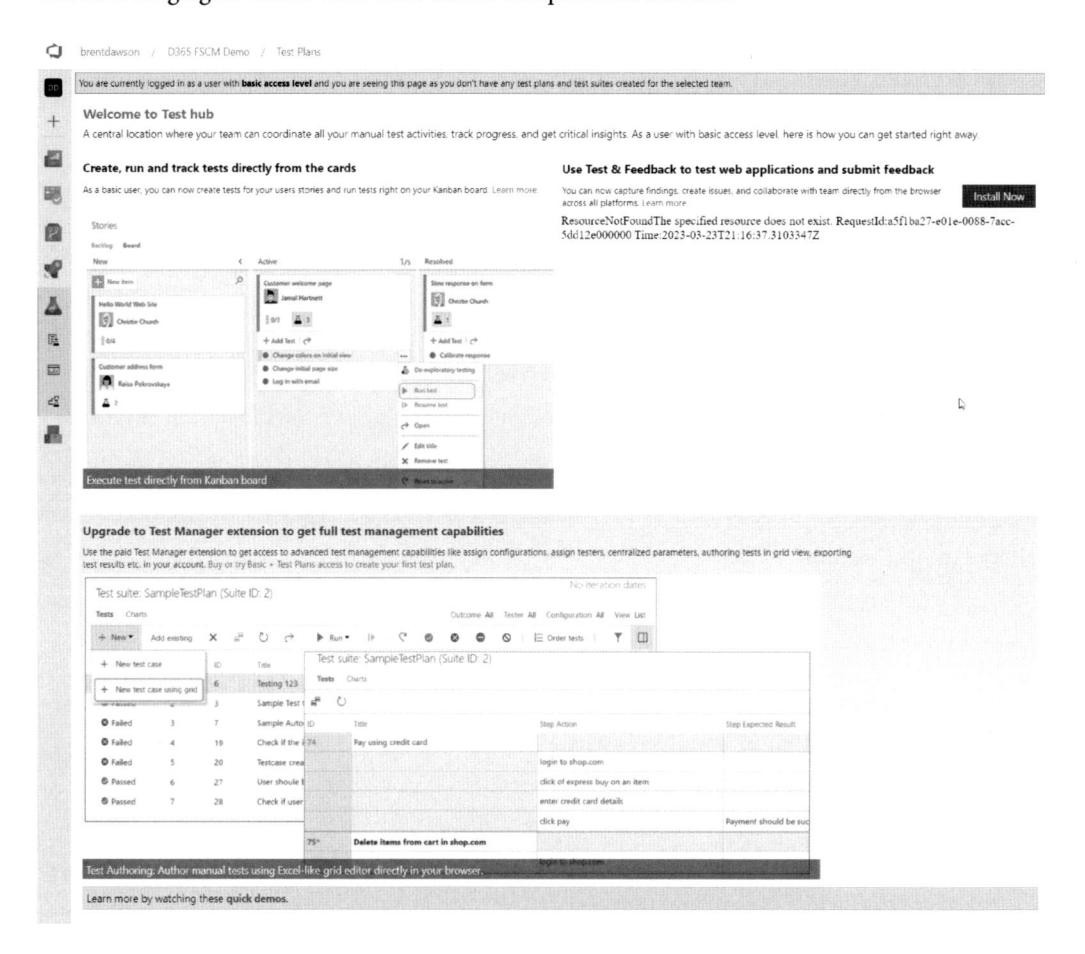

Figure 10.9: Azure DevOps Test hub

Best practices

When working on a Dynamics 365 F&SCM project, there are several best practices to consider when using tools. These practices can help improve efficiency, collaboration, and overall project success. Here are some key recommendations:

- **Requirements gathering and documentation**: Use tools such as Microsoft Word, Excel, or SharePoint to capture and document project requirements. Maintain a centralized repository for easy access and version control.
- **Project management**: Utilize project management tools such as Microsoft Project, Azure DevOps, or Jira to plan and track project tasks, milestones, and dependencies. These tools enable effective communication and collaboration among team members.
- **Source code management**: Implement a version control system such as Git, and leverage code repository platforms such as Azure DevOps, GitHub, or Bitbucket. This ensures proper versioning, code branching, and collaboration during development.
- **Testing and bug tracking**: Employ test management tools such as Azure DevOps Test Plans, Zephyr, or QTest to manage test cases, track test execution, and report defects. These tools streamline the testing process and facilitate bug tracking and resolution.
- **CI/CD**: Use tools such as Azure DevOps, Jenkins, or TeamCity for CI/CD automation. This helps maintain a robust and reliable release pipeline, allowing for frequent and reliable software updates.
- **Data migration**: Leverage D365 F&SCM's **Data Management Framework** (DMF) for data migration. It provides import/export capabilities, data transformation, and validation rules. Additionally, tools such as Microsoft Excel or Azure Data Factory can assist with data manipulation and **Extract, Transform, and Load** (ETL) processes.
- **Business intelligence and reporting**: Utilize tools such as Power BI, **SQL Server Reporting Services** (SSRS), or Jet Reports to create insightful dashboards and reports for stakeholders. These tools enable data visualization and analysis, providing valuable insights into business performance.
- **Collaboration and communication**: Employ collaboration tools such as Microsoft Teams, SharePoint, or Slack to facilitate communication and document sharing among project stakeholders. These platforms enhance real-time collaboration, knowledge sharing, and issue resolution.
- **Documentation and training**: Develop comprehensive project documentation using tools such as Microsoft Word, SharePoint, or Confluence. Additionally, consider using e-learning platforms or authoring tools (e.g., Articulate Storyline or Adobe Captivate) to create interactive training materials for end users.
- **Change management**: Implement change management tools such as Azure DevOps, ServiceNow, or Jira to effectively manage and track change requests, approvals, and their impact on the project. These tools ensure proper control and visibility of changes throughout the project life cycle.

Remember, the specific tools to use may vary depending on project requirements, team preferences, and organizational standards. It's important to evaluate the available options and select the ones that align best with your project's needs.

Conclusion

In this chapter, we looked at the tools that are available to assist the team with successfully completing a project. Using these tools makes the project much easier and learning how to use these tools early on, will also make you more productive.

In the next chapter, I'm going to talk about what I think is probably the most important topic in this book, human change management. If you do this well, your project is guaranteed to be a success.

11
Human Change Management

One of the biggest struggles that an organization can face is preparing its employees for changes coming down the line. In this chapter, we will discuss many issues that can occur when proper corporate change management is excluded from a project. We'll look at how to best prepare a company for coming changes.

As we move through the chapter, we'll discuss the following:

- What is human change management?
- Why must employees need to know what's coming?
- Human change methodologies
- Who's best to lead change?

At the end of this chapter, I'll give you two different case studies that respectively show a well-run project and a project that was, frankly, terrible. It's important to remember that change management is not just a phase in the project, but an activity that should be executed every day of the project, even past go-live.

What is human change management?

If you've been in IT for less than half a day, you'll have heard the phrase "change management." Human change management refers to the process of planning, implementing, and monitoring changes within an organization, with a specific focus on how those changes will impact the people within the organization. This process involves understanding how individuals and groups will be affected by the changes, and then developing strategies to help them adapt to those changes.

At its core, human change management is about ensuring that organizational changes are implemented successfully by minimizing resistance from employees and promoting their engagement and commitment to the new ways of working. This involves a variety of activities, including communication and training, stakeholder engagement, leadership support, and ongoing monitoring and evaluation.

Ultimately, the goal of human change management is to help employees embrace change and understand how it can benefit them and the organization as a whole, while minimizing any negative impacts that may arise from the change process. By effectively managing human change, organizations can increase their chances of success when implementing new initiatives, systems, or processes.

Human change management is a crucial aspect of project management that involves understanding, planning for, and implementing changes in human behavior that occur during the project life cycle. It is the process of preparing, equipping, and supporting individuals, teams, and organizations to adopt new processes, policies, systems, and behaviors necessary to achieve project objectives.

In project management, human change management is critical because successful project outcomes often depend on people embracing and adopting the changes that the project introduces. Without effective human change management, individuals may resist new ways of working, leading to delays, increased costs, or even project failure.

Human change management involves several key steps, including the following:

1. **Identifying stakeholders and their needs**: Understanding who will be affected by the project and how they will be impacted
2. **Developing a change management strategy**: Developing a plan that outlines the specific actions, timelines, and resources required to support the adoption of new processes, policies, and behaviors
3. **Communicating the change**: Communicating the benefits of the change, how it will be implemented, and what the impact will be on individuals and the organization
4. **Training and development**: Providing the necessary training, coaching, and support to enable individuals to develop the skills and knowledge required to adopt the new processes and behaviors
5. **Reinforcement and sustainability**: Developing processes to ensure that the changes are sustained over time and embedded into the culture of the organization

Human change management is an essential component of project management. It helps project managers to plan for and manage the people side of change, which is often the most challenging and critical aspect of project success.

Let's break this list down and talk about these steps individually.

Identifying stakeholders and their needs

Identifying stakeholders and their needs is an essential step in human change management. The first step is to identify all the stakeholders who will be impacted by the change. This includes employees, managers, customers, vendors, and other relevant parties. It is important to cast a wide net and identify all relevant stakeholders. Once you have identified all the stakeholders, prioritize them based on their level of influence and impact on the change. Some stakeholders may have a higher level of influence or a greater impact on the change than others.

Now that we have prioritized the stakeholders, you need to determine their needs. This can be done by conducting interviews and surveys, using focus groups, and via other methods of gathering feedback. It is important to understand what each stakeholder wants and needs from the change. You need to gather feedback from the stakeholders and analyze their needs to identify common themes and areas of overlap. This will help you to develop a comprehensive understanding of the needs of all the stakeholders. Lastly, based on the needs of each stakeholder, develop a stakeholder management plan that outlines how you will communicate with them, address their concerns, and involve them in the change process. The plan should be tailored to the needs of each stakeholder and should be reviewed and updated regularly.

By following these steps, you can identify the stakeholders and their needs, and develop a plan to manage their involvement in the change process. This will help to ensure that the change is successful and that all stakeholders are engaged and satisfied with the outcome.

Developing a change management strategy

Developing a change management strategy involves a series of steps that aim to ensure that changes are implemented successfully within an organization. The following are the key steps you can follow to develop a change management strategy:

1. **Define the change**: Start by identifying what needs to change within your organization. Determine what the current state is, what the desired future state is, and what needs to be done to bridge the gap between the two.
2. **Identify stakeholders**: Identify who will be affected by the change and who will need to be involved in the change process. This includes individuals, groups, and departments within the organization, as well as external stakeholders such as customers, suppliers, and partners.
3. **Assess the impact**: Evaluate the impact of the change on different stakeholders and assess their readiness for change. This will help you to identify potential risks and resistance to the change and to develop strategies to mitigate them.
4. **Develop a communication and engagement plan**: Create a plan for how you will communicate the change to different stakeholders and engage them in the change process. This should include the message you want to convey, the channels you will use, and the timing of your communication.
5. **Develop a training and support plan**: Develop a plan for how you will train and support employees through the change process. This should include identifying the skills and knowledge they will need, developing training materials, and providing ongoing support.
6. **Monitor and evaluate**: Monitor the progress of the change and evaluate its effectiveness. This will help you to identify any issues or challenges that need to be addressed and to make any necessary adjustments to your change management strategy.

By following these steps, you can develop a comprehensive change management strategy that will help ensure the successful implementation of changes within your organization.

Communicating the change

In human change management, communication is a critical factor for successful change. When introducing change, it's essential to communicate the change effectively to ensure that everyone understands what's happening, why it's happening, and how it will affect them. The following are some tips for effective communication during the change management process:

- **Be transparent**: Be honest about the changes taking place and why they're necessary. This builds trust and helps to reduce uncertainty and resistance.
- **Tailor your message**: Different stakeholders may have different concerns and interests. Tailor your message to address their specific needs and concerns.
- **Choose the right channels**: Use multiple channels, such as face-to-face meetings, emails, and social media, to reach all stakeholders.
- **Repeat your message**: People need to hear a message multiple times to understand it fully. Repeat your message consistently to ensure it is understood.
- **Encourage feedback**: Create opportunities for stakeholders to ask questions and provide feedback. This helps to identify concerns and address them proactively.
- **Be timely**: Communicate changes as early as possible, so stakeholders have time to adjust and prepare for the change.

By following these tips, you can help ensure that the communication of change is effective and successful.

Training and development

In human change management, training and development are crucial components of a successful change initiative. Training refers to the process of providing employees with the knowledge and skills necessary to perform their job tasks effectively. Development, on the other hand, involves a more long-term and strategic approach to building the capacity and potential of employees.

During a change initiative, training and development are essential for several reasons. First, they help employees understand and adapt to new systems, processes, and technologies. Second, they help build employee skills and competencies, which are critical for success in the new environment. Third, training and development can help build a culture of learning and continuous improvement, which can contribute to the long-term success of the organization.

To effectively manage training and development during a change initiative, it is important to have a comprehensive plan in place. This plan should include an assessment of current employee skills and competencies, as well as an analysis of the skills and competencies needed for success in the new environment. The plan should also include a schedule for training and development activities, as well as a system for evaluating the effectiveness of these activities.

In addition to providing training and development opportunities, it is also important to create a supportive environment for employees during a change initiative. This can include providing resources such as mentors, coaches, and support groups, as well as creating a culture that values learning and growth. By investing in training and development and creating a supportive environment, organizations can increase the likelihood of success during a change initiative.

Reinforcement and sustainability

In human change management, reinforcement and sustainability are two critical elements that can significantly impact the success of the change effort.

Reinforcement refers to the actions taken to encourage and support the desired behaviors and actions that are part of the change. Reinforcement can take many forms, such as positive feedback, recognition, rewards, or incentives. The purpose of reinforcement is to create an environment where the desired behaviors are encouraged and reinforced, making them more likely to continue.

Sustainability, on the other hand, refers to the ability for the change to be maintained over the long term. Sustainable change is change that lasts and becomes part of the culture and the way things are done. Sustainability is achieved by embedding the change into the organization's systems, processes, and culture, making it a part of the fabric of the organization.

Reinforcement and sustainability are closely related, as sustained change requires ongoing reinforcement. Reinforcement helps to create a culture where the desired behaviors are recognized and rewarded, making them more likely to become habitual. This, in turn, makes the change more sustainable over the long term.

To ensure successful change management, it's essential to design reinforcement and sustainability plans early in the change effort. This requires careful planning and implementation to ensure that the desired behaviors are consistently reinforced and embedded into the organization's culture and systems. By doing so, organizations can achieve sustainable change that lasts and delivers real results.

Why do employees need to know what's coming?

It is essential for employees to know about changes in the software applications used to fulfil tasks as part of their jobs because it directly affects their work processes and productivity. There are several reasons why it is crucial for employees to know about changes in software applications:

- **Preparedness**: Knowing about the upcoming changes allows employees to prepare themselves for the new software applications. This preparation can include attending training sessions or learning how to use the new software to ensure a smooth transition.
- **Increased efficiency**: When employees are aware of the changes in software applications, they can adapt their work processes accordingly, which can help to increase their efficiency and productivity.

- **Better collaboration**: Knowing about new software applications can facilitate better collaboration between team members. By being aware of the new tools and features, employees can collaborate more effectively with each other.
- **Improved morale**: When employees are kept in the loop about changes in their job, it helps to create a culture of transparency and openness. This, in turn, can improve employee morale and engagement.
- **Avoidance of errors**: If employees are not aware of the changes in software applications, they may make mistakes that could affect the quality of their work. By keeping employees informed, they are less likely to make errors or waste time on tasks that are no longer relevant.

Informing employees about upcoming changes in software applications is essential for ensuring a smooth transition and maximizing productivity. As well as the aforementioned benefits, let's look at the importance of keeping employees in the know when it comes to corporate changes.

Employees who feel informed about changes in their job tend to have a higher level of job satisfaction. When employees understand how their work will be impacted by new software applications, they are more likely to feel like they have control over their job and are not blindsided by unexpected changes. But it's not just end users who can be positively impacted by being well informed. Support teams are always stuck in the middle between the user and the company. Changes in software applications can impact how IT support interacts with users, especially in customer service roles. By informing employees about these changes, they can provide better service to users, which can lead to higher user satisfaction and loyalty.

Change can also be difficult for employees, especially if they are not given enough information or preparation. By informing employees about upcoming changes and providing them with the necessary training, they are less likely to resist changes, which can save time and resources. When a user is more accepting of change, it also makes them better at how to work with the software, which ultimately makes them better at problem-solving. When employees are familiar with new software applications, they can use them to their full potential, including using new tools and features to solve problems more efficiently. By being informed about changes, employees can better identify and solve problems, leading to improved productivity and work quality.

Generally, in most organizations, when a new software application is released, it often comes with new policies and procedures that employees need to follow. By keeping employees informed about these changes, they are more likely to comply with the new policies, reducing the risk of compliance issues and potential legal problems.

In summary, informing employees about changes in software applications is critical for ensuring a smooth transition, reducing resistance to change, and improving job satisfaction, customer service, problem-solving, and compliance with company policies.

The Change Curve

The Change Curve is a popular model used to understand the process of personal or organizational change. It describes the various stages people go through as they cope with and adapt to a significant change in their lives or work environment. The Change Curve model has been widely applied to change management, organizational development, and psychology.

The Change Curve model typically consists of four to six stages, depending on the particular version of the model. The most common stages are the following:

1. **Denial/resistance**: This stage is characterized by a sense of shock and disbelief about the change. People may deny that the change is happening or resist it out of fear, anger, or confusion.
2. **Anger/blame**: In this stage, people may begin to express their frustrations and concerns about the change. They may blame others for the situation or become defensive.
3. **Bargaining/negotiation**: This stage involves attempts to find ways to adapt to the change while minimizing its impact. People may try to negotiate with others or find compromises.
4. **Depression/despair**: This stage is characterized by a sense of loss and sadness. People may feel overwhelmed by the change and the challenges it presents.
5. **Acceptance/integration**: In this final stage, people begin to accept the change and adapt to the new reality. They may find new ways to cope and develop new skills or strategies.

It's important to note that not everyone will experience each stage of the Change Curve, and people may move through the stages at different rates. Additionally, people may move back and forth between stages, and it's not always a linear process.

Overall, the Change Curve model is a useful tool for understanding how people respond to change and how to support them through the process of adapting to new situations.

The following figure lays out how The Change Curve affects the average worker.

The Change Curve

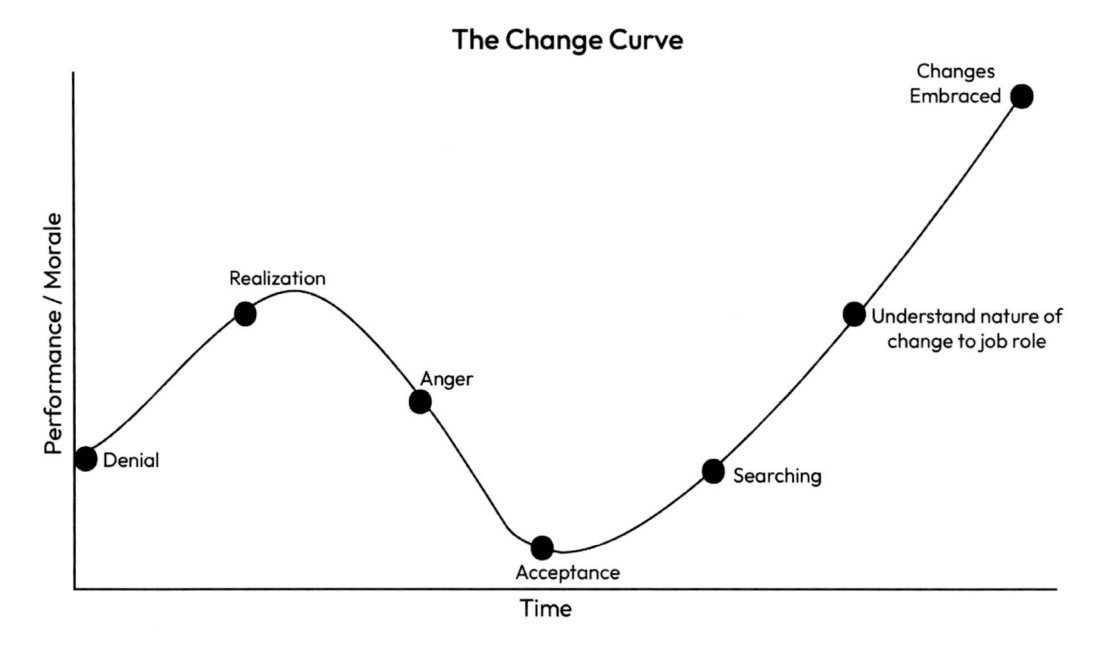

Figure 11.1: The Change Curve

Human change methodologies

Human change management methodologies are approaches used to help individuals, teams, and organizations successfully navigate and adapt to changes in the workplace. These methodologies aim to address the human aspects of change, including resistance, uncertainty, and anxiety.

Some commonly used human change management methodologies include the following:

- **ADKAR model**: The ADKAR model is a step-by-step approach to change management that focuses on individual change. It stands for **Awareness**, **Desire**, **Knowledge**, **Ability**, and **Reinforcement**.
- **Lewin's Change Management Model**: This model suggests that change involves three stages – *unfreeze*, *change*, and *refreeze*. In the unfreeze stage, individuals must be made aware of the need for change. In the change stage, the actual changes are implemented. In the refreeze stage, the changes are embedded and become part of the organization's culture.
- **Kotter's 8-Step Change Model**: This model involves eight steps that organizations can follow to successfully implement change. The steps include creating a sense of urgency, forming a powerful coalition, creating a vision for change, communicating the vision, empowering

others to act on the vision, creating short-term wins, consolidating gains, and anchoring new approaches in the organization's culture.

- **Bridges' Transition Model**: This model focuses on the psychological and emotional aspects of change. It suggests that individuals go through three stages during a transition – *ending*, *neutral zone*, and *new beginning*. The ending stage involves letting go of the old way of doing things. The neutral zone is a period of uncertainty and discomfort. The new beginning involves embracing the new way of doing things.
- **Prosci ADKAR Model**: This model is similar to the original ADKAR model but focuses more on organizational change management. It involves creating awareness of the need for change, building a desire for the change, developing the knowledge and ability to support the change, reinforcing the change, and ensuring that the change is sustainable over the long term.

Each of these methodologies has its own strengths and weaknesses, and the best approach will depend on the specific situation and the needs of the organization or individuals involved.

Prosci ADKAR Model

The Prosci ADKAR Model is a goal-oriented change management framework that provides a structured approach for individuals and organizations to navigate change. It is the most commonly used model for large projects. The model focuses on the five key building blocks necessary for successful change under **AKDAR**.

Each of the five components of the ADKAR model represents a stage in the change process that must be addressed in order to achieve successful change:

1. **Awareness**: This stage involves creating an understanding of why the change is necessary and what the implications of the change will be. This includes communicating the need for change and the consequences of not changing.
2. **Desire**: This stage is about creating a desire for change. It involves addressing the emotional factors that might cause resistance to the change and showing people how the change will benefit them personally.
3. **Knowledge**: In this stage, people need to be equipped with the knowledge and skills necessary to make the change. This might involve providing training, coaching, and other resources.
4. **Ability**: This stage focuses on ensuring that people have the ability to implement the change. This might involve removing any obstacles or barriers that might be preventing people from making the change.
5. **Reinforcement**: This stage involves reinforcing the change so that it becomes a permanent part of the organizational culture. This might involve providing ongoing support, recognition, and rewards for those who have made the change.

The ADKAR Model provides a roadmap for organizations to navigate the change process and achieve successful outcomes by addressing the individual factors that influence behavior. By addressing each of the five stages in the model, organizations can minimize resistance, promote adoption, and increase the likelihood of success.

The following diagram shows the progression of the ADKAR model.

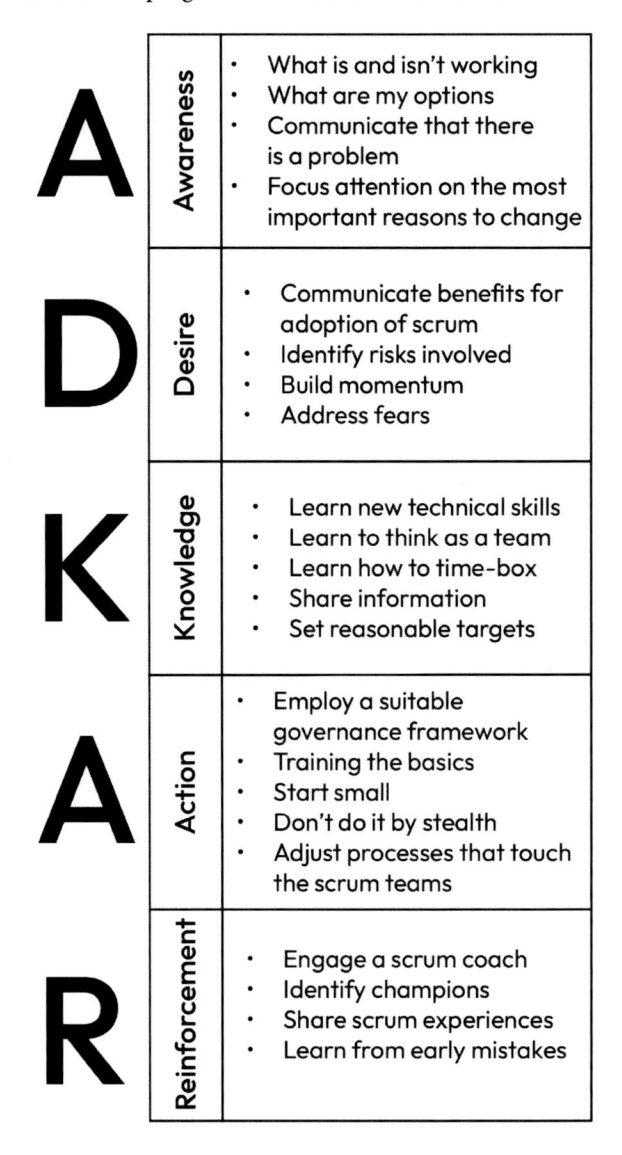

A	Awareness	• What is and isn't working • What are my options • Communicate that there is a problem • Focus attention on the most important reasons to change
D	Desire	• Communicate benefits for adoption of scrum • Identify risks involved • Build momentum • Address fears
K	Knowledge	• Learn new technical skills • Learn to think as a team • Learn how to time-box • Share information • Set reasonable targets
A	Action	• Employ a suitable governance framework • Training the basics • Start small • Don't do it by stealth • Adjust processes that touch the scrum teams
R	Reinforcement	• Engage a scrum coach • Identify champions • Share scrum experiences • Learn from early mistakes

Figure 11.2: ADKAR Change Management steps

Let's look at an example of how we can implement the ADKAR model. Let's say a company is implementing a new software system across the organization. Here's an example of how the Prosci ADKAR Model could be applied to this change initiative:

1. **Awareness**: The company communicates the need for the new software system and the benefits it will provide, such as improved efficiency and productivity.
2. **Desire**: The company emphasizes how the new system will benefit individual employees by making their jobs easier and more streamlined. They also address any concerns or fears employees may have about the change.
3. **Knowledge**: The company provides training sessions and resources to ensure that employees have the necessary knowledge and skills to use the new software system.
4. **Ability**: The company ensures that all necessary hardware and software is in place and any technical issues have been addressed to ensure that employees will be able to use the new system without any obstacles.
5. **Reinforcement**: The company reinforces the adoption of the new system by providing ongoing support, recognition, and rewards for those who have successfully transitioned to using the new system. They also gather feedback and make any necessary adjustments to ensure continued success.

By applying the Prosci ADKAR Model, the company can minimize resistance to change, promote adoption, and increase the likelihood of successful implementation of the new software system.

Who is best to lead change?

As human change management involves organizational change, it's best that someone who works in the company leads the process of change. In a company, the best person to lead human change management is typically a dedicated change management professional or a human resources professional with expertise in change management. This person should have a deep understanding of the organization's culture, values, and vision, as well as the knowledge and skills needed to effectively manage the people's side of change.

In some cases, the CEO or other senior executives may also play a significant role in leading human change management. However, it's important to have a dedicated person or team focused on this area to ensure that change is managed effectively and that employees are properly supported throughout the transition.

Change management is a structured approach to managing the people side of organizational change, including changes in processes, systems, technologies, and organizational structures. Effective change management can help ensure that the changes are implemented successfully and that employees are able to adapt to the new ways of working with minimal disruption.

The role of the change management professional or HR professional in leading human change management comprises several tasks that must be executed. Firstly, we need to plan and prepare for the change. This involves identifying the goals of the change initiative, assessing the potential impact on employees, and developing a detailed plan for managing the people side of the change. This may include developing communication plans, training programs, and other support mechanisms to help employees navigate the change.

Once we've made the plan, we next need to prepare for communication and engagement with the users. One of the most important aspects of effective change management is ensuring that employees are informed and engaged throughout the process. This may involve regular communication about the reasons for the change, the expected outcomes, and how employees can contribute to the success of the initiative. Next, we need to prepare the employees by setting up training and development of the software. Change often requires new skills and knowledge, and it's important to provide employees with the training and support they need to be successful in the new environment. This may include providing on-the-job training, e-learning courses, or other resources to help employees learn the new processes and systems.

Lastly, throughout the change process, it's important to monitor employee engagement and satisfaction, identify any areas of resistance or confusion, and adjust the change management plan as needed. This may involve conducting surveys, focus groups, or other feedback mechanisms to gather input from employees and track progress toward the goals of the initiative.

Overall, the role of the change management professional or HR professional in leading human change management is critical to the success of any change initiative. By focusing on the people side of change and providing the support and resources employees need to adapt to new ways of working, companies can ensure that change is implemented effectively and that employees are able to continue delivering value to the organization.

Change tools

There are several tools and techniques that can be used to assist in human change management. Here are some examples:

- **Change readiness assessment**: This tool is used to assess the organization's readiness for change and identify potential obstacles or resistance to the change initiative. It may involve surveys, focus groups, or interviews with employees and stakeholders to gather input on their perceptions of the change and their level of readiness to embrace it.

- **Stakeholder analysis**: This tool is used to identify key stakeholders in the change initiative, assess their level of influence and interest in the change, and develop strategies for engaging and communicating with them throughout the process.

- **Communication plan**: This tool outlines the key messages, communication channels, and timing of communication for the change initiative. It may include regular updates, town hall meetings, email communications, or other methods of keeping employees informed and engaged.

- **Training and development plan**: This tool outlines the training and development needs of employees affected by the change initiative, as well as the resources and methods for delivering the training. It may include e-learning courses, on-the-job training, or workshops to help employees develop the skills and knowledge they need to succeed in the new environment.

- **Resistance management plan**: This tool outlines strategies for identifying and addressing resistance to the change initiative. It may involve developing a communication plan to address common concerns, identifying and addressing specific areas of resistance, or providing support and resources to employees who may be struggling with the change.

- **Metrics and evaluation plan**: This tool outlines the key metrics and evaluation criteria for the change initiative, as well as the methods for tracking progress and evaluating the effectiveness of the change management plan. It may involve conducting surveys, focus groups, or other feedback mechanisms to gather input from employees and track progress toward the goals of the initiative.

These tools and techniques can help ensure that the human side of change is effectively managed and that employees are properly supported throughout the transition. By using these tools, companies can increase the likelihood of a successful change initiative and minimize disruption to employees and the organization.

Case studies

In my experience, human change management is a vital part of any **Enterprise Resource Planning (ERP)** project. In this next section, we'll look at two different projects I participated in. In one project, the company did a really good job of preparing the staff for the upcoming changes. In the other, the company wasn't as good.

Case study 1 – the bad project

A medium-sized manufacturing company decided to deploy a new ERP system to streamline their operations. The company's IT department spent months evaluating different ERP software options and decided to implement a cloud-based ERP system. Specifically, they decided on D365 F&SCM. They also selected a couple of different ISV solutions to extend the capabilities of the D365 system.

The company already had an outdated and very heavily customized ERP system. They had no system for warehouse management on their manufacturing lines, and no simple way to know where any items were located in the manufacturing buildings. The project also contained a sub-project where a regional sales office and warehouse, located in Europe, was included. The project was devised in such a way that the sale office project was completed first. The project had several staff members who were involved during the project stages.

However, the company did not involve the end users, including the employees who would be using the system, in the decision-making process. The company's IT department assumed that the new system would be easy to use and that the employees would be able to adapt to it quickly.

On the day of the deployment, the IT department pushed the new ERP system to all company computers without any training or guidance. The employees were left to figure out how to use the new system on their own, and many struggled with the new interface and features.

As a result, the company experienced a significant decrease in productivity and an increase in errors and frustration among employees. Some employees even refused to use the new system, causing further delays and inefficiencies.

In this example, the company failed to involve end users in the decision-making process, provide proper training and guidance for the new software, and manage the change effectively. This led to a negative impact on the company's operations and employee morale.

Case study 2 – the good project

I don't want this to be a purely negative discussion. Even though many companies don't do human change management well, that doesn't mean a company can't do a better job during the project, once it's identified the risk. In contrast to the previous example, let's talk about a project I was involved in that was an excellent example of how to do human change management well.

I was involved in a project back when Dynamics AX 2012 was the most recently released version. At the very beginning of the project, a member of the Human Resources department was responsible for managing human change management. The HR representative used several of the methods and tools mentioned in this chapter to help prepare the staff for upcoming changes.

At the very beginning of the project, the staff were notified via email that the project was starting, the impact that the project would have, and the timeline of the project. Then, at the next employees' meeting, there was a short demo and discussion about the project. After that, throughout the course of the project, there were emails, notice boards, and milestone walkthroughs of different business processes, such as how to fill out an expense report.

After every meeting, there was a survey of all the staff to find out whether the information was useful and whether there was anything that they needed further clarification on. The other advantage was that the people completing the demos were staff members that were well known to the rest of the organization. They were identified as the "champions" for each of the business units. They were assigned to the project full-time and were always available to help staff understand the changes coming down the line.

The other key part of the role that these individuals played was to help create and present training to staff on how to complete the new business rules. They created clear and easy-to-follow documentation and used that documentation to assist in getting all the staff ramped up to use the new tools prior to the go-live of the software.

Once go-live happened, there were very few issues in relation to how the system worked and how employees were to complete tasks. Overall, the work that was completed by the Human Resources department, the project team, and corporate leadership to prepare the staff for the new system was a textbook example of how to properly prepare employees for an upcoming change.

Conclusion

I know I've said it in other places so far, but this chapter is one of the most important in the book. If done right, human change management will compensate for many deficiencies in other places of a project. If you can get the staff excited about the change, it makes the work of the project much easier. Human change management is a critical process that helps organizations successfully navigate changes in their structure, processes, and technology. It involves understanding how people react to change, designing strategies to minimize resistance, and fostering a culture of openness and collaboration. Effective change management can help organizations achieve their goals more efficiently, reduce costs, and increase employee engagement and satisfaction. It is important because change is inevitable in today's fast-paced and ever-changing business environment, and organizations that fail to adapt risk falling behind their competitors. By investing in change management, organizations can ensure that they remain agile and responsive to the changing needs of their stakeholders and can continue to grow and thrive over the long term.

As the solution architect, you have the responsibility and opportunity to guide the company toward the implementation of proper human change management throughout the organization. You can work with the company's internal operations teams or hired contractors to get the business ready and excited for any change that comes.

In the next chapter, we'll look at how to deploy a system from a finalized blueprint solution.

12
Building a Blueprint Solution

Once you have been through all the client discovery and requirements-gathering sessions, it's up to the **solution architect** (**SA**) to create a viable solution for their project. Knowing what the client needs and how it should be implemented is an important step to a successful project. A good blueprint will be easily explained and defended. That, in turn, makes the sign-off by the client on the design a simple formality.

In this chapter, we'll look at the following key topics:

- Knowing what goes into a solution blueprint
- Expressing user requirements
- Documents to include in the blueprint
- How to maintain a living document

Knowing what goes into a solution blueprint

In today's fast-paced world, businesses and organizations need to adapt and implement solutions quickly to stay competitive. One popular approach to achieving this is by using blueprints. These blueprints are essentially templates that enable organizations to accelerate their processes by leveraging pre-built solutions, best practices, and guidelines.

However, to ensure long-term success, it's crucial to create a supportable solution based on these blueprints. In this chapter, we will discuss the steps and considerations involved in building a supportable solution from a blueprint.

Understanding the blueprint

Before delving into the process of building a supportable solution, it's crucial to understand the structure and components of a blueprint. A *Success by Design* solution blueprint typically includes the following components:

1. **Goals and objectives**: The first step in creating a Success by Design solution blueprint is to clearly define the goals and objectives of the project. This includes identifying the problem that needs to be solved, the desired outcomes, and the metrics for success.

2. **Strategy**: The next step is to develop a strategy for achieving the desired outcomes. This may involve identifying key stakeholders, determining the necessary resources, and outlining a plan of action.

3. **Implementation plan**: Once the strategy is developed, an implementation plan is created. This outlines the specific steps that will be taken to implement the strategy, including timelines, budgets, and responsibilities.

4. **Risk management**: A risk management plan is also included in the Success by Design solution blueprint. This identifies potential risks and outlines strategies for mitigating them.

5. **Performance metrics**: In order to track progress and ensure success, performance metrics are identified and monitored. This includes both quantitative and qualitative measures of success.

6. **Communication plan**: Finally, a communication plan is developed to ensure that all stakeholders are informed and engaged throughout the process. This includes identifying key messages, communication channels, and a timeline for communication.

Overall, a Success by Design solution blueprint is a comprehensive plan that outlines the steps necessary to achieve a specific goal or objective while also identifying potential risks and strategies for mitigating them.

Assess the suitability of the blueprint

Before adopting a blueprint, evaluate its suitability for your specific project or organization. To assess the suitability of the blueprint for a project solution, you need to review some of the points that will help you to make a valid decision. Start by understanding the project requirements and objectives. This will help you determine whether the blueprint is suitable for the project. Next, study the blueprint and evaluate its suitability for the project. Consider the scope, deliverables, and timelines of the blueprint.

An important step is to identify any gaps between the project requirements and the blueprint. Determine whether the blueprint needs to be customized or whether it can be used as is. If the blueprint does fit, you need to look at resourcing. Evaluate the resources available for the project, including the team's skills, budget, and technology requirements. Determine whether the blueprint can be executed with the available resources. As a new or junior SA, you may need to consult with experts in the field who have experience with blueprints or similar project solutions. Gather their feedback and insights to determine the suitability of the blueprint.

Another consideration is what types of risks will be integrated into the blueprint. Evaluate the risks associated with implementing the blueprint for the project. Determine whether the risks are manageable and whether the benefits outweigh the potential risks. Based on your analysis and evaluation, decide on whether the blueprint is suitable for the project. If not, consider alternative project solutions that may be better suited to the project's requirements and objectives.

Assessing the suitability of the blueprint for a project solution requires careful analysis and evaluation of the project requirements, the blueprint, available resources, potential risks, and expert feedback.

Customize the blueprint

While the blueprint provides a solid foundation, it is essential to customize the blueprint to meet your specific business needs. Here are some steps to follow when customizing the blueprint:

1. **Identify your specific business needs**: Before you start customizing the blueprint, you need to identify your specific business needs. What are your business goals? What are the challenges you are facing, and how can the blueprint help you overcome them? Knowing your specific business needs will help you tailor the blueprint to meet your unique requirements.

2. **Determine the scope of the customization**: Once you have identified your business needs, you need to determine the scope of the customization. What parts of the blueprint do you need to customize? Is it the entire Blueprint or just specific sections? By determining the scope of the customization, you can avoid unnecessary work and ensure that your efforts are focused on areas that will provide the most value.

3. **Modify the blueprint**: With the scope of the customization defined, you can begin to modify the blueprint to meet your specific requirements. This may involve adding new content, removing sections that are not relevant, or modifying existing content to better align with your business needs. You may also need to customize the implementation plan and timeline to reflect your specific requirements.

4. **Test and validate the customized blueprint**: Once you have made the necessary modifications to the blueprint, you need to test and validate the customized blueprint. This involves checking that the modifications meet your business requirements, ensuring that the implementation plan is realistic, and identifying any potential issues that may arise during implementation.

5. **Communicate the customized blueprint to stakeholders**: Once you have validated the customized blueprint, you need to communicate it to all relevant stakeholders. This includes employees, partners, and other stakeholders who will be involved in the implementation process. By communicating the customized blueprint, you can ensure that everyone is on the same page and understands the changes that have been made.

Customizing the blueprint involves the following steps:

1. Identifying your specific business needs.
2. Determining the scope of the customization.

3. Modifying the blueprint.
4. Testing and validating the customized blueprint.
5. Communicating the customized blueprint to stakeholders.

By following these steps, you can tailor the blueprint to meet your unique business requirements and ensure a successful implementation of Microsoft cloud technologies.

Establish a strong governance structure

It is incredibly important to establish strong governance in a blueprint. It is essential for ensuring successful implementations. The governance structure gives the framework for how decisions are made and processed, task accountability, and overall oversight of the project. If you have a well-designed governance structure, everyone who is a part of the project, from the application testers to the executive sponsor of the project, will understand their role in the project, what their specific responsibilities will be, and how any decisions related to them are to be made to allow for efficiency and effectiveness.

There are some specific reasons why a well-designed governance structure is necessary for a blueprint. A governance structure that includes representatives from key stakeholders can help ensure that everyone has a say in the implementation process and feels heard. This can help build support and buy-in for the blueprint, which is crucial for success. The governance structure should also identify potential risks and establish processes for mitigating them. This can help minimize disruptions and ensure that the blueprint stays on track.

A governance structure can establish metrics for tracking progress and ensure that everyone is held accountable for meeting milestones. This can help identify potential delays early on and allow for timely course corrections. And lastly, a governance structure can help ensure that resources (e.g., funding, personnel, technology) are allocated in a way that supports the blueprint's objectives. This can help avoid conflicts and ensure that everyone is working toward the same goals.

Develop a detailed implementation plan

The implementation plan should be detailed enough to provide a supportable solution. When putting together the plan, you need to keep in mind that you need to define project milestones to determine how the project is progressing. It can also be used as a method to inform staff of what the project will produce once it goes live. The plan will also have a list of all the tasks and their dependencies. Also, the plan can allow for multiple tasks to be executed in parallel, so in theory, you could complete some of the project tasks faster. This will depend on how many resources you have allocated to your project.

The plan will also let you identify who will be needed during the execution of the project. As an example, **subject matter experts** (**SMEs**) will be needed during the requirements-gathering phase of the project and when the testing phase is executed. They will only be needed sparingly during the design and build phases of the project. Because of this, you might not need to backfill their positions for as long as the entire length of the project. Lastly, the plan will assist you in avoiding and mitigating risks that might appear during the project (and frankly, that's really the whole point of this entire book!).

Ensure adequate training and skill development

To build a solution, you need to validate that your project team has the correct skills required to produce a valid solution. Early on, identify the skills gap on the team and solve any issues through technical training, localized workshops, and a buddy system.

Implement monitoring and evaluation mechanisms

Monitoring the project is how you can tell whether you're on the right track. Identify what your **key performance indicators** (**KPIs**) will be so you can validate the success of your solution. From these KPIs, you'll generate your progress reports.

Foster collaboration and knowledge sharing

Way back at the beginning of the book, I mentioned that from my point of view, the job of the SA is to be a cheerleader. If the SA can get the team to work like a team, such as sharing information and learning from each other, your success rate will be incredibly high. And it's not just in the sense of sharing information. It's also getting everyone to do things together. Some suggestions include some sort of team-building exercise (on one project, we went axe throwing), giving everyone a 20-minute chair massage once a month, and team potluck lunches. I like to bake, so I always bring in things such as cheesecake, cookies, or loaves. It also explains why I'm overweight and need to exercise.

Plan for long-term support and maintenance

The plan needs to lay out what steps will be needed to plan for long-term stability and maintenance. You need to create processes for addressing issues and bugs, how and when the software will be updated, and what process to follow to complete regular system audits.

Review and iterate

Lastly, a regularly scheduled set of reviews of the solution needs to be planned and executed so that the SA can adjust the project in real time. Feedback from stakeholders, testing and performance data, and lessons learned are ways to help the SA understand where the project is.

Building a supportable solution from a blueprint requires a comprehensive understanding of the blueprint, customization to fit the organization's unique needs, and a focus on long-term sustainability. By following the steps and considerations discussed in this chapter, organizations can effectively leverage blueprint blueprints to create robust and supportable solutions that drive success and remain adaptable to changing business environments.

Project roles

Implementing **Dynamics 365 Finance and Operations (D365 F&O)** is typically a complex project requiring a variety of roles with unique responsibilities and deliverables.

Here are some key roles that typically exist in a D365 F&O project and their main responsibilities/deliverables in the solution blueprint phase:

- **Project manager**: Responsible for overseeing the entire project. They set the timeline, coordinate resources, and manage risk. Their deliverable is usually the overall project plan, which includes the timeline, budget, resource allocation, and risk management plan.
- **Business analyst (BA)**: They are responsible for understanding the business needs, processes, and requirements. The BA's deliverable is the requirement documentation, which includes user stories, use cases, and business process flow diagrams.
- **SA**: The role of the SA is to design the overall solution. They should understand both the business requirements and the capabilities of D365 F&O. Their deliverable is the solution design document outlining how D365 F&O will be configured and customized to meet business requirements.
- **Functional consultant**: The functional consultant works closely with the business analyst and the solutions architect. Their role is to understand the business process in detail, map it to D365 F&O functionalities, and configure the system accordingly. Their deliverable is the configured system and also the functional design documents outlining the system configurations and the mapping with the business process.
- **Technical consultant**: The technical consultant is responsible for any required system customizations, integrations, or data migrations. They work closely with the solutions architect and functional consultant. Their deliverable is the technical design document outlining any system modifications, customizations, data migration strategy, and the actual customized system.
- **Data analyst**: The data analyst is responsible for understanding the data requirements and preparing for the data migration. They usually produce a data migration plan and a data mapping document.
- **Quality assurance (QA) analyst**: The QA analyst is responsible for testing the system to ensure it meets business requirements and doesn't contain critical bugs. They develop a test plan and test cases and carry out system testing.
- **Change manager**: The change manager is responsible for managing the changes in the organization due to the implementation of D365 F&O. They create change management, communication, and training plans.
- **Training coordinator**: Responsible for coordinating and delivering training to end users. The deliverable is the training plan and training material, and they may also be involved in training sessions.

This list is not exhaustive, as roles and responsibilities can vary depending on the size and complexity of the project, as well as the specific needs of the organization.

Expressing user requirements

The collection and expression of user requirements are essential to Success by Design. There are several methods an SA can use to assist in gathering user requirements. The types of methods used depend on the type of project, how many resources you have at hand, and the types of users in the organization. These are some of the more common methods available.

The most popular method used to collect information is the **survey**. Surveys can be conducted online or in person and can collect both quantitative and qualitative data, which in turn is used to help consolidate the results. These surveys can also be used to gather other types of data, including demographics, end-user needs, specific application preferences, and satisfaction levels.

Another successful method is the **interview**. Interviews allow for a more in-depth method of collecting user requirements. They can be conducted in one-on-one interactions or as a group, such as in a focus group setting. The insights that can be gained by using interviews allow the SA and functional consultants to have a more detailed understanding of the reasons for a specific process or their motivation for the types of decisions they make daily. You can also dive deeper into the pain points the company is currently dealing with, so you can better design a solution to resolve those issues.

A third method to collect information is through **observation**. This method allows the data collector to follow users around to see how they complete their tasks in their existing systems. Observations can be conducted in person or remotely, using video recordings or screen-sharing tools. Workshops allow for a more collaborative method of collecting requirements. Workshops can be used to set requirement priorities, generate ideas that can lead to a solution, and create prototypes that can be tested during the build phase of a project. Workshops don't have to be completely structured, as unstructured discussions often lead to more interesting data and better solutions.

Card sorting is a method that can be used for gathering and grouping user requirements. Users are presented with a set of cards that contain a separate requirement and then asked to organize or sort them in the order that they think is the priority. You can also get them to sort them into different categories. Once this sorting exercise has been completed, the SA can identify patterns in the user requirements.

Analytical tools can also be used to collect data about how users work with the existing systems. This data can include user behaviors on websites, apps, or any other digital platform. This data can then be analyzed to show user satisfaction and usage patterns.

Lastly, **user testing** can be used to observe how users interact with a specific product or service. This method can be used to identify user issues, collect feedback on how the product or service has been designed, and validate that it answers as many user requirements as possible. Again, this testing doesn't necessarily need to be conducted in person. It could easily be collected remotely by using screen-sharing software.

Now that we've collected information, let's look at ways that we can clearly express the information that we collected back to the customer as a blueprint. The following list details some of the techniques I've used previously to help with this task:

- **Research**: We've collected the user requirements and the information needed to successfully create a solution that fixed their pain points.

- **Use clear and concise language**: This might sound rather obvious, but it's not hard to start getting into the "technical" weeds when creating your solution. Remember, most of the people this solution is intended for aren't as technical as you, so keep your language simple.

- **Prioritize requirements**: Inevitably, sometimes a user story isn't important. Remember, user stories will define all the processes the business has, but you need to filter out the ones that are standard or out of the box and only focus on the ones that you will need to do a fit-gap analysis on to resolve. You can use methods such as prioritization matrices or user story mappings. Either way, you'll focus on the stories that have the most impact on the project and the satisfaction of all the users.

- **Collaborate with stakeholders**: You can't create a successful solution in isolation. You need to work with the correct stakeholders and collaborate on the solution. You should include other users, such as product managers, developers, and designers. Engage stakeholders throughout the process to ensure that requirements are feasible, that they align with business objectives, and can be implemented within constraints such as time or budget.

- **Use visual aids**: Visual aids such as diagrams, flowcharts, or wireframes can help to communicate user requirements in a more accessible and engaging way. Use these tools to illustrate complex concepts or show how different requirements relate to each other. Using swim lane diagrams drawn in Visio is extremely effective.

- **Validate requirements**: Before you finalize a requirement and add it to the solution, make sure you validate and test it with users to ensure that it accurately reflects the users' needs and expectations. This may include making a proof of concept and having the users give it a try.

These are by no means the only ways to communicate with the users all their requirements, but these are the ones that I've found help the most. I'm sure that many of you have all sorts of other ways to help in this process. All that matters is that the solution you create for the client covers all their pain points and gives them what they need to be successful.

What to include in the blueprint

The blueprint solution in Success by Design is a comprehensive strategy for achieving successful software deployment. Depending on the context of the project, the sections of the document may vary based on the modules needed. There are some common sections that should be included in every solution document.

- **Executive summary**: Give a brief overview of the entire solution. You should highlight the main goals and objectives of the project. Keep this to about a page in length.
- **Background and problem statement**: This section should contain a detailed explanation of the problem or challenge the blueprint solution aims to solve, along with any relevant background information.
- **Goals and objectives**: You need to provide a clear statement of the goals and objectives of the solution and should include any specific targets or metrics that will be used to measure the success of the project.
- **Scope and limitations**: This section needs a description of the scope of the solution and needs to include all the limitations and constraints that will affect the implementation of the project.
- **Strategy and action plan**: This will include a detailed description of the strategies and actions that will be taken to achieve the goals of the project and the objectives of the solution.
- **Resource requirements**: Of all the sections in the document, I think this is the most important. Here you will provide an assessment of the resources required to implement the project. This resources list will include both partner and customer human resources, equipment, such as computers, projectors, and so on, and all funding needs for the project.
- **Risk assessment and management**: You need to provide an analysis of any potential risks and challenges that will be associated with the implementation of the solution. You also need to lay out methods to help resolve any unforeseen risks, including a risk register. You'll also need to define how those risks will be mitigated. (It might be a bit cheeky but keep this book handy!)
- **Monitoring and evaluation plan**: A description of how the success of the solution will be monitored and evaluated over time. This needs to include any metrics or indicators that will be used to measure the progress of the project and to make sure you're hitting all the defined milestones.
- **Conclusion**: This section is a short summary of the key points made in the previous sections of the document. You may also want to include any final recommendations for the project team.

Besides these sections of the blueprint solution document, there are a few other documents that should be included with the solution. These documents will be created during the process of the project and may end up being edited several times prior to the project delivery has been completed. Some common documents that are often included are as follows:

- **Project scope**: The project scope document defines the boundaries of the project, including what is included and what is not included. It outlines the goals, objectives, and deliverables of the project, as well as the timeline and budget. The project scope document helps to ensure that everyone involved in the project understands what is expected of them and what they need to deliver.

- **Business requirements document (BRD)**: The BRD outlines the specific needs of the organization and its stakeholders. It describes the business processes that the solution will support, the data that will be used and the reporting requirements. The BRD helps to ensure that the solution meets the needs of the business and its users.

- **Functional design document (FDD)**: The FDD describes the functional requirements of the solution. It outlines the features, functions, and capabilities of the system, including any technical constraints or limitations. The FDD helps to ensure that the solution is technically feasible and meets the requirements of the project. There will be an FDD for all the business processes.

- **Technical design document (TDD)**: The TDD describes the technical requirements of the solution. It outlines the features, functions, and capabilities of the system, including any technical constraints or limitations. The functional specifications document helps to ensure that the solution is technically feasible and meets the requirements of the project. There will be a TDD for each customization created in the project.

- **Architecture design document (ADD)**: The ADD describes the overall architecture of the solution, including the hardware and software components, as well as the interactions between them. It outlines the system topology, the integration requirements, and the security considerations. The architecture design document helps to ensure that the solution is scalable, secure, and reliable.

- **User interface design document**: The user interface design document describes the visual and interaction design of the solution. It outlines the layout, navigation, and visual design of the system, as well as any usability guidelines or standards. The user interface design document helps to ensure that the solution is intuitive, easy to use and meets the needs of the users. This is an optional document.

- **Test plan document**: The test plan document outlines the testing strategy for the solution. It describes the test cases, scenarios, and acceptance criteria that will be used to validate the system. The test plan document helps to ensure that the solution is thoroughly tested and meets the requirements of the project.

- **Implementation plan document**: The implementation plan document outlines the plan for deploying the solution. It describes the deployment strategy, the timeline, and the resource requirements. The implementation plan document helps to ensure that the solution is implemented smoothly and efficiently.

In the next section, let's look at how we identify who is responsible or who leads what tasks in the project. We also need to have a way to track the project costs. We'll discuss **responsible, accountable, consulted, and informed** (**RACI**) charts and project budget documents.

Responsible, accountable, consulted, and informed

A RACI document is a project management tool that defines and clarifies the roles and responsibilities of team members involved in a particular project or process. The four main categories of team member roles are shown in the following list:

- **Responsible**: This is the person who is responsible for completing the task or work item
- **Accountable**: This is the person who is ultimately accountable for the successful completion of the task or work item
- **Consulted**: This is the person who is consulted for their expertise or input on the task or work item
- **Informed**: This is the person who needs to be kept informed about the progress of the task or work item

A RACI document typically lists all the tasks or work items involved in the project or process, and for each task, it identifies which team members are responsible, accountable, consulted, and informed. This helps ensure that everyone knows their roles and responsibilities, which can improve communication, reduce confusion, and increase accountability.

As we mentioned, a RACI chart helps define roles and responsibilities in a project, in this case, a D365 F&O **Enterprise Resource Planning** (**ERP**) project.

The RACI chart for a D365 F&O ERP project might look like this:

Key:

- **R = Responsible**: The person who performs an activity or does the work
- **A = Accountable**: The person who is ultimately accountable and has yes/no/veto powers
- **C = Consulted**: The person who needs to provide input, they have the information or capability necessary to complete the work
- **I = Informed**: The person who needs to be kept informed about progress or decisions

Task/Processes	Project Manager	Functional Consultant	Technical Consultant	Testing Team	Training Team	Stakeholders
Project Plan Creation	A	C	C	R	R	I
Requirement Gathering	R	A	C	I	I	C
FDD Creation	R	A	C	I	I	C
TDD Creation	R	C	A	I	I	C
Code Development	R	C	A	I	I	C
Testing (Unit, Integration, UAT)	R	C	C	A	I	C
Training Material Creation	R	C	I	I	A	C
User Training	R	C	I	I	A	C
Go-Live Preparation	A	C	C	R	R	C
Post-Go-Live Support	A	C	C	R	I	C

Table 12.1 – RACI chart

Next, we need to have a budget document that will define how and where project costs will be allocated.

Project budget document

A project budget document typically includes a detailed breakdown of all the costs associated with a project. The document may include the following sections:

- **Introduction**: This section outlines the purpose of the budget document and provides an overview of the project.
- **Project scope**: This section describes the scope of the project and the specific deliverables that will be produced.

- **Assumptions**: This section lists all the assumptions that were made when creating the budget, such as the cost of materials or labor.
- **Budget summary**: This section provides a high-level summary of the project budget, including the total cost of the project and the funding sources.
- **Cost breakdown**: This section provides a detailed breakdown of all of the costs associated with the project. It may include categories such as personnel costs, equipment costs, materials costs, and travel costs.
- **Budget justification**: This section provides a detailed explanation of how each of the budget items was calculated and why it is necessary for the project.
- **Contingency plan**: This section outlines a contingency plan in case the project goes over budget or unexpected expenses arise.
- **Conclusion**: This section summarizes the budget document and may include any final recommendations or conclusions.

Overall, the project budget document is a crucial tool for project managers and stakeholders to understand the financial aspects of a project and ensure that it stays on track.

These documents are all important components of a Success by Design solution blueprint. By providing a comprehensive understanding of the project, its requirements, and the proposed solution, these documents help to ensure that the project is delivered on time, on budget, and to the satisfaction of all stakeholders.

Living documents

Maintaining a living document used in a technical project can be crucial for the success of the project. Here are a few ways to keep a document up to date:

- **Assign ownership**: Assigning ownership of the document is crucial to ensure that someone is responsible for maintaining and updating it. This person or team should have a clear understanding of the project goals and objectives, as well as the technical aspects of the project.
- **Version control**: Version control software helps to track changes made to the document over time and ensures that the latest version is always available to the team. This can be done using software such as GitHub, Bitbucket, or GitLab.
- **Regular updates**: Regular updates to the document are essential to ensure that it reflects the latest developments in the project. A schedule should be established for updates, and team members should be notified when changes are made.
- **Use templates**: Using templates helps to ensure consistency across the document and makes it easier to maintain. Templates can be used for various aspects of the document, including formatting, content, and style.

- **Review process**: Establishing a review process ensures that the document is accurate and up to date and that it meets the needs of the project. The review process should involve team members who have expertise in the technical aspects of the project.
- **Automation**: Automation tools can be used to streamline the process of updating the document and ensure that updates are made in a timely manner. This can include automated alerts when changes are made, automated version control, and automated backups.
- **Communication**: Communicating changes to the document to the relevant stakeholders is essential to ensure that they are aware of any changes that may affect the project. This can be done through emails, project management tools, or regular meetings.
- **Training**: Training team members on how to use the document is important to ensure that they understand its purpose and to encourage them to provide feedback and suggestions for improvement. This can include providing training on the use of templates, version control software, and review processes.

Best practices

Microsoft Success by Design is a program that offers guidance and best practices for creating successful solutions using Microsoft technologies. When it comes to creating a solution blueprint, Microsoft recommends the following best practices:

- **Clearly define the problem or opportunity**: Before you start designing your solution, you need to have a clear understanding of the problem or opportunity you're trying to address. Clearly define the scope of the problem and the desired outcome you want to achieve.
- **Involve stakeholders**: Involve all relevant stakeholders in the process of creating the solution blueprint. This includes end-users, technical experts, business leaders, and anyone else who will be impacted by the solution.
- **Use a structured approach**: Use a structured approach to create the solution blueprint, such as a design thinking process. This will help you to identify user needs, define requirements, and generate ideas for the solution.
- **Prioritize requirements**: Prioritize requirements based on their importance to achieving the desired outcome. This will help you to focus on the most critical features and functionality of the solution.
- **Leverage existing technologies**: Leverage existing technologies and platforms to accelerate the development process and reduce costs. This can include using Microsoft Azure services, Microsoft Power Platform, or other Microsoft technologies.
- **Design for scalability and maintainability**: Design the solution blueprint with scalability and maintainability in mind. This will ensure that the solution can grow and evolve as the business needs change and can be easily maintained over time.

- **Test and iterate**: Test the solution blueprint and iterate as necessary to ensure that it meets the requirements and achieves the desired outcome. This includes user testing, technical testing, and other forms of validation.

By following these best practices, you can create a comprehensive and effective solution blueprint that meets the needs of your organization and delivers real value to your users.

Are you still with me? I hope that I haven't put you to sleep at this point. We are almost near the end, I promise. This chapter's purpose was to show how to prepare the solution, how to express user requirements, and how to maintain the solution as a living document.

Conclusion

So far in this book, we've looked at areas that can cause issues, how to set up a project to be successful, what types of tools to use, and what should be included in a solution. In the next and final chapter of the book, we're going to put it all together. We will look at how to take our solution, build the solution blueprint, and prep the system from build to go live.

13
Deploying the Project Solution

Now that we've looked at everything that needs to be completed, let's get to work. This chapter will put everything we discussed into a logical cheat sheet that you can use to get the project off on the right foot. We'll look at the timelines you should follow so the project starts off and stays on track until the final go-live. We will present a final project structure based on the FastTrack process.

We'll look at the following:

- Building the blueprint solution
- Go-live preparation
- How should it look

At the end of the chapter, we'll look at how to prepare for pre- and post-go-live.

Building the blueprint solution

Creating a solution blueprint based on Success by Design involves planning, strategic thinking, and the application of a structured process. The aim is to design for success from the start, ensuring that every component of the blueprint is built to contribute to the final goal.

Here are some steps that we should follow to create a solution blueprint:

1. The first step in any successful design is to understand what success looks like. What are the ultimate goals you're trying to achieve in this project? These should be clearly defined; they need to be measurable and should be agreed upon by all stakeholders. The goals to be measured may include increasing sales, improving customer satisfaction, or helping to reduce production costs. They could also be technical goals such as reducing downtime, increasing system capacity, or improving data security.
2. Once the goals are defined, identify the key success factors. These include the elements that will most directly and significantly influence the achievement of the goals. These could be things such as user engagement, system performance, cost controls, and so on. Each success factor should be measurable so that you can track progress and adjust as needed.

3. With a clear understanding of the goals and the key success factors, you can now start to define the solution. This involves identifying the main components of the solution, their interactions, and their dependencies. This might include software systems, hardware, processes, roles, responsibilities, and so on. Each component should be clearly defined, and its role in achieving the success factors should be understood. Now you can start to create the blueprint. This is a visual representation of the solution, showing all the components and their interactions. It should be detailed enough to provide a clear understanding of the solution, but not so detailed that it becomes overwhelming. It should also be flexible enough to allow for adjustments and improvements as the solution is implemented and tested.

4. Once the blueprint is created, it should be validated against the goals and the success factors. Does it provide a clear path to achieving the goals? Does it address all the key success factors? Are there any gaps or potential issues that need to be addressed? Validation should involve all stakeholders to ensure that everyone is on board with the solution. With a validated blueprint, you can now start to implement the solution. This should be done in a controlled and measurable way, with regular testing and adjustment to ensure that the solution is working as expected and moving toward the goals. Even after the solution is implemented, the job isn't done. It's important to monitor the solution, measure its performance against the success factors, and make improvements as needed. This is a continuous process that ensures the solution remains effective and continues to deliver success.

The preceding steps, when followed, allow an SA to create a solution blueprint that is designed for success from the start of the project. This proactive approach will help to prevent problems, help to reduce risks that could derail the project, and ensure that whatever solution you come up with, the solution will deliver the results that the client requires.

Design pillars of solution architecture

Microsoft has set out a list of design pillars as part of Success by Design. Specifically for Dynamics 365, the pillars include the following:

- **Technical architecture**: Technical architecture defines the technical infrastructure and components of the solution. This includes the hardware, software, networks, and other infrastructure that will be used to support the solution. The technical architecture should be designed to meet the performance, security, and scalability requirements of the solution.

- **Security**: Security is essential for protecting the solution from unauthorized access, use, disclosure, disruption, modification, or destruction. This includes implementing security controls at the infrastructure, application, and data levels. The security controls should be designed to meet the security requirements of the solution and the organization.

- **Business alignment**: Business alignment is critical to ensure that the solution meets the business requirements and objectives. This includes understanding the business needs, identifying the gaps between the current state and the desired state, and developing a solution that addresses those gaps.

- **Performance**: Performance is important to ensure that the solution meets the performance requirements of the business. This includes ensuring that the solution can handle the expected volume of transactions and users. The performance of the solution should be monitored and adjusted as needed to ensure that it meets the requirements.
- **User experience** (**UX**): UX ensures that the solution is easy to use and meets the needs of the users. This includes designing the **user interface** (**UI**) to be intuitive and easy to use. The UI and UX should be designed to meet the needs of the users and the business.

Strategies

There are several decisions that need to be made early in the project to help to drive how the project is executed. These decisions are made during strategy meetings. The following sections will tell us the different types of strategy sessions you will need to complete to get the correct information needed to successfully plan and execute the project.

ALM, tools, and deployment

The point of an **application life cycle management** (**ALM**) strategy is to design an appropriate ALM approach. The data that is collected may vary depending on the objectives of the workshop, and the type of organization it's being used in. There are some common types of data that need to be collected during this workshop.

Before we go too far, first and foremost, we need to understand what ALM practices the organization already has:

- Participants will be asked to describe the tools, processes, and methodologies they currently have in place. With this data, you can identify a starting point for the workshop and determine what challenges currently exist. Knowing this can help you make decisions to improve these processes.
- Workshop organizers may gather information about the stakeholders involved in the ALM process. This includes identifying key individuals or teams responsible for different stages of the application life cycle, such as development, testing, deployment, and maintenance.
- Understanding the organization's overall business objectives is crucial for aligning the ALM strategy. Data related to business goals, priorities, and strategic initiatives may be collected to ensure the ALM strategy supports and enhances these objectives. Information about the organization's application portfolio may be gathered. This includes details about the existing applications and their architecture, technologies, dependencies, and criticality to the business. This data helps identify areas that require special attention during the ALM strategy formulation.
- Understanding the organization's resource availability is important when formulating an ALM strategy. Data related to the availability of skilled personnel, budget, infrastructure, and tools may be collected to ensure the strategy aligns with the available resources.

- Depending on the industry and regulatory landscape, data related to industry standards, compliance requirements, and security considerations may be gathered. This ensures that the ALM strategy addresses these specific needs and adheres to relevant guidelines.

- As a part of the workshop, participants may be asked to provide feedback and suggestions on the ALM strategy discussed. This feedback helps refine and improve the strategy based on the insights and perspectives of the participants.

- During this workshop, we also need to identify what project management tool will be used and how the project will be created and managed in Azure DevOps and Dynamics Lifecycle Services. This information should include who will be responsible for creating new D365 environments, who will be responsible for managing and updating environments, and how partner users will access the D365 environments.

To review all the tools and how they are used, please refer to *Chapter 10*.

Data management

The Dynamics FastTrack data management strategy workshop is designed to help organizations effectively implement and optimize their use of Microsoft Dynamics 365. The workshop typically involves collaboration between stakeholders, business users, and Dynamics 365 experts to define the organization's objectives, identify key challenges, and develop a tailored data management strategy. The purpose of the workshop is to align business goals with the capabilities of Dynamics 365, establish best practices, and create a roadmap for successful implementation.

When working through the workshops, there are several types of data that we need to look at, as well as how that data should be collected, so that the project team has a detailed understanding of how the data usage impacts the organization. These types of data points include business process and workflow data, data sources and legacy systems, corporate data governance, data quality, data for reporting and analytics, how users will access the data, and lastly how data influences integrations and data migrations:

- **Business processes and workflows**: Understanding the organization's existing business processes, workflows, and data flows is crucial. This includes mapping out how different departments or teams currently manage and interact with data, identifying pain points and exploring opportunities for automation and streamlining.

- **Data sources and systems**: Identifying the various data sources and systems within an organization is important for data integration and consolidation. This involves documenting the existing systems, databases, applications, and data repositories that are relevant to the organization's operations and decision-making processes.

- **Data governance requirements**: Collecting information on data governance policies, regulatory requirements, and internal compliance standards helps ensure that the data management strategy aligns with legal and ethical guidelines. This includes identifying any data privacy or security regulations that must be adhered to, as well as internal policies for data access, retention, and sharing.

- **Data quality and cleansing needs**: Assessing the quality of the existing data is essential for an effective data management strategy. This includes identifying data inconsistencies, duplicates, inaccuracies, and gaps that need to be addressed during the implementation process. Gathering information on the data cleansing requirements helps prioritize data quality improvement efforts.
- **Reporting and analytics requirements**: Understanding an organization's reporting and analytics needs is crucial for designing an effective data management strategy. This includes identifying the **key performance indicators** (**KPIs**), report templates, data visualizations, and analytical capabilities required to support decision-making at different levels of the organization.
- **User roles and permissions**: Gathering information on user roles, responsibilities, and permissions helps define access controls and security settings within Dynamics 365. It involves understanding the different user types, their data access needs, and any specific role-based requirements for data management and system usage.
- **Integration and data migration**: If the organization is transitioning from existing systems to Dynamics 365, it is important to collect data migration requirements. This includes identifying the data to be migrated, data mapping, transformation rules, and any integration points with external systems.

This workshop collects the data that will serve as a foundation for creating a data management strategy within the scope of the D365 project. It also informs the project team on how the data should be collected, migrated between systems, and processed, including any data transformations and whether there are any customizations that need to be made to the data so that it will fit into the data structures of D365.

Integrations

If data is the most important part of a project, integrations are a close second. This strategy will collect various pieces of information that will give a detailed understanding of the requirements of the organization, the end goals of the project, and how integrations should be implemented. The following list comprises the data points that need to be considered when putting together the plan:

1. Organization details:
   - The company name, size, and industry
   - Key stakeholders and their roles
   - The existing systems, tools, and technologies used
   - Any specific integration requirements or constraints
2. Project goals and objectives:
   - Clearly defined objectives for the integration project
   - KPIs or metrics to measure success
   - The desired outcomes and benefits of the integration

3. Business processes and requirements:
    - Current business processes and workflows
    - Pain points, bottlenecks, and areas for improvement
    - Future state requirements and how the integration will support them
    - Compliance, security, and data privacy considerations

4. Data and system integration:
    - The data sources and types to be integrated
    - Data quality, cleansing, and transformation requirements
    - Any data migration or conversion needs
    - Integration touchpoints between systems and applications
    - APIs, connectors, or middleware to be used for integration

5. User requirements and change management:
    - User roles and access requirements
    - UX expectations
    - Training and onboarding needs for end users
    - Change management strategies to address user adoption

6. Timelines and milestones:
    - Project start and end dates
    - Key milestones and deliverables
    - Dependencies and critical path activities
    - Resource allocation and availability

7. Risks and mitigation strategies:
    - Potential risks and challenges
    - The impact and likelihood of each risk
    - Strategies for mitigating and addressing risks

8. Budget and resources:

    - The available budget for the integration project
    - Resource allocation (internal or external teams)
    - Infrastructure requirements (hardware, software, and cloud services)

9. Stakeholder engagement and communication:

    - Stakeholders and their communication preferences
    - A stakeholder engagement plan
    - Regular communication channels and an updated cadence

10. Success criteria and evaluation:

    - Define success criteria for the integration project
    - Determine how the success will be evaluated
    - Plan for post-implementation reviews and feedback gathering

The previous list will provide detailed information for the SA to use to properly design the strategy for integrations.

Types of integrations

An SA needs to have a complete understanding of the types of integrations that can be used with D365. Back in *Chapter 3*, we looked at the different types of integrations available, but let's take a quick look at the different options available:

1. **Common Data Service (CDS)**:

    - CDS allows for seamless integration between various Dynamics 365 applications and other Microsoft services
    - It provides a unified data platform for storing and managing data across different applications
    - It supports data synchronization, sharing, and real-time collaboration

2. Connectors and APIs:

    - Dynamics 365 provides a range of connectors and **Application Programming Interfaces (APIs)** to integrate with external systems and services
    - Connectors enable easy integration with popular applications such as SharePoint, Outlook, Power BI, and more
    - APIs allow for custom integration development to connect with third-party systems

3. Power Automate (formerly Microsoft Flow):

    - Power Automate is a cloud-based service that enables workflow automation across multiple applications and services
    - It offers pre-built connectors for Dynamics 365, allowing users to create automated workflows and integrate data and processes

4. Azure Logic Apps:

    - Azure Logic Apps is a cloud-based service that allows for building and deploying integration workflows
    - It provides a visual designer to create logic workflows and supports a wide range of connectors for integrating with Dynamics 365 and external systems

5. Azure Service Bus:

    - Azure Service Bus provides a robust messaging infrastructure for connecting distributed systems across different platforms
    - It supports reliable message queuing and publish-subscribe patterns, allowing for asynchronous communication and integration

6. The Data Export service:

    - The Data Export service enables the seamless integration of Dynamics 365 with Azure Data Lake Storage and Azure SQL Database
    - It allows you to export data from Dynamics 365 entities to Azure for further analysis and reporting or integration with other systems

7. Azure Functions:

    - Azure Functions provides serverless computing capabilities that can be leveraged for integration scenarios
    - With Azure Functions, you can develop custom code snippets to process data, trigger actions, and integrate with Dynamics 365

8. Custom development:

    - Dynamics 365 provides extensive development capabilities using common programming languages such as C#, JavaScript, and TypeScript.
    - Developers can use the Dynamics 365 **Software Development Kit** (**SDK**) and other development tools to build custom integrations

The choice of integration method that you select depends on the specific requirements, the systems that will be connected, the age of those systems, and the complexity of the integration scenario that needs to be executed.

Security

D365 F&SCM is a cloud-based deployment. Due to the cloud features Microsoft supports, they have created the Microsoft Trusted Cloud Principles. The Microsoft Trusted Cloud Principles are a set of guiding principles and commitments that Microsoft follows to ensure the security, privacy, compliance, and transparency of its cloud computing services. These principles are designed to build trust among customers and users of Microsoft's cloud platform, known as Azure. Here's an explanation of each principle:

- **Security**: Microsoft is committed to providing a highly secure cloud infrastructure. This involves implementing robust security measures to protect data and systems from unauthorized access, ensuring physical security at data centers, employing encryption technologies, and continuously monitoring and mitigating security risks.

- **Privacy**: Microsoft is dedicated to protecting the privacy of individuals and organizations that use its cloud services. It adheres to privacy laws and regulations, including the **General Data Protection Regulation** (**GDPR**). Microsoft offers customers control over their data and provides transparency regarding how data is collected, used, and stored.

- **Compliance**: Microsoft is committed to meeting the compliance requirements of various industries and regulatory bodies. It provides customers with the tools and resources needed to comply with applicable regulations, such as the **Health Insurance Portability and Accountability Act** (**HIPAA**) for healthcare data or the **Federal Risk and Authorization Management Program** (**FedRAMP**) for US government agencies.

- **Transparency**: Microsoft aims to be transparent about its cloud services and practices. It provides customers with visibility into how their data is handled and stored, as well as information on security measures, incident response protocols, and data breach notifications. Microsoft also publishes compliance reports and undergoes independent audits to demonstrate its adherence to industry standards.

- **Resilience**: Microsoft is committed to ensuring the availability and reliability of its cloud services. It employs redundant systems and data centers to minimize service disruptions and maintain business continuity. Microsoft also conducts regular testing, monitoring, and disaster recovery exercises to mitigate potential risks and quickly recover from any issues.

- **Intellectual property**: Microsoft respects the intellectual property rights of its customers and partners. It does not access customer data for its own purposes or use it for advertising. Microsoft recognizes that customers own their data and provides them with the tools and capabilities to manage and control their data.

The Security Framework

The D365 F&SCM Security Framework is designed to ensure the confidentiality, integrity, and availability of data within the D365 F&SCM application. It provides a comprehensive set of security features and controls to protect sensitive information and prevent unauthorized access. Here are some key components and features of the D365 F&SCM Security Framework:

- **Authentication**: Users are required to authenticate themselves before accessing the system. Authentication methods can include a username and password, multi-factor authentication, or integration with external identity providers such as Azure Active Directory.

- **Role-based security**: The framework utilizes a **role-based access control** (**RBAC**) model, where access to system features and data is granted based on predefined roles. Roles define the permissions and privileges associated with different job functions or responsibilities within the organization.

- **User provisioning**: The framework allows administrators to manage user access by provisioning and deprovisioning user accounts. This ensures that only authorized individuals have access to the system and its resources.

- **Segregation of duties (SoD)**: D365 F&SCM supports the principle of SoD by allowing organizations to define and enforce separation between incompatible job functions. This helps prevent conflicts of interest and reduces the risk of fraud or misuse of privileges.

- **Data encryption**: Sensitive data, both at rest and in transit, can be encrypted using industry-standard encryption algorithms. This helps protect data from unauthorized access or interception.

- **Auditing and logging**: The framework provides robust auditing and logging capabilities, allowing administrators to track user activities, system changes, and data access. Audit logs can be used for forensic analysis, compliance reporting, and detecting any potential security breaches.

- **Data isolation**: D365 F&SCM ensures the logical separation of customer data through tenant isolation. Each organization's data is stored in a dedicated database, providing data privacy and security.

- **Security updates and patches**: Microsoft regularly releases security updates and patches to address vulnerabilities and protect against emerging threats. These updates can be applied to the D365 F&SCM application to ensure a secure and up-to-date environment.

- **Compliance and certifications**: D365 F&SCM complies with various industry standards and regulations, such as **the GDPR**, ISO 27001, and **Service Organization Controls** (**SOC**) reports. These certifications demonstrate the platform's commitment to maintaining a secure environment.

- **Monitoring and threat detection**: The framework supports proactive monitoring and threat detection mechanisms to identify potential security incidents. It may include features such as anomaly detection, security event correlation, and integration with **security information and event management** (**SIEM**) systems.

It's important to note that the D365 F&SCM Security Framework is continuously evolving to address new security challenges and adapt to changing threat landscapes. Organizations using the platform should regularly review and update their security configurations to ensure the optimal protection of their data and systems.

Testing strategies

The testing strategies that D365 uses are a comprehensive set of testing types that help to ensure the project produces a quality and reliable software tool. These tests will help the business determine whether the solution provided resolves its pain points and properly executes its business processes. This strategy involves various types of testing methodologies and techniques to identify and resolve any issues or bugs in the system.

Here are the key elements typically included in the testing strategy for Microsoft D365 F&SCM:

- **Functional testing**: This type of testing focuses on verifying whether the system meets the functional requirements specified for the application. It involves testing various functionalities such as finance, supply chain management, sales, procurement, and human resources to ensure they work as expected.

- **Integration testing**: Integration testing is performed to validate the interaction and data flow between different modules and external systems integrated with D365 F&SCM. This includes testing the integration with other Microsoft products such as Office 365, Power Platform, and Azure services.

- **Performance testing**: Performance testing aims to assess the system's responsiveness, scalability, and stability under different load conditions. It involves testing scenarios with varying numbers of concurrent users, transactions, and data volumes to ensure the system can handle the expected workload efficiently.

- **Security testing**: Security testing is crucial for identifying vulnerabilities and ensuring the protection of sensitive data within the D365 F&SCM application. It includes testing access controls, authentication mechanisms, data encryption, and vulnerability assessments to mitigate security risks.

- **User Acceptance Testing (UAT)**: UAT involves testing the system from the end user's perspective. It typically involves users or business stakeholders who validate the system's functionality, usability, and overall performance in real-world scenarios. UAT helps ensure that the application meets the business requirements and user expectations.

- **Regression testing**: Regression testing is performed to verify that existing functionality has not been negatively impacted by any changes or enhancements introduced during development. It involves retesting previously tested scenarios to ensure that no new issues have been introduced and that the application continues to function correctly.

- **Automated testing**: Automation plays a vital role in reducing testing effort and increasing test coverage. It involves developing automated scripts to perform repetitive and time-consuming tests, such as regression testing and performance testing. Automated testing tools such as Selenium, Coded UI, or Microsoft's own testing framework can be utilized for this purpose.

- **Data migration testing**: Data migration testing is performed when migrating data from legacy systems or other sources to D365 F&SCM. It involves validating the accuracy, integrity, and completeness of the migrated data, ensuring it is correctly transformed and loaded into the new system.

- **Localization testing**: D365 F&SCM is used by organizations worldwide, and localization testing ensures that the application functions correctly in different languages, currencies, and regional settings. It involves validating language translations, date and time formats, regional taxation rules, and other localized requirements.

- **Accessibility testing**: Accessibility testing ensures that the application can be used by individuals with disabilities, conforming to accessibility standards such as the **Web Content Accessibility Guidelines** (**WCAG**). It involves testing screen readers, keyboard navigation, color contrast, and other accessibility features.

It's important to note that the testing strategy may vary depending on the specific project requirements and an organization's preferences. Organizations may also include additional testing types or methodologies based on their needs.

Test planning and execution

Testing planning and execution are crucial steps in the implementation and maintenance of this software to ensure its stability, accuracy, and reliability. Let's break down the process of testing planning and execution for D365 F&SCM:

1. Test planning:

    A. **Requirement analysis**: The testing process begins by analyzing the functional and technical requirements of the system. This involves understanding the business processes, system configurations, and customizations.

    B. **Test strategy**: Based on the requirements, a test strategy is developed, which outlines the overall approach, scope, and objectives of the testing process. It also defines the roles and responsibilities of the testing team.

    C. **Test plan**: A detailed test plan is created, specifying the test scenarios, test cases, test data, and the expected results. This includes information about the testing environment, test schedule, and resources required.

2. Test execution:

   A. **Test case preparation**: Test cases are developed based on the test scenarios defined in the test plan. These test cases cover various aspects of the system, including functional workflows, integrations, data validations, and performance testing.

   B. **Test data setup**: Test data is prepared to simulate real-world scenarios. This includes creating sample customers, vendors, transactions, and other relevant data necessary for testing.

   C. **Test environment setup**: A dedicated testing environment is prepared, mirroring the production environment, to ensure accurate testing and minimize any impact on the live system.

   D. **Test execution**: The test cases are executed systematically, following the predefined test plan. The test results, including any defects or issues encountered, are documented for further analysis and resolution.

   E. **Defect tracking**: If any issues or defects are identified during testing, they are logged in a defect tracking system. This helps in tracking and managing the issues until they are resolved.

   F. **Test reporting**: Regular test reports are generated to provide stakeholders with an overview of the testing progress, including test coverage, test results, and any critical issues that require attention.

3. **Test management**:

   A. **Test monitoring and control**: The testing process is monitored to ensure that it stays on track and meets the defined objectives. Test progress is tracked, and any deviations or risks are identified and addressed promptly.

   B. **Test coverage evaluation**: The test coverage is assessed to ensure that all critical functionalities and business processes are adequately tested. Any gaps or areas of improvement are identified and addressed.

   C. **Regression testing**: Whenever changes or updates are made to the system, regression testing is performed to ensure that existing functionality has not been affected. This helps maintain the system's stability.

   D. **UAT support**: Assistance is provided to end users during the UAT phase. This involves addressing any issues, providing training, and ensuring a smooth transition to the live system.

Overall, the testing planning and execution process for D365 F&SCM involves careful planning, thorough test case preparation, systematic test execution, defect tracking, and effective communication with stakeholders. By following this process, organizations can ensure the successful implementation and ongoing stability of their D365 F&SCM system.

Performance testing

Performance testing is a critical aspect of ensuring that the system can handle the expected workload and operate efficiently. It involves evaluating the system's responsiveness, scalability, stability, and resource usage under different conditions.

When it comes to performance testing in D365 F&SCM, the primary objectives are to assess the system's ability to handle concurrent user activities, process large volumes of data, and meet response time requirements. Here are some key considerations:

- **Workload modeling**: Performance testers need to analyze and understand the system's usage patterns and business processes to create realistic workload scenarios. This involves identifying the most critical user activities, transaction volumes, and data sizes.
- **Load testing**: Load testing involves subjecting the system to increasing levels of simulated user activity to determine its performance limits. Testers typically use load-testing tools to generate virtual users and mimic real-world usage patterns. The tests measure KPIs such as response times, throughput, and resource utilization.
- **Stress testing**: Stress testing pushes the system to its limits by simulating extreme conditions, such as high transaction volumes, peak loads, or unexpected spikes in user activity. The goal is to identify potential bottlenecks, performance degradation, or system failures and assess the system's ability to recover from such situations.
- **Scalability testing**: Scalability testing determines how well the system can handle increasing workloads by adding additional resources, such as servers or processing power. Testers assess the system's ability to scale horizontally (adding more servers) or vertically (increasing resources on existing servers) while maintaining performance and stability.
- **Performance monitoring**: During testing, performance metrics are collected and monitored to identify any performance issues or anomalies. This includes monitoring server resource utilization, database performance, network latency, and response times. Monitoring tools and performance counters are often used to gather this data.
- **Performance tuning**: Based on the test results and performance monitoring, performance bottlenecks and areas for improvement are identified. Performance tuning may involve optimizing database queries, configuring server settings, or fine-tuning the system's configuration to enhance performance.
- **Reporting and analysis**: After completing the performance testing process, testers compile test reports summarizing the findings and observations. These reports provide insights into the system's performance characteristics, identified issues, recommendations for improvement, and overall system readiness.

It's important to note that performance testing is an iterative process and should be performed at different stages of the application life cycle, including development, testing, and production. This helps ensure that any performance-related issues are identified and resolved early on, minimizing the impact on end users and the business.

By conducting thorough performance testing in D365 F&SCM, organizations can validate the system's ability to handle the expected workload, optimize its performance, and deliver a seamless UX.

Business intelligence

A **business intelligence** (**BI**) strategy focuses on leveraging data to provide insights, enhance decision-making, and optimize operations within an organization.

Here are some key aspects of D365 F&SCM's BI strategy:

- **Data integration**: The system collects and integrates data from various sources, including financial transactions, supply chain activities, customer interactions, and more. This integration ensures a holistic view of the organization's operations and enables comprehensive analysis.

- **Real-time analytics**: D365 F&SCM offers real-time analytics capabilities to provide up-to-date information and enable timely decision-making. Users can access dashboards, reports, and visualizations that display KPIs, financial metrics, inventory levels, production statuses, and other relevant data.

- **Advanced reporting and visualization**: The solution incorporates powerful reporting and visualization tools to present data in an intuitive and meaningful way. Users can create custom reports, interactive dashboards, and graphical representations of data to analyze trends, identify patterns, and gain actionable insights.

- **Predictive analytics**: D365 F&SCM also supports predictive analytics, leveraging machine learning algorithms and statistical models to forecast future trends and outcomes. These predictive capabilities can aid in demand forecasting, inventory optimization, cash flow projections, and other strategic planning activities.

- **Self-service BI**: The solution promotes self-service BI, allowing users to explore data independently and create personalized reports and visualizations. This empowers business users with the ability to access relevant information and perform ad hoc analysis without relying solely on IT or technical resources.

- **Integration with Power BI**: D365 F&SCM seamlessly integrates with Microsoft Power BI. This integration enables organizations to leverage Power BI's advanced capabilities for data visualization, data modeling, and collaboration, further enhancing the BI strategy.

- **Mobile access**: D365 F&SCM supports mobile access, enabling users to access BI insights and reports from their smartphones or tablets. This ensures that decision-makers can stay informed and act on the go, enhancing productivity and responsiveness.

- **Data security and governance**: The BI strategy of D365 F&SCM emphasizes data security and governance. Access controls, data encryption, and auditing mechanisms are in place to protect sensitive information and ensure compliance with regulatory requirements.

By adopting these components, D365 F&SCM's BI strategy empowers organizations to make data-driven decisions, optimize processes, identify cost-saving opportunities, improve forecasting accuracy, and enhance overall operational efficiency.

Now that we know what needs to be included in the solution blueprint document from the point-of-view of strategies to execute the project, we'll next focus on the process of go-live.

Go-live preparation

Now that we have completed all the other phases of the project, testing has been completed, and we all agree that the project is ready for deployment, we now start the go-live phase. Here, we develop a detailed go-live plan that outlines the sequence of activities and tasks required to transition from the current system to Microsoft Dynamics. Consider factors such as data freezing, the cutover strategy, downtime minimization, and contingency plans. Also, we need to submit our go-live plans to Microsoft for its approval. This approval is the kick-off of getting the production environments created. Microsoft will use the gold image that you have created after all your project work to create the production environments.

They will also use previous performance testing results to determine the number of production environments that will be created. This date for go-live will be negotiated with Microsoft. Once that date has been reached, the customer will be able to start adding users to the system, assign their security roles, and start entering outage data.

When executing the go-live, we will follow the go-live plan, execute the necessary tasks, and transition users to the new Microsoft Dynamics system. Monitor the system closely during the initial period to address any issues promptly. Once we have successfully completed the go-live, there will be post-go-live support. This support provides ongoing support and assistance to users following the go-live. Address any post-implementation challenges, questions, or issues. Continuously monitor the system's performance, gather feedback, and make necessary improvements.

Remember that each implementation project may have unique requirements, so it's important to tailor these steps to your specific context. Microsoft Dynamics FastTrack provides additional resources and guidance throughout the implementation process to help ensure a successful go-live.

Case study

When preparing for the go-live of a completed D365 F&SCM project, we need to determine what will happen during the cut-over phase. The cut-over allows the company to get everything ready for the new system to be used by the staff. One of the decisions that needs to be made with the business is how any new transactions that need to be completed during the cut-over will be executed.

In the previous project, the client was worried about how to maintain the business while the project cutover occurred. Their main concern was how they would record new purchase requisitions and purchase orders. Also, they needed to figure out how to process vendor invoices so that they didn't get any unhappy vendors. To solve this problem, we added three things to the go-live/cutover plan.

First off, we got the business units to agree to reduce the number of items they were ordering. Luckily, we completed the cutover during a slower time of year, so it made it easier to accomplish this requirement. All of the buyers recorded all new purchases in Excel. Again, there weren't many due to the time of year.

Once the cutover was completed, all of the new purchases that were recorded in Excel were entered into the new system by hand prior to all the other users being given access to the system. This also allowed the staff to make all of the entries without any interruption and got through the list of entries very quickly.

The second part of the cutover was to keep vendors happy while these changes were occurring. We agreed with the AP group to contact all of the main vendors to let them know that the company was bringing in a new finance system and asked them to please be patient when looking for payments. All of the vendors agreed to the delays. We only had to delay payments by one week, again due to the time of year in which the cutover took place. All of the vendors were impressed with the speed of the migration, and they were all kept happy in terms of the payments.

This project was one of the best that I've been involved in when going live. One thing to keep in mind – the SA helps to plan the cutover, and there needs to be a cutover practice run so that everyone knows what is to happen during that phase, but ultimately, it's the client that is responsible for making it happen successfully. The SA needs to be 100% confident that everyone knows their roles in the cutover.

How should it look?

At this point, you're most likely wondering what an actual document would look like. Here's a sample blueprint solution for a Dynamics 365 **Finance and Operations** (**F&O**) project:

1. Project overview:

    - Provide a brief description of the project objectives, scope, and timeline
    - Identify the key stakeholders and their roles in the project

2. Business process analysis:

    - Conduct a thorough analysis of the existing business processes and identify areas for improvement
    - Document current pain points, bottlenecks, and inefficiencies
    - Define the desired future state and outline the benefits of implementing Dynamics 365 F&O

3. Solution architecture:

    - Design the solution architecture based on the business requirements
    - Identify the modules and features of Dynamics 365 F&O that align with the organization's needs
    - Determine any customizations or integrations required to meet specific business requirements
    - Define the data migration strategy to transfer existing data into the new system

4. System configuration:

    - Configure the Dynamics 365 F&O environment according to the solution architecture
    - Set up the chart of accounts, financial dimensions, and organizational structure
    - Configure modules such as the General Ledger, Accounts Payable, Accounts Receivable, Inventory Management, and Purchasing
    - Define security roles and access permissions for different user groups

5. Custom development and integration:

    - Identify any custom development requirements not covered by out-of-the-box functionality
    - Develop customizations, extensions, or integrations using appropriate development tools (e.g., X++, C#, or Power Platform)
    - Conduct thorough testing to ensure the customizations meet the defined requirements

6. Data migration:

    - Extract and cleanse data from legacy systems or spreadsheets
    - Define data mapping rules to map data from the source to the target system
    - Perform data transformation and validation
    - Execute data migration using tools or APIs provided by Dynamics 365 F&O

7. User training and change management:

    - Develop a comprehensive training plan and materials for end users
    - Conduct training sessions to familiarize users with the new system
    - Provide ongoing support and assistance during the transition period
    - Implement change management strategies to ensure user adoption and minimize resistance

8. Testing and quality assurance:

    - Develop test scripts and scenarios covering various business processes
    - Conduct unit testing, integration testing, and UAT
    - Perform system performance and security testing
    - Address and resolve any issues or bugs identified during testing

9. Deployment and go-live:

    - Prepare a detailed deployment plan with minimal disruption to business operations
    - Conduct a final data migration and validate the accuracy of migrated data
    - Coordinate with the IT team to ensure infrastructure readiness
    - Execute the deployment plan, including system configuration, custom development, data migration, and user training
    - Monitor the system closely during the go-live phase and provide immediate support for any critical issues

10. Post-implementation support:

    - Provide post-implementation support to address user questions and issues
    - Monitor system performance and identify opportunities for optimization
    - Conduct periodic system reviews and ensure alignment with evolving business requirements
    - Plan for future enhancements or updates to the Dynamics 365 F&O system

Remember, this is just a sample blueprint solution, and the actual requirements and approach may vary based on the specific project and organization.

Conclusion

I'm hoping now that you've completed this book you have a better idea of the types of tasks you need to complete to become a successful DA in D365 and how to run a successful D365 F&SCM project. Many of the examples I've provided are not just unique to my experiences. I have several contacts and friends in this industry who have passed many of these stories to me that I've included. However, I've been in this business a long time, and even though I have a lot of experience both as an SA and as an admin and analyst, I don't know everything. As with everything else in technology, things change regularly. Your own experience is the best way to help guide you to completing a successful project.

Good luck, and I hope that I've been of some help to you. And keep an eye open. You never know, there might have to be a second edition of this book.

Index

A

Accounts Payable (AP) 110
active listening 154
  performance 154, 155
  techniques 155
ADKAR Model 194
agile method 22
analytical tools 209
Apache JMeter 172
Appium 171
Application Integration Framework 131
application life cycle management (ALM) 221
Application Programming Interfaces (APIs) 225
architecture design document (ADD) 212
as-is business process 136
  mapping process 137
Asset Management 105
assigned license 97
asynchronous transfers 86
attached license
  versus base license 97
authentication 52
authorization 52

Azure DevOps 143, 167
  Test hub 184
Azure DevOps, Agile project management keys
  backlog management 169
  CI/CD 170
  daily stand-up meetings 169
  sprint planning 169
  user feedback and retrospectives 170
Azure DevOps, keys
  Agile Project Management 169
  CI/CD 169
  IaC 169
  monitoring and feedback 169

B

base license
  versus attached license 97
baseline business processes 136
batch API 40
Batch data API 86
behavior-driven development (BDD) 171
Bill of Materials (BOM) 47, 131, 144
  creating, from LCS 132

blueprint solution
  architecture, design pillars 220, 221
  building 219, 220
  business intelligence (BI) strategy 233, 234
  performance testing 232
  strategies 221
  view 235-237

blueprint solution, strategies
  ALM 221, 222
  data management 222, 223
  deployment 221, 222
  integrations 223-225
  security 227
  testing 229, 230
  test planning and execution 230, 231
  tools 221, 222

Bridges' Transition Model 195
bring your own database (BYOD) 84
business analyst (BA) 208
Business Central (BC) 4
business intelligence (BI) 233
business processes 144
  acquiring 153
  case study 158
  identifying 132-134
  initiating 130
  turning, into solution blueprint for D365 project 153

Business Process Modeler (BPM) 141, 142, 150
  benefits 142

business process modeling tools 151
business process optimization 136-139
  fit-gap analysis 139-141
  solution, modeling 139

business requirements document (BRD) 212

C

card sorting 209
case studies, human change management 199
  bad project 199
  good project 200

Change Curve 193, 194
  acceptance/integration stage 193
  anger/blame stage 193
  bargaining/negotiation stage 193
  denial/resistance stage 193
  depression/despair stage 193

change management professional 197, 198
change management strategy
  communication 190
  developing 189

change manager 208
client
  listening to 154

clients business process, with Success by Design
  obtaining 129, 130

cloud-first 20
cloud security 52, 53
Coded UI Test 171
code testing 34
Common Data Service (CDS) 225
configuration data 78
continuous integration and continuous delivery (CI/CD) 165
Create, Read, Update, and Delete (CRUD) 86
customization 149
custom security
  creating, in D365 Finance and SCM 102

custom services 40, 86

Index   241

D

D365 F&O Enterprise Resource Planning (ERP) project 213

D365 Finance and Supply Chain Management (D365 F&SCM) 5
  extended data security model 54
  performance testing, consideration 232
  security 53
  security architecture 61, 64
  security model hierarchy 53, 54
  security reports 54
  security, setting up 60
  testing strategy 229, 230

D365 F&SCM components, with BPM
  business events 142
  business rules 142
  forms 142
  implementation phases 143, 144
  integrations 143
  process tasks 142
  project, best practices 185
  project, creating 180-184
  reports 143
  workflows 142

D365 F&SCM environments 173
  cloud-hosted environments 173
  OneBox 173
  Sandbox 173
  Tier-1 Production 173
  Tier-2 Production 173

D365 F&SCM's BI strategy
  aspects 233

D365 F&SCM, security architecture
  security privilege, creating 67-74
  security role, creating 65, 66

D365 F&SCM Security Framework 228
  components and features 228, 229

D365 F&SCM, security reports
  Role to user assignment report 57
  Security duty assignments report 58, 59
  Security role access report 56, 57
  segregation of duties report 59
  User role assignments report 54, 55

D365 F&SCM, security reports locations
  databases 60
  LCS 60

D365 project
  business language 131
  checklists 126
  governance 118

D365 project management 113-115
  layout 115
  tools 116

data analyst 208

data entities 82

data-first 21

data framework 81

data integration patterns 39

data locations 78, 79

data management 80
  data entities 82
  data framework 81
  data mapping 83
  data tools 84

Data Management Framework (DMF) 185

data management workspace 84

data mapping 83

data migration 77, 78
  best practices 88-90
  data locations 78, 79
  data types 78
  methodologies 79, 80

data migration strategy
  creating 84
  cutover plan 87

data import and export 86
data output, validating 86
preparing 85
data tools 84
data types 78
Dataverse 41
   data integrators 41
   DW 41-43
Dell Boomi© 47
development 149
   working, in D365 F&SCM 149
device licenses 98
diagrams
   using 156
digital transformation
   impact, on creation of business processes 139
dual-write (DW) 88
   for racing team 47
Dynamics 365 applications 143
Dynamics 365 (D365) 3-5
   implementing 5-14
   issues, preventing 15, 16
Dynamics 365 Finance and Operations (D365 F&O) project 208
   business analyst (BA) 208
   change manager 208
   data analyst 208
   functional consultant 208
   project manager 208
   quality assurance (QA) analyst 208
   solution architect (SA) 208
   technical consultant 208
   training coordinator 208
Dynamics 365 for Finance and Supply Chain Management (D365 F&SCM) 137
Dynamics 365 F&SCM Target Operating Model 134

Dynamics 365 F&SCM Target Operating Model, components
   business processes 134
   change management 135
   data management 134
   governance and compliance 135
   organizational structure 134
   performance measurement 135
   technology architecture 135
Dynamics 365 Licensing Guide 100
dynamics license types
   assigned license 97
   unassigned license 97
Dynamics Lifecycle Services (LCS) 172
   D365 F&SCM environments 173
   key roles 172
Dynamics Lifecycle Services (LCS), business process tools
   BPM 141, 142
   Process Configuration 142
   Process Documentation 142
   Process Library 141

E

Enterprise Agreements (EA) 96
Enterprise licenses 97
Enterprise Resource Planning (ERP) 4, 199
ERP project
   preparing 116
   team 116, 118
ERP project, types
   analysts 117
   BI analysts 117
   data analyst 117
   developer 117
   ISV consultants 117
   partner representative 116

program manager 117
project manager 117
project Manager (PM) 116
solution architect (SA) 117
Subject Matter Experts (SMEs) 118
technical architect 117
Excel spreadsheets 151
extensions 149
external users
versus internal users 105
Extract, Transform, and Load (ETL) 185

F

FastTrack engagement
case study 30
initiate phase 31
FastTrack engagement, initiate phase
implementation 33, 34
operate 35
preparation 34, 35
workshops 32, 33
FastTrack for Dynamics 365 5
FastTrack Recognized Solution Architects (FTRSA) 29
Federal Risk and Authorization Management Program (FedRAMP) 227
Finance and Operations (F&O) 235
fit-gap analysis 139-141, 150
fit-gap analysis, for D365 F&SCM
tools and techniques, using 140
functional consultant 208
functional design document (FDD) 212

G

General Data Protection Regulation (GDPR) 227
general ledger (GL) 44
Git 167
go-live
preparation 234
preparation, case study 234, 235

H

Health Insurance Portability and Accountability Act (HIPAA) 227
historical data 78
human change management 187, 188
case studies 199, 200
change, communicating 190
change management professional 197, 198
change management strategy, developing 189
key steps 188
methodologies 194, 195
reinforcement 191
stakeholder needs, identifying 189
stakeholders, identifying 188
sustainability 191
tools 198, 199
training and development 190

I

implementation plan document 213
Independent Software Vendor (ISV) licenses 104
integrated development environment (IDE) 178

integration issues
   fixing 48-50
integrations 38, 223-225
   components, for creating 38, 39
   types 225-227
integrations, components
   batch API 40
   custom services 40
   data integration patterns 39
   Dataverse 41
   OData 40
   virtual entities 43, 44
integrations failure 44
   client and project teams 45
   data dependency 44
   interface complexity 45
   negative impact 46
   resistance to change 45, 46
   working, in silos 44
integrations failure, case study 46
   DW, for racing team 47
   Power Automate tools 48
   solidworks, to D365 47, 48
   two ERP systems, integrating 46, 47
internal users
   versus external users 105
interview method 209

J

JavaScript Object Notation (JSON) 86
JMeter 171

K

key performance indicators (KPIs) 135, 207, 223
Kotters 8-Step Change Model 194

L

Lewin's Change Management Model 194
licenses
   assigning 106
   determining, to obtain 99
   obtaining 96
   real-world example 109
   reporting 107, 109
Lifecycle Services (LCS)
   Bill of Materials (BOM), creating 132
living documents
   maintaining, tips 215, 216
LoadRunner 171

M

master data 78
methodologies, human change management
   ADKAR Model 194
   Bridges' Transition Model 195
   Kotters 8-Step Change Model 194
   Lewin's Change Management Model 194
   Prosci ADKAR Model 195,-197
Microsoft Azure DevOps 165
   CI/CD 166
   project, creating 166, 167
   project management 166
   project management tool 169
   release pipelines 168
   source control management 165
   testing 166
   testing, types 170
   tools 165
   version control 167
Microsoft Certified Technology Specialist (MCT) 95
Microsoft Dynamics NAV 4

Microsoft FastTrack for Dynamics 365 24
  customer requisites 24
  engagement requisites 25, 26
  implementation guide 26
  methodology 29
  partner requisites 25
  SA role 30
  types 26
Microsoft FastTrack for Dynamics 365, implementation guide
  organizational change management 26
  solution design 27, 28
Microsoft FastTrack for Dynamics 365, tasks 28
  customer tasks 28
  Microsoft tasks 29
  partner tasks 28
Microsoft licensing model 95
  dynamics license types 97
  licenses, obtaining 96
Microsoft Power Platform 143
Microsoft Products and Services Agreement (MPSA) 96
Microsoft Test Manager 171
Microsoft Trusted Cloud Principles (MTCP) 52
Microsoft Visio 143
Multi-Factor Authentication (MFA) 53
multiplexing 105, 106

O

observation 209
OData 40, 86
Office integration 84
operations licenses 98
out-of-the-box solution
  Dynamics 365, providing 148

P

personalization 149
per-user license 105
phased approach 21
  implementation phase 23
  initiate phase 22, 23
  operate phase 24
  prepare phase 24
  process 22
Postman 171
Power Automate 48, 143
Process Configuration tool 142
process diagram review
  factors, consideration 138, 139
Process Documentation tool 142
Process Library 141
process mapping tools 150, 151
project budget document 214
  assumptions 215
  budget justification 215
  budget summary 215
  conclusion 215
  contingency plan 215
  cost breakdown 215
  introduction 214
  project scope 214
project manager 208
project scope document 212
Proof of Concept (POC) 156
Prosci ADKAR Model 195
  ability stage 195
  awareness stage 195
  desire stage 195
  implementation example 197
  knowledge stage 195
  reinforcement stage 195
purchase orders (POs) 97

Q

quality assurance (QA) analyst 208

R

Regression Suite Automation
    Tool (RSAT) 176, 177
release pipelines 168
    setting up 168
Representational State Transfer (REST) 86
requirement gathering templates 150
Requirements Traceability
    Matrix (RTM) 151
    collecting information 151, 152
        displaying information 151
        displaying, information 152
responsible, accountable, consulted, and
    informed (RACI) charts 213
return on investment (ROI) 136
Robot Framework 171
role-based access control (RBAC) 109, 228

S

security 227
Security configuration diagnostics 109
Security duty assignments report 58, 59
security information and event
    management (SIEM) 228
security privilege
    creating 67-74
security role
    creating 65, 66
segregation of duties (SoD) 59, 228
Selenium 171
Service Organization Controls (SOC) 228
Simulation 0/Sim 0 148

SoapUI 171
software applications changes
    communication with employees,
        need for 191, 192
Software as a Service (SaaS) application 149
Software Development Kit (SDK) 226
solution architect (SA) 15, 203, 208
    client agreement 157
    roles 16, 17
    user requirements expressing 209, 210
    working, relationship with client 156
solution blueprint 203
    adequate training and skill
        development, ensuring 207
    background and problem statement 211
    conclusion 211
    containing, components information 162
    creating 158, 159
    customizing 205, 206
    detailed implementation plan,
        developing 206
    evaluation mechanisms 207
    executive summary 211
    foster collaboration 207
    goals and objectives 211
    information types 160-162
    iterate 207
    knowledge sharing 207
    Microsoft recommended best
        practices 216, 217
    monitoring and evaluation plan 211
    monitoring, implementing 207
    plan, for long-term support
        and maintenance 207
    resource requirements 211
    review 207
    risk assessment and management 211
    scope and limitations 211

strategy and action plan 211
strong governance structure,
    establishing 206
suitability, assessing 204
swim lane diagram 162
SpecFlow 171
SQL Server Reporting Services (SSRS) 185
Statement of Work (SOW) 22
Subject Matter Experts (SMEs) 22, 117, 206
Subscription estimator 102, 104
subscription requirements
    planning 100
Success by Design 129
    using 130
Success by Design, methodology 20
    cloud-first 20
    data-first 21
    phased approach 21
Success by Design, solution blueprint 204
    communication plan 204
    goals and objectives 204
    implementation plan 204
    performance metrics 204
    risk management 204
    strategy 204
Supply Chain Management (SCM) 96
Sure Step 19
surveys 209
synchronous transfers 86
System Administration
    Users page 101
system administrator (sys admin) 99
system license 105

T

Target Operating Model (TOM) 133
    success, reasons 135, 136
Task Recorder 64, 173, 174
    for security configuration 174-176
    RSAT 176, 177
    usage, purposes 175, 176
    Visual Studio 178, 179
Team Foundation Version
    Control (TFVC) 167
    models 167
Team/Team Member licenses 98
technical consultant 208
technical design document (TDD) 212
Telerik Test Studio 172
TestComplete 171
testing phase four 34
testing phase one 34
testing phase three 34
testing phase two 34
testing, types
    automated testing scripts 170
    manual testing scripts 170
test plan document 212
test scripts
    managing, steps 170, 171
The Five Diamond Method 136
    processes 137
tools, for human change management
    change readiness assessment 198
    communication plan 198
    metrics and evaluation plan 199
    resistance management plan 199
    stakeholder analysis 198
    training and development plan 199

tools, with D365 Business process modeler
  Azure DevOps 143
  Dynamics 365 applications 143
  Microsoft Power Platform 143
  Microsoft Visio 143
  Power Automate 143

training coordinator 208

transactional data 78

transportation management system (TMS) 44

two ERP systems
  integrating 46, 47

U

unassigned license 97
unit testing 34
use case diagrams 151
User Acceptance Testing (UAT) 50, 118, 229
user assignment role 57
user experience (UX) 221
user interface design document 212
User role assignments report 54-57
Users page
  in System Administration 101
user stories 152, 153
user testing 209

V

version control 167
version control, options
  Azure DevOps 167
  Git 167
  TFVC 167
virtual entities 43, 44
Visual Studio 178, 179
  features and capabilities 178
  using, to create customization for D365 F&SCM 179
Visual Studio Test Professional 171

W

Web Content Accessibility Guidelines (WCAG) 230
workbook designer 84

Z

Zero Trust 52

‹packt›

packtpub.com

Subscribe to our online digital library for full access to over 7,000 books and videos, as well as industry leading tools to help you plan your personal development and advance your career. For more information, please visit our website.

Why subscribe?

- Spend less time learning and more time coding with practical eBooks and Videos from over 4,000 industry professionals
- Improve your learning with Skill Plans built especially for you
- Get a free eBook or video every month
- Fully searchable for easy access to vital information
- Copy and paste, print, and bookmark content

Did you know that Packt offers eBook versions of every book published, with PDF and ePub files available? You can upgrade to the eBook version at packtpub.com and as a print book customer, you are entitled to a discount on the eBook copy. Get in touch with us at customercare@packtpub.com for more details.

At www.packtpub.com, you can also read a collection of free technical articles, sign up for a range of free newsletters, and receive exclusive discounts and offers on Packt books and eBooks.

Other Books You May Enjoy

If you enjoyed this book, you may be interested in these other books by Packt:

Extending Microsoft Dynamics 365 Finance and Supply Chain Management Cookbook Second Edition

Simon Buxton

ISBN: 978-1-83864-381-2

- Understand the importance of using patterns and frameworks for creating unique solutions
- Write code that can make your solution extendable
- Leverage new frameworks that allow your solution to adapt as your business grows
- Design the UI and business logic to fit standard patterns
- Understand how to not only write unit tests, but also perform efficient unit testing to automate the testing process
- Design your security model and policies to provide code access privileges

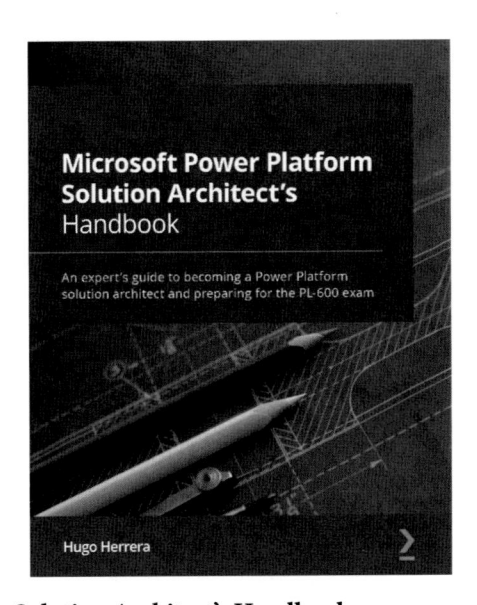

Microsoft Power Platform Solution Architect's Handbook

Hugo Herrera

ISBN: 978-1-80181-933-6

- Cement the foundations of your applications using best practices
- Use proven design, build, and go-live strategies to ensure success
- Lead requirements gathering and analysis with confidence
- Secure even the most complex solutions and integrations
- Ensure compliance between the Microsoft ecosystem and your business
- Build resilient test and deployment strategies to optimize solutions

Packt is searching for authors like you

If you're interested in becoming an author for Packt, please visit `authors.packtpub.com` and apply today. We have worked with thousands of developers and tech professionals, just like you, to help them share their insight with the global tech community. You can make a general application, apply for a specific hot topic that we are recruiting an author for, or submit your own idea.

Share Your Thoughts

Now you've finished *Becoming a Dynamics 365 Finance and Supply Chain Solution Architect*, we'd love to hear your thoughts! Scan the QR code below to go straight to the Amazon review page for this book and share your feedback or leave a review on the site that you purchased it from.

`https://packt.link/r/1804611492`

Your review is important to us and the tech community and will help us make sure we're delivering excellent quality content.

Download a free PDF copy of this book

Thanks for purchasing this book!

Do you like to read on the go but are unable to carry your print books everywhere? Is your eBook purchase not compatible with the device of your choice?

Don't worry, now with every Packt book you get a DRM-free PDF version of that book at no cost.

Read anywhere, any place, on any device. Search, copy, and paste code from your favorite technical books directly into your application.

The perks don't stop there, you can get exclusive access to discounts, newsletters, and great free content in your inbox daily

Follow these simple steps to get the benefits:

1. Scan the QR code or visit the link below

   `https://packt.link/free-ebook/9781804611494`

2. Submit your proof of purchase
3. That's it! We'll send your free PDF and other benefits to your email directly

Made in the USA
Middletown, DE
06 March 2024